Under Siege:
P.L.O. Decisionmaking
During the 1982 War

Under Siege:
P.L.O. Decisionmaking
During the 1982 War

Rashid Khalidi

Columbia University Press
New York   **1986**

Library of Congress Cataloging in Publication Data

Khalidi, Rashid.
Under siege.

Bibliography: p.
Includes index.
1. Lebanon—History—Israeli intervention, 1982–
2. Munazzamat al-Tahrir al-Filastiniyah. 3. Palestinian
Arabs—Lebanon—Politics and government. I. Title.
DS87.53.K48   1985   956.92′044   85-17046
ISBN 0-231-06186-2

Columbia University Press
New York   Guildford, Surrey
Copyright © 1986 Columbia University Press

Printed in the United States of America

This book is Smyth-sewn and printed on permanent and durable acid-free paper

Contents

Preface

It is rare that a historian has the opportunity to observe the events he later chronicles. It is perhaps rarer still that an account by a contemporary observer merits the title of history. I make no such claim for this work; but I did witness the events of the summer of 1982 in besieged West Beirut, and this gives it a special and, I hope, a valuable perspective.

The writing of this book was made possible by the kindness of many individuals and institutions: those who afforded me access to the documentary material on which it is primarily based; those who gave generously of their time and of their sometimes painful recollections in the interviews listed in the bibliography; and those whose financial support was indispensable throughout.

It is unusual that sensitive diplomatic correspondence of such recent origin is opened to the researcher, particularly without any conditions or limitations being imposed in the process. Permission to utilize the P.L.O. Archives for the first time was generously given by the Chairman of the P.L.O. Executive Committee, Yasser 'Arafat. To him, and to the dedicated individuals working in the Office of the Chairman, the P.L.O. Archives, and the Palestine News Agency (WAFA), who extended every possible assistance to me on three trips to Tunis, I owe deep thanks.

Among those interviewed, it is necessary to record in particular my debt to those unable to be cited by name, but who nevertheless contributed detailed on-the-record accounts of their experiences. I must also thank the many individuals: American, Israeli, French, Palestinian and Lebanese; diplomats, politicians, journalists and scholars; friends, colleagues, and co-workers, who were kind enough to discuss key aspects of this subject with me or provided important data, but whose names cannot be mentioned.

The initial work on this book was done during the 1982–83 academic year at the American University of Beirut, whose courageous President, the late Malcolm Kerr, strongly encouraged me in my work and provided help in difficult circumstances. My colleagues in the Political Studies and Public Administration Department, particularly its Chairman, Professor Adnan Iskandar, and the Acting Dean of the School of Arts and Sciences, Professor Landry Slade, were supportive throughout, and kindly allowed me the leave of absence for the two academic years during which this volume was completed.

During that period, generous support was extended by the Ford Foundation, Georgetown University's Center for Contemporary Arab Studies, where I spent a stimulating year, the American Middle East Peace Research Institute, and the Institute for Palestine Studies. I owe a debt of thanks to all of these institutions and their officers and employees, in particular to Dr. Ann Lesch, who was instrumental in securing the initial funding for this project.

The idea for writing this book came during the war from my friend and colleague, Sami Musallam, who later gave me much valuable assistance. Many other people who lived through that terrible summer in Beirut helped me with the reconstruction of events or by providing their expertise on specific points. Among them were Ramzi Khouri, Sami'al-Banna, 'Abd al-Hadi Khalaf, Muhammad 'Ali al-Khalidi, Camille Mansour, Noha Tadros, my brother Raja and my wife Muna. All provided valuable insights, which in some cases greatly improved the manuscript.

Others read all or part of the manuscript, providing much helpful advice. In particular, I would like to thank Professor Michael Hudson and Joe Stork, whose many observations were much appreciated. Yazid Sayigh, Julie Peteet, 'Imad al-Hajj, and Ahmed al-Khalidi also provided useful comments.

It remains for me to thank those who helped this book along in various stages of its production, including Miss Muna Nsouli and the librarians at the Institute for Palestine Studies in Beirut and Georgetown University's Lauinger Memorial Library; the staff of Columbia University Press, particularly, Kate Wittenberg, Assistant Executive Editor, and the talented Leslie Bialler, Manuscript Editor; my mother, for her essential moral support; and finally Professor Edward Said and Professor Tarif Khalidi, both of whom, as always, provided invaluable advice and help.

None of those mentioned by name, or who contributed in any way to this book, bear any share of responsibility for its shortcomings or errors: they are my own. However, much of the credit for any merits it may have belongs to them.

In conclusion, I and many others owe the greatest debt of gratitude to those who gave their lives during the summer of 1982 in order that others might live, and in defense of the cause of Palestine and the independence of Lebanon. To those who died; to those in Beirut and South Lebanon who survived to face an uncertain future; and to those dispersed by the war, I dedicate this book.

Rashid Khalidi
Washington, D.C., April 1985

Under Siege:
P.L.O. Decisionmaking
During the 1982 War

Introduction

I A War Without Victors

It is now apparent that the 1982 war has taken its place with those of 1948, 1967 and 1973 as a watershed in modern Middle Eastern history. This is clear from its drastic effects on all the parties to the conflict, and from the extensive literature devoted to it.

Israel, the war's initiator, was bogged down in Lebanon for three years, spending about $1 million per day on the costs of occupation. Since June 6, 1982, over 650 Israeli soldiers have been killed and almost 4000 wounded.[2] In spite of this high cost, the invasion of Lebanon has not measurably helped Israel to achieve its primary goals vis-à-vis the Palestinians, Lebanon, or Syria, or to advance its security.

For over two months in the summer of 1982, the Israeli army, which on the eve of the invasion was widely and rightfully feared throughout the Arab world, appeared impotent before the gates of Beirut. This impression has been powerfully reinforced by its inability to quell resistance activity in South Lebanon since then.

As a result of this novel demonstration of Israeli military incapacity, and of the questioning inside of Israel of the war's justifiability, there is now doubt whether Israel can sustain its former role of preeminent regional superpower. Israelis would undoubtedly come to the defense of their country if it were threatened, but they are unlikely to allow themselves once again to be dragged into the kind of adventure launched by former Prime Minister Menachem Begin and former Defense Minister Ariel Sharon in 1982.

As for the Palestinians, they too have been major losers. In spite of their resistance to the Israeli attack, which was more prolonged than anyone could have predicted, the war had few positive results for them. The Palestine Liberation Organization (P.L.O.) was driven out of South Lebanon, and then forced to leave Beirut in August 1982. It did so without obtaining either binding guarantees for the Palestinian civilians left behind, or the political quid pro quo it sought for the evacuation. The result was a bloody massacre at Sabra and Shatila, and a marked decline in the Organization's visibility and effectiveness.

In the three years which followed, the P.L.O. has suffered dispersion, profound internal dissension, and a bitter dispute with Syria, which led to its forced evacuation from Tripoli. Although the loyalty to it of Palestinians in the West Bank and Gaza Strip has not wavered, they remain under intense pressure from the Israeli authorities, while the situation of Palestinians in Lebanon since 1982 has been precarious.[3] In all of this, the Palestinians' national cause has not been measurably advanced.

Lebanon was the arena and a major victim of the 1982 war. Its situation, bad to begin with, is considerably worse than when the invasion began. Aside from massive losses to life and property in much of the country during and since the invasion, a resolution of the long-lasting Lebanese crisis seems no closer than it was before June 1982. Instead, the precarious internal balance which had prevailed since 1976 has been shattered, as new conflicts have erupted and old ones have reappeared.

Most depressing to the Lebanese people, the war and its bitter aftermath have shown that many of their pre-war hopes for the future—whether for a purely Lebanese solution, or for external intervention—were in vain. The resulting state of despair is reflected in an economic crisis without precedent since fighting began in 1975, massive emigration, and a state of near total public insecurity.[4]

Most external powers intervening in Lebanon have fared nearly as badly. Following Israel's invasion, the United States fell into the trap in its turn, with the Marines eventually becoming little more than another militia on the Lebanese chessboard, while providing easy targets for shadowy enemies. American prestige in the Middle East has suffered measurably as a result of this involvement.

The reasons why are easy to discern. America is held responsible in the region for not having restrained Israel during the war, for not living up to its solemn commitments by preventing the Sabra and Shatila massacres, and for not immediately getting Israel out of Lebanon. Thereafter, U.S. power was committed on the Western rim of Asia for nearly 18 months in support of a narrowly based and weak regime. It confronted a fiercely committed and battle-hardened local majority enjoying strong external backing. This situation was strangely reminiscent of the United States position for so many years on the southeastern rim of the same continent.

Originally, it was Israel's failure to achieve its 1982 war aims which forced Washington to choose between the two unwelcome options of continuing costly U.S. military involvement, while increasing aid to a weaker Israel in the context of a closer alliance, or allowing Syria to gain a predominant position in Lebanon, and the region, with resulting benefits for the USSR.[5] Events finally imposed the latter on the Reagan administration, with the withdrawal of the Marines from Lebanon in February 1984, but even then the chapter of U.S. involvement in Lebanon was not ended.

As for the Soviets, in the wake of the crushing defeat of their Syrian ally during the war, they reluctantly had to commit several thousand of their own combat personnel and advanced new weapons systems to a highly independent Syria. The USSR was thereby faced with the possibility of a direct confrontation with the U.S. in a situation over which it had little control, and where clients of clients often seemed to be be calling the tune.

Their new and more exposed posture in the region was all the more dangerous for the Soviets, since an enraged U.S. tended to blame its predicament in Lebanon partly on them. In fact, the Soviet Union had done little more than benefit from gross errors made by the U.S. and Israel, while extending the support demanded by Syria, its sole remaining regional client of importance.

Among other negative outcomes of the war for the USSR was the fate of the P.L.O., whose defeat in Lebanon, followed by its quarrel with Syria and the resulting internal dissension, paralyzed an important Soviet regional client. On balance, however, and notwithstanding the problems inherent in their position, the Soviets have probably benefited overall from the results of Israel's invasion.[6]

The numerous Arab rivals of Syria have all been discomfited by the preeminence in Arab affairs which it has managed to achieve through its perseverence in Lebanon. Whereas one of the initial results of the war seemed to be a diminution of Syrian power and prestige, that is clearly no longer the case. Syria successfully stood up to both the U.S. and Israel, while backing the winning side in the internal Lebanese conflict.

Syria would seem so far to have escaped the unenviable fate of all other external actors involved in Lebanon for the past decade.[7] However, it is now in the potentially dangerous position of appearing to be on top in Lebanon, with a host of determined and powerful enemies nursing their resentment against it. It will moreover be held largely responsible for events in that country, although it cannot control them. Syria's experience from 1976–1982, when it was ostensibly the dominant power in Lebanon, show that that is not always a desirable position to be in.

The summer of 1982 thus marked the end of an era in the Middle East, where the United States has long managed to maintain its dominance, while only rarely having to flex its own muscles. This anomaly was largely due to its special relationship with a powerful Israel. Following the joint Israeli-U.S. debacle in Lebanon of 1982-83, it will be considerably harder for both to maintain their former regional predominance without a level of willingness higher than ever before to intervene directly—with all the perils that entails.

For all the powers involved, the 1982 war was a turning point, with the predicament of each since then firmly grounded in the events of that summer. Although this central reality has been largely ignored in the prevalent ahistorical blindness in the United States regarding the Middle East, that makes it no less true.

II Perspective and Rationale

Little written so far about the 1982 war has used documents or interviews to illuminate the actions of the parties involved. The reasons are easy to find. In Israel, the war has been a matter for bitter, partisan dispute since it began, coloring the large amount of material which has been published so far. Lebanon is still torn by war, while the Palestinian movement has been riven by dissension. As a result, few Lebanese or Palestinians have had the chance to record their view of events in 1982.[8]

As for other actors such as the U.S., the USSR, and Syria, none is in the habit of releasing sensitive documents on still vital issues very quickly (if ever). At the same time, relatively little has been said for publication by those individuals who were in positions of responsibility in 1982. At the time of this writing most of them were still at their posts, and still engaged in dealing with the direct consequences of their decisions during that summer.[9]

More has probably been written from the American and Israeli perspectives than from that of the victims of the invasion, the Palestinians and Lebanese. Most of this material has been devoted to discerning Israel's precise objectives in invading Lebanon, the degree of American acquiescence in its decision, the course of relations between the United States and Israel during the war, and the domestic impact of the invasion and its bitter aftermath on both countries.

Harder to answer, and less fully dealt with, have been questions about why the P.L.O. and its allies were defeated so relatively swiftly in South Lebanon while the siege of Beirut was thereafter so prolonged, exactly when and why the P.L.O. decided to leave Beirut, what was the exact nature of the contacts between the U.S. and the P.L.O. to this end, and what were their results.

Full access to the P.L.O. archives[10] has made it possible to shed light on these subjects, and provide answers to many of these questions. This was in large measure the raison d'être for this study: to clarify, from the point of view of those under siege—and using as much of the contemporary diplomatic correspondence as possible—what the P.L.O. did, and why, in the summer of 1982. A better understanding of this conflict, and of its sad aftermath, may well do something to avert similar future ones.

During this war, many Israelis began to realize for the first time that the Palestinians and Lebanese they had been fighting for so long were ordinary human beings. Therefore, one of the main objectives of this book has been to give these men and women a little more substance by describing their actions during the summer of 1982 through the imperfect medium of diplomatic telex messages and recollections recorded over a year after the event.

III The Problem of Sources

Three main categories of primary sources were used in this study: (A) documents from the P.L.O. archives; (B) material published in Beirut during the siege; (C) interviews with individuals involved.

A. The first category includes two groups of unpublished confidential sources:

1. Situation reports sent by the P.L.O. Central Operations Room to units in the field and offices abroad on a regular daily basis starting June 29, two weeks after the siege of Beirut had begun. Drafted by the top leadership of the P.L.O. (usually by Commander-in-Chief and Executive Committee Chairman Yasser 'Arafat), these reports reflect their mood and their view of the state of the conflict.

2. Diplomatic dispatches sent via telex by the P.L.O. leadership to its envoys abroad, or received from them. These include more confidential and revealing information than the situation reports, and are the main source for the analysis of the negotiations for the P.L.O.'s withdrawal from Beirut.

B. The second category comprises publications issued in Beirut during the siege, including the daily al-Safir, the only newspaper to continue publishing without interruption from the beginning of the war on June 4 until the lifting of the siege in late August; the leading Lebanese daily al-Nahar; the daily news bulletin issued by WAFA, the P.L.O.'s news agency; and selected issues of Filastin al-Thawra (the P.L.O.'s daily newspaper), and of other short-lived news-sheets which emerged during the siege such as al-Ma'raka and al-Mitras.

C. Finally, those interviewed include most members of the top Fateh leadership in Beirut during the siege, and several who played important roles outside. Also interviewed were a number of middle-level P.L.O. cadres and officers in key positions, P.L.O. envoys abroad, and a number of Western diplomats and officials involved in dealing with the crisis.

Clearly, the material in all three categories suffers from a variety of potentially serious drawbacks. The first is the most obvious: most of it reflects exclusively the perspective of one party to the conflict, a party which was besieged and cut off from normal contact with the outside world, and which was under the most extreme military, political, and psychological pressure throughout the war.

While this feature of most of the sources must be borne in mind throughout, in no way does it detract from the value of this material or from the validity of the perspective it represents: that of a main participant in the conflict. Where possible, it has been checked against other sources, and against recollections of non-Palestinian participants in the events, which diminishes this problem somewhat.

Another more specific drawback resides in the nature of the P.L.O. situation reports. These were intended to inform, but also served to exhort combatants and cadres to remain steadfast. They thus often contained rhetoric, verses from the Qur'an, and other material meant to raise morale (although the translations sent by telex and used in this study were considerably less inflated than the originals transmitted in Arabic by the P.L.O. military radio network).

These reports were also at times imprecise, and lacked detail when compared with the diplomatic telex traffic, or even with published WAFA communiques. This is notably true regarding details of the withdrawal negotiations. However, since they were meant for units in the field, there was always a high measure of accuracy in their description of the military situation. It would have been foolish to tell the combatants in the front lines anything but the truth about events occurring before their eyes on a circumscribed battlefield.

As for the diplomatic dispatches sent by telex, their use is associated with all the normal pitfalls facing the diplomatic historian: the bias of those sending them, the possibility that the envoy abroad is not being told the whole story by his superiors (or vice versa), and the chance that truly vital communications are going via another channel.

The latter consideration presents a problem, since telex traffic represented only a portion of the P.L.O.'s wartime diplomatic communications. These also included indirect negotiations which took place in Beirut; radio messages (to those P.L.O. missions with full diplomatic status, and entitled to employ wireless communications); and telephone conversations with foreign leaders and P.L.O. officials abroad, which were frequent at decisive stages of the war.

Little from the latter categories was used in this study. This was unavoidable as regards both telephone and verbal communications. The P.L.O., which usually made transcripts of these, could no do so under conditions of siege (although *procès-verbales* of certain key meetings were drawn up.) The memory of some of those involved had to serve as an imperfect substitute in these cases.

In the case of the radio traffic, transcripts of the material are neither as easily accessible nor as well organized and indexed as the telex traffic. Careful checking determined that most of it duplicated the telex material. Where it did not, little light would have been shed on the key issues in question, as they were generally not treated in these radio communications with P.L.O. offices in Arab, East bloc, and third world states. Certain things mitigate the importance of the gaps resulting from the absence of this material. In the first place, it emerges from a study of the telex traffic that after an early date during the war, virtually all significant messages, whether sent originally by radio, telephone, or telex, were routinely repeated in serial form via telex to important offices abroad.

In addition, key communications with P.L.O. offices in a number of centers (particularly Paris and New York) took place largely by telex. This was due to the need for a written record of what was communicated and for a high degree of textual accuracy regarding documents which were the focus of negotiations, such as Security Council draft resolutions, and the agreement on P.L.O. withdrawal from Beirut. At least one P.L.O. envoy involved stated later that he consciously avoided use of the telephone for these reasons.[11]

Also diminishing the extent of this problem is material gathered during interviews with several of the principals involved. This has provided information on some of what passed verbally during face-to-face negotiations in Beirut and elsewhere, and in diplomatic discussions on the telephone (which was the chosen medium in dealings with some parties).

One further problem with the telex traffic is that it went out *en clair* in English on international telecommunications networks, and was thus definitely subject to interception by the United States and Israel.[12] Those sending and receiving them were aware that their confidential communications were probably being read by the very people they were negotiating with. There is thus at times a certain reticence, or careful circumlocution, about important points in these telexes. On the other hand, this knowledge on the part of the senders often meant that they were drafting their messages as much for their effect on those doing the evesdropping as on the intended recipients.[13]

In spite of these drawbacks, the resulting picture of the negotiations is complete in several respects, although gaps remain. It reveals that the complex quadrilateral diplomacy between the P.L.O., the Lebanese government, the United States, and Israel to end the conflict took place on many levels. While U.S. Presidental envoy Philip Habib was its main focus throughout, there were several complicating factors.

The most serious complication was the multiplicity of channels used in the negotiations, due to the self-imposed prohibition on direct P.L.O.-U.S. contacts, and Habib's frequent relaying of Israeli positions or acting on behalf of Israel, which also refused to recognize the P.L.O. Thus Habib had to negotiate via several intermediaries, generally Lebanese government officials located in West Beirut and in contact with the P.L.O. leadership, or Lebanese military officers. Former Lebanese Premier Sa'eb Salam was also an important conduit for Habib's diplomacy. On the Palestinian side, there were a number of different negotiators at different phases. However, after the initial contacts, all of them belonged to a committee authorized to carry out this task, and all were acting on instructions from the combined P.L.O. leadership, which regularly met to review the talks and issue instructions to its emissaries.[14]

Another complication which was revealed in the course of this research was the existence of a second line of communications between the U.S. and the P.L.O., supplementing the "Habib channel." Starting on June 25 (as far as can be ascertained), the U.S. State Department sent certain important messages for the P.L.O. via the French government. Occasionally other powers and private individuals were used as intermediaries in relaying messages to and from the P.L.O.

Frequently the French alternate channel seems to have been used only for the repetition of messages Habib was delivering in Beirut. But at times it carried either original messages not sent via any other route; or messages which arrived in West Beirut faster than similar ones relayed by Habib via his Lebanese interlocutors; or messages whose content differed slightly from what was being sent via Habib. This was perhaps due to the latter being transmitted through (and presumably distorted by) several sets of mediators.

It is easier to understand why the messages Washington sent Habib, or which he originated or brought with him from Israel, might have been distorted by the time they reached the P.L.O. leadership if the route they took is described. The U.S., or Israeli, or U.S./Israeli, position was generally first transmitted by Habib to officials of the Lebanese government either at the U.S. Ambassador's residence in Yarzé, or at the nearby Presidential Palace in Ba'abda. It was then passed, often by telephone (which was subject to constant breakdowns) to other ministers or to former Premier Salam in West Beirut. This roundabout means of transmission between Lebanese was necessitated by the fact that neither Habib, nor President Elias Sarkis, nor his Foreign Minister Fuad Butros went to West Beirut during the war. At the same time, Premier Shafiq al-Wazzan, Minister Marwan Hamadeh, other Muslim ministers, as well as Sa'eb Salam, often could not or would not go up to Ba'abda after its occupation by the Israelis for reasons of principle, or because heavy fighting blocked roads.

However a message reached Lebanese intermediaries in West Beirut, it was then passed to the P.L.O. official delegated to receive it, who would then take it back to the entire leadership for consideration. During major escalations of the fighting when it was impossible for messengers to go up and down to Ba'abda, or when time was short, the telephone was used for the negotiation of ceasefires and other crucial accords. If the phones were not working and the roads were impassable as a result of the intensity of the combat, as was the case at least three times in August, negotiations ground to a halt.

The potential for distortion in such an extended and tenuous chain of transmission was great, particularly given the extreme strain on those involved in the process. Moreover, most of the Lebanese intermediaries had a major stake in the results of these contacts,[15] while the members of the P.L.O. negotiating team had conflicting views on what should be done and differing understandings of the propositions they had received. This inevitably colored the transmission process, particularly when messages were passed verbally.

In addition to all the above sources of unconscious or unintentional deformation of the original messages, there was also always the possibility of conscious deception, concealed duplicity, and intentional procrastination by any link in the complicated chain of transmission. Possibilities of distortion on the Washington–Paris–West Beirut channel, while clearly less great, also existed. On the one hand, it is perfectly possible that changes of emphasis were added when messages came through Paris, just as they certainly were added, consciously or unconsciously, by the various interested Lebanese parties who served as intermediaries in Beirut. France—a regional power with major interests in Lebanon, and which was deeply engaged in its own dialogue with the P.L.O. leadership throughout the war—was able at the very least to express its opinion on what it was transmitting. It frequently availed itself of this opportunity, often in the strongest terms.

On the other hand, while it was the Americans who initially chose to use the French channel, in time resentment seems to have developed on their part at the special position France had thereby acquired. This resentment was undoubtedly fueled by the overt conflict which developed soon after the war began between the U.S. and French positions on most of the key questions at issue during the conflict. American diplomats thus at times strove to demonstrate that the French were unreliable or were distorting communications. Their apparent intention was to discourage too great P.L.O. reliance on, or confidence in, France. They thus utilized the Paris channel as an emergency backup to Habib's efforts, but did not want it to take precedence over them. This reflected the fear that negotiations would move even slightly out of American hands, where Washington was determined to keep them centered.

As the siege went on, however, the Americans had to reconcile themselves to the fact that at times it was essential, if only for reasons of speed and reliability, that messages sent via Paris play a key role. They had to accept this even if it tended to diminish the importance of Habib, enhance the French role, and bring the P.L.O. ever so slightly closer to its objective of direct contacts with the U.S.

IV Structure and Organization

The P.L.O.'s evacuation from Beirut was not solely a function of defeats on the battlefield, or a result of the unfavorable regional and international balance of forces. Its decision to leave was also strongly influenced by the lack of support from the Lebanese, particularly those in West Beirut, at the outset of the war. Their attitude can be understood only by tracing its roots to the poor state of Lebanese–Palestinian relations in the years immediately preceding the war. This is the subject of chapter 1.

The military situation was a key factor in the decisions taken by the P.L.O., but it is wrong to assume that because the odds against them were so one-sided, and Israel's defeat of their forces in South Lebanon so relatively swift, that the course of the siege of Beirut had little impact on these decisions, and that the P.L.O. was summarily forced to leave, with the only question ever at issue being when and how.[16] This assumptions ignores both the length of time it took to reach a supposedly inevitable conclusion (70 days of fighting, from June 4 until August 12) and the effect on negotiations, time and again, of decisive events on the battlefield. This topic is dealt with in chapters 2 and 3.

Chapters 4 and 5 approach the major issues facing the Palestinian leadership in Beirut chronologically and thematically. These involved demands in mid-June for the P.L.O.'s departure from Beirut, as stipulated in the plan offered by Philip Habib; whether some quid pro quo could be obtained in exchange for acceptance of Habib's proposals, or whether better terms could be negotiated, as was hoped until late July; and after that, whether relatively minor modifications could be made in the plan to meet basic P.L.O. requirements.

Chapter 4 deals with the P.L.O.'s late-June decision to accept the principle of leaving Beirut, and the factors shaping it. These included the poor state of P.L.O.–Lebanese relations, the grave situation on the battlefield during the war's first week, and the absence of external aid for the P.L.O. The chapter then explores the controversy among the besieged sparked by the growing perception in late June that the war was not yet lost, and that better terms could perhaps be obtained. This was closely linked to the efforts of France to achieve a settlement more favorable to the P.L.O.

Chapter 5 examines the decline of P.L.O. hopes, culminating in the decision late in July to accept the Habib terms. It explores the crucial influence on this decision of the actions of Syria and Saudi Arabia, and the role of other factors in leading the P.L.O. to accept an outcome it had resisted for so long. This chapter also focuses on contacts with the U.S. after the P.L.O.'s decision to leave had been taken in principle, and what remained was a question of the terms under which the evacuation would take place. The effect of Israeli actions on the battlefield on the negotiations is also examined.

In conclusion, chapter 6 discusses the aftermath of the war, focusing on the extent of U.S. responsibility for the Sabra/Shatila massacres, on the basis of its commitments to the P.L.O. These included both provisions contained in the published evacuation agreement, and others worked out in the course of the secret contacts. In all the attention devoted to the responsibility of Israel, the Phalangists, and the Lebanese state for the massacres, this U.S. role was largely ignored. The telex correspondence on this matter, together with other documents, show that this tragedy could have been prevented, had repeated explicit P.L.O. warnings been heeded by the United States.

This chapter concludes an account of events which transformed the politics of Lebanon, the Palestinians, and Israel. In Lebanon, the war seemed to give Bashir Gemayel a chance at supreme power. But after his death, hopes of a Maronite ascendancy based on reliance on Israel and the U.S. were shattered, as the country was wracked by continued war and foreign intervention. Yasser 'Arafat and Fateh confronted the first serious challenge to their leadership after the P.L.O. lost its Lebanese base, while facing the daunting problems of the over four million Palestinians it represents. In Israel, major governmental changes were only one effect of the war. Others include a grave economic crisis and a new skepticism among many Israelis regarding an adventurous foreign policy. The chapter is a somber prelude to any study of the consequences of all these changes for U.S. policy and for the region, as well as of possible future implications of this most recent Arab-Israeli war, the first between Israelis and Palestinians.

Chapter 1

The P.L.O.
and the Lebanese
Before the 1982 War

I Turbulence Before the Storm

If the relationship between a successful guerilla army and the society it operates within is accurately described by Mao Zedong's metaphor of "fish swimming in the water," the P.L.O. was flopping helplessly on dry land in Lebanon on the eve of the 1982 war.[1] Pre-war Lebanese alienation from the P.L.O. cannot be measured precisely, but it had certainly become considerable. At the same time, Lebanese public opinion was volatile and subject to constant shifts. As an example, many Lebanese who were bitterly critical of the P.L.O. before June 1982 fought alongside it against overwhelming odds during the war.[2] Nevertheless, the poor state of pre-war Palestinian-Lebanese relations had a vital impact on the P.L.O. when the Israeli invasion began and its foes demanded that it leave Lebanon.

It was of particular importance that immediately before the war this alienation had begun to affect communities and groups traditionally well disposed to the Palestinians and which benefited politically from the P.L.O.'s presence. These included the leftist, nationalist, and Muslim parties of the coalition called the "Lebanese National Movement" (LNM), as well as many Shi'a in south and northeastern Lebanon, Druze in the Shouf Mountains, and Sunnis in the coastal cities.

An indication of how serious the situation had become is that in the months preceding the invasion, there were battles between local factions and P.L.O. units in two strategically vital areas. These were the mainly Sunni port city of Sidon, capital of the muhafaza, or province, of South Lebanon, and several Shi'a villages along the coast road between Sidon and Tyre. Central to P.L.O. defensive dispositions against Israel, both regions were the scenes of fierce fighting when the war broke out. The fighting in the coastal area around Sarafand and 'Adloun first started between militias of the Shi'ite Amal movement and the Lebanese Communist Party, but P.L.O. forces became involved, and were accused of shelling several villages in the course of the battle. Great bitterness was engendered by these and similar incidents in the south and in Shi'a suburbs of Beirut in which P.L.O. factions and Amal were involved, often as a result of fighting between Amal and groups of the LNM such as the Communists or the Iraqi Ba'th party.

In Sidon, clashes between small local groups affiliated with different LNM and P.L.O. factions became endemic in the Old City and the port area. The most serious outbreak in Sidon was in late May between two groups, one linked to Fateh and the other to the LNM, and caused massive property damage in the Old City. The P.L.O.'s promise to pay reparations did not assuage the outrage felt by the population of Sidon. It was little comfort that after the occupation, a few of those responsible for initiating the incidents on both sides were revealed to have been collaborators with the Israelis. Although local Lebanese were involved on both sides of these disputes, and often initiated them, they left the ugly and lasting impression that in South Lebanon, Palestinians were fighting Lebanese. This was exactly the belief hostile propaganda had been assiduously trying to create for many years. The intensely negative impact of these clashes paved the way perfectly for the Israeli invasion of Lebanon.

By this time, traditional Muslim politicians and religious figures had repeatedly made clear their intense irritation with many actions of the P.L.O., as had leaders of the LNM and Amal. One of the most damaging aspects of the May P.L.O.– Amal clashes was the harsh criticism of the P.L.O. by Shaykh Muhammad Mehdi Shams al-Din, Vice Chairman of the Shi'ite Higher Council, broadcast on Lebanese state television just after the fighting ended.[3] As a result, when war began, the P.L.O. found itself opposed by the Maronite militias of the "Lebanese Forces" (LF), and without the support of important sectors of the formerly sympathetic Sunni, Shi'a, and Druze communities.

However, there were major differences between the attitude of the Maronite right and the other forces in the country. While the former had been in open, armed opposition to the Palestinians since the late 1960s, and had ultimately entered into alliance first with Syria and then with Israel to defeat them, most members of the other sects originally looked favorably on the P.L.O.'s presence in Lebanon.

This distinction had practical consequences. On the whole, non-Maronites were reluctant to take up arms against the P.L.O. in spite of grievances against them. This was partly because of the widespread perception that the P.L.O. was needed to balance the power of the dominant Maronites. In addition, there was strong sympathy among Muslims and the left for the Palestinians as refugees and freedom-fighters; the strength of P.L.O. military forces stationed in Muslim areas; and intermarriage between Lebanese and Palestinians, which made relative by marriage loath to resort to arms against one another. The constant pressure of Israel on both Palestinians and Lebanese in South Lebanon reinforced this reluctance.

In view of all this, the clashes in Sidon and the villages along the coastal road on the eve of the war took on great significance: they meant that the P.L.O. had gravely alienated its last allies in Lebanon, and augured badly for its ability to resist the much-awaited Israeli offensive.

II The P.L.O. and the Lebanese Crisis

How had it come about that the P.L.O. was virtually without friends on the eve of its most decisive battle in Lebanon? Welcomed by large sectors of the Lebanese population in the late 1960s, the P.L.O. originally enjoyed extensive popular support. By 1969, however, it had already become deeply involved in Lebanese politics, where its presence polarized even further an already weak and unstable system.[4] While P.L.O. involvement in Lebanese politics was often the result of its own choice it was just as frequently due to its being dragged into internal quarrels by its local allies.

The net effect for Lebanon of the Palestinian armed presence was inevitably negative in the long run, not only because this presence was so destabilizing to the internal Lebanese status quo, but also because it exposed the host country to great danger in view of Israel's enormous power.

Israel had soon after 1967 begun to apply what amounted to a scorched-earth policy in areas of Jordan and Syria where Palestinian commandos were based. Although this approach was firmly rooted in the Israeli military doctrine of punitive retaliation (as this had been refined far earlier than 1967), it was now applied on a much larger scale than ever before.[5] This policy was increasingly applied to South Lebanon as the P.L.O. established itself there. It involved relentless artillery, air, naval and ground attacks, resulting in heavy Lebanese and Palestinian civilian casualties, and generally in negligible losses to the presumed targets, P.L.O. combatants.

The reason for these apparently anomalous results is simple: Israeli attacks were often directed at civilians, with the objective of alienating them from the P.L.O. and exacerbating Palestinian–Lebanese tensions. Israeli attacks on civilians were nothing new. Responding to a reporter's question about attacks on civilians during the 1978 invasion of Lebanon, then-Chief of Staff Gen. Mordechai Gur emphatically affirmed that Israeli forces had carried out such attacks regularly for 30 years, whether in 1948, in 1967–70 along the Canal Zone and the Jordan River Valley, or in Lebanon. He added: "Since when has the population of South Lebanon become so sacred? They knew perfectly well what the terrorists were doing."[6]

Initially, this potentially grave situation did not pose a major problem for the P.L.O. The southerners shared the Arab world's post–June 1967 enthusiasm for the commandos, who were seen as the first Arabs to strike back at Israel. Moreover, the south of Lebanon was bound by traditional ties of trade, shared history, and proximity to northern Palestine. To this was added a special sympathy for the Palestinians, who were perceived by many Shi'a as having taken up arms for a just cause. In the words of a Shi'a shaykh (who preached resistance to the P.L.O., and after 1982 to Israel), initially the Palestinians "were Moslems and fought for a right cause."[7]

As a result, the southerners were generous in their support of the commandos. For many years, the impoverished villagers of the south, neglected by the Lebanese state, continued to shelter and help the P.L.O. in spite of Israel's massive reprisal raids. This welcome eventually wore out, but the increasingly effective partisan warfare waged against Israeli occupation forces in this same region since 1982 can only be understood against the background of these fifteen years of coexistence in adversity.[8]

Although by 1982 the P.L.O. faced a major problem in South Lebanon, opposition to its presence did not originate with the initially supportive southerners. It started with the Maronite-dominated political establishment, which rapidly perceived that the P.L.O. was a formidable potential ally for the disadvantaged, and thus a threat to the status quo. To conservative Lebanese, the P.L.O.'s emergence in the wake of the 1967 defeat suggested a form of politics antithetical to the existing traditional structures which they dominated. The radical ideologies of many Palestinian groups only enhanced this effect.[9]

Not surprisingly, members of have-not sects tended to be more attracted by this vision than were those from sects that benefited the most from the status quo. Further distinctions must be made in this broad scheme. On the whole, the Shi'a and Druze communities, which rightly perceived themselves to be more radically disadvantaged then the Sunnis, were more affected by the impact of the P.L.O.

At the same time, the traditional upper-classes of all three Muslim sects responded quite differently from their rank-and-file followers. The old politicans saw the P.L.O. as an asset in their conventional bargaining process with the Maronite segment of the elite. They thus sought to exploit this new card in the game, although most were to find it hard to control, and came to regret their attempt to do so.

The P.L.O. leadership bore much responsibility for what followed. For while many Lebanese politicians actively sought their aid, at the outset Palestinian leaders were no less active in involving their organizations in Lebanese politics. This was a considered decision, although most failed to realize its full impact on the Lebanese political arena.

However serious its consequences for the P.L.O. and Lebanon, theirs was not an irrational decision. Members of the P.L.O. had arrived in Lebanon after their traumatic expulsion from Jordan in 1970–71 deeply imbued with the idea that the only way to avoid a repetition of what had happened was to surround themselves with sympathetic formations of the Lebanese left. The theory was that these groups would side with them in any confrontation with the authorities or the Israelis. The theory proved correct, at least initially; but not surprisingly, this approach eventually led to problems.

Clashes with the Maronite militias began as early as 1969. Palestinian leaders were soon convinced that a repetition of "Black September" in Jordan was being planned against them in Lebanon. Whatever truth there may have been to such fears, the frantic expansion and intensive armament of the right-wing militias was largely a response both to the growing P.L.O. armed presence, and to the galvanizing effect this had on their local Muslim and leftist rivals.

Naturally, an arms race was soon launched: as time went on the Palestinians and their allies expanded their own militias and increased their level of armament in response to similar preparations on the Maronite side. The country quickly became an armed camp, with both sides training men and importing and distributing arms feverishly.

However, it was not only on the level of arms that the P.L.O. had an effect. Many Lebanese disenchanted with traditional Lebanese politics saw that it provided new avenues to effect their aims, and joined its ranks. A number were idealistic intellectuals, who perceived in the P.L.O. things that were not there. Some were eventually alienated by its failure to live up to their high hopes. Their abandonment of it led to a serious erosion in Lebanese support, while their renewed adhesions in times of crisis (as in 1975–76, 1978, and 1982) brought sudden, unexpected accretions of strength.[10]

Certain others who flocked to the P.L.O.'s banners were less principled, seeing it as an irresistible force, and allying themselves with it on the time-tested principle of "ma al-hait al-waqif" (with the standing wall). In time, as the wall looked less solid, some among them would abandon their support, or even move rapidly to the opposite end of the spectrum. As a result of these two trends, Lebanese popular support for the P.L.O. would often swing up and down dramatically.

This brings us to the heart of the P.L.O.'s problem in Lebanon: any growth of its local strength only multiplied its enemies. At an early stage, its presence was supported by a majority of Lebanese: nearly half a million people, most of them Lebanese, had marched in the funeral cortege of three P.L.O. leaders, Kamal Nasser, Kamal 'Adwan, and Abu Yusuf Najjar, after their assassination by the Israelis in the heart of

Beirut on April 10, 1973.[11] In a country of under three million, such a demonstration constituted an expression of popular emotion which the P.L.O.'s foes could not ignore.

The killing of the three leaders contributed both directly and indirectly to the outbreak of clashes one month later between the commandos and the Lebanese army. Immediately after the Israeli attack, there was violent recimination between Premier Sa'eb Salam and President Suleiman Frangieh over the army commander's refusal to obey Salam's orders to confront the Israelis. Salam resigned in protest, after he had been castigated for the inaction of the state security services by an angry crowd of citizens on the site of one of the attacks.

The existence of widespread mass support for the P.L.O. which the funeral demonstrated was particularly explosive, given that discontent within the Lebanese system was growing. Maronite leaders were deeply disturbed, and began to speak openly of the inevitability of an armed confrontation with the P.L.O. Against this background, the Israeli raid of April 1973 finally pushed the Lebanese army onto the offensive. In May 1973, it surrounded and bombarded the Palestinian refugee camps around Beirut, with negligible results.

Thereafter, the Maronite leaders seem to have felt they had no alternative but to fall back upon their own militias for the task of confronting the P.L.O. They undoubtedly realized the limitations of these forces. However, they apparently hoped that the prospect of "ghuraba" (foreigners) battling Lebanese would bring the army into the conflict in force and on their side. Failing that, the only remaining recourse was the intervention of some foreign power in their favor.

This was the background to the 1975–76 conflict.[12] During its first phases, the Maronite militias repeatedly took the offensive against the stronger P.L.O. and its Lebanese allies. They achieved no decisive result, managing only to overrun, destroy, and depopulate isolated neighborhoods located in predominantly Christian regions and inhabited by poor Lebanese and Palestinians, such as Haret al-Ghawarneh,

Sibnaye, Karantina/Maslakh, and the Dbaye refugee camp. In all of this, the army failed to intervene.

These repeated massacres in the fall and winter of 1975–76, and the January 1976 siege of the large Palestinian refugee camp of Tal al-Za'tar, provoked the P.L.O. and its allies into a counteroffensive. For the first time during the war, regular P.L.O. commando forces moved toward Beirut from Syria and South Lebanon, reaching Kahhale just east of the capital along the Damascus road, and simultaneously opening the coast road closed by the right-wing militias. In the process, the town of Damour was overrun by P.L.O. and LNM forces, with attendant destruction and the shedding of much innocent blood in a cruel massacre.

The "Joint Forces" (JF) of the P.L.O. and LNM had won the military initiative. Their offensive was halted not by Maronite resistance, but by forceful Syrian diplomatic intervention. By the time fighting resumed in the spring of 1976, after a brief lull, the Lebanese Army had shattered under conflicting pressures: its high command and mainly Christian units insistently exhorted by the right to intervene in its favor, and its Muslim units pressed by the LNM to support it.

The JF now carried the war northward toward the Maronite heartland, launching an offensive into the Metn. Success in their quest to rid the country of the Palestinians eluded the Maronite right wing until, by a sort of Phyrric dialectic, its successive defeats led to a severe power imbalance and triggered the intervention of Syria and Israel (respectively overt and covert), in its favor.[13]

The Maronite leaders may have hoped that they could play these two regional rivals off against one another, and thereby make them do their bidding. For a time both powers were willing to go along with them in limiting the ambitions of the P.L.O. and its Lebanese allies. But both soon showed the Maronites how wrong they had been to imagine they could maintain a privileged position in this unwieldy troika.[14]

Contrary to all expectations, the P.L.O. survived the

joint Syrian-Maronite-Israeli onslaught. Indeed it came out of it stronger in some ways. This was in part because it managed to retain the support of much of the Lebanese population in the areas where its forces and offices were located, extending services as government institutions sweemed to wither away.

Already at this early stage, there were mutterings from some Lebanese of P.L.O. heavyhandedness or favoritism. But in the war with the right-wing Maronite parties, the Palestinians were generally seen as aggressed against, and were valued as natural allies, since most of the population perceived these parties to be a threat to them as well. Indiscrimate massacres of Lebanese Muslims, such as the bloody "Black Saturday" killings in the heart of Beirut in December 1975, or the bombardment of residential neighbourhoods (practiced by both sides) only reinforced such attitudes.

Even the Syrian intervention did not not seem to undermine Lebanese popular support for the P.L.O. Many Lebanese were impressed by the ability of the JF to stand up to the combined Syrian-rightist offensive for five months in 1976 while enduring an Israeli naval blockade, and to emerge intact with a narrower but still ample margin within which to maneuver. In spite of its defeat, the P.L.O. was seen by a sizable constitutency as a powerful independent force deeply involved in the Lebanese system, which could be relied upon to help right any imbalance caused by Maronite dependence on external help, and to balance the powerful Syrian presence.

However, the war was by no means a victory for the P.L.O. and the LNM, and resulted in a new situation. The postwar settlement was hammered out in October 1976 at the Riyad mini-summit (attended by the Saudi, Kuwaiti, Egyptian, Syrian, P.L.O. and Lebanese leaders) and then consecrated at the subsequent Cairo summit. By its terms, Syria's position in Lebanon was legitimized and its forces became the "Arab Deterrent Forces" (ADF). Regular P.L.O. commando units were withdrawn from Lebanon's cities, where they had been moved beginning in January 1976, and sent back to the south. On their arrival there, the JF found that Israel had set up a militia under former Lebanese Army Major Sa'ad Haddad as local surrogates, which were expanding their area of control into mainly Shi'a areas so as to create a buffer zone north of the Israeli border. In view of this alarming development, the P.L.O., the Syrians, and the LNM were impelled to reconcile their differences.

There were still scores to settle, however. Heavy fighting occurred in Beirut in February 1977 between Syrian and P.L.O. forces. Kamal Jumblatt, head of the LNM, was assassinated the following month; and Colonel Sa'id Musa (Abu Musa), commander of the JF in their defense of Sidon against the Syrians, was shot and wounded in Nabatiyeh, both allegedly at Syrian instigation. Nevertheless, in view of the growing Israeli presence in the south, relations between the three parties were soon normalized, at least to the point that minimal cooperation between them became possible.[15]

III The War for South Lebanon Begins

With the end of the 1975–76 fighting, a new phase commenced. This was the war for South Lebanon, which was still raging at the time of this writing. It was during this post-1976 phase that the P.L.O.'s problems with its Lebanese allies became acute. These problems developed for many reasons. The most basic was that in time most Lebanese, especially those exposed to the brunt of Israel's firepower, ceased to believe that the P.L.O. was achieving anything positive with its presence in the south, or whether this was worth its high cost.

This was not always the case. After the 1967 war, most Lebanese accepted the presence of the commandos, who were perceived as being in the vanguard of a pan-Arab war of attrition against Israel. Even after Black September in 1970 closed the Jordanian frontier to attacks against Israel, after that of Syria was closed by the 1974 disengagement accord, and after Sadat moved toward peace with Israel, there was little diminution of Lebanese support for the P.L.O. This was partly because it came to be a valuable ally for some Lebanese in their internecine conflicts.

But the five years after the return of P.L.O. forces to South Lebanon in the fall of 1976 were bitter ones for its people. In one period of under six months in 1979, there were 175 Israeli land, sea, and air attacks on the area. Villages were hit repeatedly, their residents made refugees time and again, and it became difficult to see what they or the P.L.O. were achieving from this war of attrition in which civilians paid the main price.

Unlike Palestinians, whether combatants or civilians, South Lebanese villagers at this time felt neither that their very existence as a people was threatened, nor that they had no choice but to fight. Israel was an enemy to be feared, but the P.L.O. presence was increasingly perceived as responsible for having brought this evil down on their heads with such force.

Southerners came in time to believe that they were being involved unwillingly in a conflict which was not their own. Unsuprisingly, their wrath was directed not at the distant, awesome Israelis who tormented them, but rather at the immediate cause of their problems, the Palestinians, who were close at hand and clearly all-too-mortal. P.L.O. failings as regards respect for life and property, which grew to alarming proportions after 1976, reinforced such attitudes.

This summary description encapsulates an agonizing five-year process as families were repeatedly uprooted, driven from their villages to Beirut, and then back again by fighting there, in an unending cycle. By 1982, most southerners were willing to accept nearly any solution which promised relief from their agony of bombardment, flight, and mortal peril.

IV The Transformation of the P.L.O. into a Para-State

Together with what was happening in the south, Lebanese had to contend with a transformation of the P.L.O. which made it harder for them to maintain their earlier supportive attitude toward it. Starting as a radical, ascetic, semiclandestine guerrilla movement, which arrived in Lebanon in the late 1960s riding a wave of popularity throughout the Arab world, the P.L.O. changed beyond recognition in less than ten years.

P.L.O. Chairman Yasser 'Arafat was now a head of state in all but name, more powerful than many Arab rulers. His was no longer a humble revolutionary movement, but rather a vigorous para-state, with a growing bureaucracy administering the affairs of Palestinians everywhere, and with a budget bigger than that of many small sovereign states. Its role in Lebanon had also changed profoundly, as had Lebanese attitudes toward it.

The initial Lebanese perception of the P.L.O. as an ally motivated by feelings of solidarity for the downtrodden sectors of Lebanese society had disappeared by the end of the 1970s. It was replaced by a view of the Palestinians as motivated by self-interest, sometimes to the exclusion of Lebanese interests, sometimes even at their expense.

Most Lebanese were disturbed by the seeming solidity of the P.L.O. "mini-state" in Lebanon, including parts of the north, the south and the Biqa' Valley, and with its "capital" in the Fakhani–Arab University area of West Beirut. These included many who remained basically well-disposed toward the P.L.O. For there was a permanence about its presence which seemed to indicate that the Palestinians contemplated an extended stay in Lebanon, and welcomed an indefinite prolongation of the existing situation.

To Lebanese who found that situation distressing, the fact that the Palestinians were relatively comfortable with it, and indeed stood to lose if it were changed, was intolerable. For Lebanese, the crisis which had begun in 1975 was the worst period in their country's history. On the other hand, in spite of the numerous dangers facing them, until 1982 Palestinians could look on their situation in Lebanon as marking a high point in the re-creation of their national identity.

Not surprisingly, given these widely differing perspectives, many in Lebanon came to accept in some measure the insidious argument that the P.L.O.'s objective in creating a "state within a state" in Lebanon was permanent settlement there. Ironically, the Arabic word used—*tawtin*—comes from the same root as that employed to describe Zionist settlement in Palestine—*istitan*.

To anyone within the P.L.O., such reasoning seemed absurd: Palestinians felt profoundly insecure in Lebanon, knew they were outsiders there, and most importantly, were deeply committed to the idea of returning to their homeland. They dismissed out of hand the idea of an "alternative homeland" in Lebanon. But in doing so, they failed to appreciate Lebanese fears fully: the basis for them could be seen in the proliferation of the P.L.O.'s offices, the growth of its para-state services, and its increasing military might.

This entity did not grow up as a result of any clear plan. A comparison of the size of the P.L.O. bureaucracy and the services it offered before and after 1975–76 reveals that the war, and the demands it imposed on the P.L.O., were the main impetus for this growth.[16] The reason was simple: as the U.N. relief agency UNRWA and the Lebanese state ceased to provide services during this prolonged conflict, and as the number of casualties mounted, it became imperative that medical and social services be extended to both Lebanese and Palestinians if morale was to be kept up and the war effort maintained.

At the same time, as vital services affecting the whole society (like telephones, electricity, security, and food and fuel supply) broke down during the war, it was increasingly the P.L.O. which moved into the breach. It often did so unwillingly, but no end of Lebanese resentment was caused by the provision of these services, even where Lebanese experts called upon by the P.L.O. did most of the actual work (as with the efforts to maintain electrical and telephone service). It is thus ironic that the 1975–76 war waged against the P.L.O. by its Lebanese and foreign foes was a primary impetus in the expansion of its presence in Lebanon, which later on became the focus of so much of their criticism.

Several strands were involved here. On the one hand, it was annoying for Lebanese to see the P.L.O. running things, although they would have complained bitterly had it not done so and the situation worsened as a result. In fact, the P.L.O. was in an acute dilemma: when the Organization was too active it provoked charges the Palestinians were taking over the country; when it was not active enough there were complaints that the deterioration of the situation was the P.L.O.'s fault.

On the other hand, the LNM, which might have been expected to provide services in the absence of the state, failed to do so. One reason was the division and disunity that prevailed in the LNM, which was made up of numerous disparate groups, parties, factions, and personalities. More serious was that its leaders could not decide whether they wanted to replace the existing state structure with a new one, take its place temporarily, reform it, or do nothing. Their indecision did not decrease Lebanese popular resentment of the P.L.O. for acting in their stead.

After the temporary calming of the situation in the fall of 1976, most of these central services reverted to the state or other Lebanese agencies, but the impact of the P.L.O.'s wartime extension of its authority lingered on.[17] Moreover, the P.L.O. was now completely in control of the provision of extensive services in the Palestinian refugee camps, and often in their environs. This provided a constant reminder of Palestinian autonomy and power, which contrasted strikingly with the weakness of the Lebanese state. Another contrast was provided by the well-financed operations of the P.L.O.

This phenomenon was of great importance. Many Lebanese were alienated from a now-prosperous movement which they had once supported partly because of its revolutionary asceticism. More important, this wealth seriously corrupted the ideals and practices of the P.L.O. itself, turning many of its cadres into employees, and further offending the Lebanese.

The flow of funds into P.L.O. coffers had increased markedly following the 1974 Rabat Arab summit resolution recognizing the Organization as sole legitimate representative of the Palestinian people, and urging Arab states to support it. As the oil boom made them wealthier, many of these states translated their support into growing financial contributions to the P.L.O., and often to Fateh in particular.[18]

The effects were twofold. On the one hand, this money, together with funds the P.L.O. generated from its own sources, such as voluntary taxes on Palestinian emigres, contributions from rich Palestinians, and extensive investments, made possible the expansion of vital services. An example was the growth of the Palestine Red Crescent Society (PRCS) from a one-hospital institution on the eve of the 1975–76 war to an extensive system centered in Lebanon but extending to other Arab countries, including Egypt and Syria. By 1980 the PRCS had nine hospitals in Lebanon, with 684 beds and 637 employees, as well as twelve camp clinics. In the first six months of the following year, it treated 425,682 patients. Over 40 percent of the unaffiliated civilian cases treated during this period were non-Palestinians.[19]

On the other hand, much money was put to considerably less worthwhile purposes. Before the 1982 war it was a prime grievance of reformers within and critics without the P.L.O. that corruption and gross waste of funds were commonplace in many branches of the Organization. Some of this was a result of the practice of throwing money at problems, which originated during the feverish wartime atmosphere of 1975–76 and continued in ensuing years, with devastating results.

Most harmful in terms of relations with the Lebanese was the spectacle of individual Palestinian officials who had grown rich, or had obtained a luxurious apartment, expensive car, and armed bodyguards because of their involvement with the P.L.O. This offended both Palestinians and Lebanese, who were being asked to accept sacrifices in the name of the

Palestine cause, and could not understand how some were not only exempt from such sacrifices, but actually prospered.

Furthermore, the disorder and insecurity in Beirut and the south after 1976 was generally blamed on the P.L.O., which admitted many of these violations (*tajawuzat*). In time, this issue was effectively picked up by the P.L.O.'s opponents, particularly the Phalange, whose powerful "Voice of Lebanon" radio had a large audience throughout the country. Its propaganda was based on reality, but many "violations," whether crimes or heavyhanded behavior by armed men at roadblocks, were the work of agents provocateurs or thugs with no relation to the P.L.O. Nevertheless it was blamed for them.

The issue of "*tajawazat*" became a major sore point with Lebanese public opinion, a legitimate, pressing concern which neither the leadership nor the cadres of the P.L.O. ever fully appreciated. This was far from being a marginal issue. It involved major structural problems of discipline, motivation, and organization attendant on the P.L.O.'s transformation into a para-state in the mid-1970s. Their persistence without any serious attempts at resolution cut deeply into Lebanese and Palestinian popular support for the P.L.O. as time went on.

In spite of P.L.O. efforts to limit its armed presence in inhabited areas, people blamed it for the prevailing near-anarchy more than they did the Syrians and the LNM, who were at least as responsible. This was inevitable in view of the P.L.O.'s clear preeminence in much of the country. It was only aggravated by the stationing of large P.L.O. standing forces in the cities awaiting an Israeli attack which P.L.O. leaders repeatedly warned was imminent.[20]

V The P.L.O.'s Military Buildup

The P.L.O.'s problems with Lebanese public opinion were compounded by its growing military power after P.L.O. main-force units had returned to south Lebanon in 1976. The situation there and around Beirut was changed fundamentally

soon afterward by a renewed confrontation between Syria and
the LF (an event linked to the cementing of their alliance with
Israel) as well as by Israel's stepped-up offensive in the
south.

After Syrian-Maronite relations soured, the Palestinian
strategic assumption had been that the ADF would provide the
primary defense of the Beirut area against any possible attack
by the LF, and that the P.L.O. could concentrate on the Israeli/
Sa'ad Haddad threat in the south. Events in 1978 changed that
asssumption. In spring of that year, Israel invaded and
occupied a large area north of its border, which it handed over
to its client forces before withdrawing. Simultaneously, relations between the Syrians and their erstwhile Maronite allies
deteriorated to the point of open fighting. The LF were
ultimately victorious, driving the Syrians out of East Beirut and
the coastal region to the north in fall of 1978. This opened the
way for full-scale Israeli–Maronite military cooperation, including the unrestricted importation of arms via the various
ports now fully controlled by the rightist militias. As a result,
the P.L.O. was now faced with the nightmare prospect which
was to haunt it until it became reality in 1982: an Israeli
hammer coming up from the south and driving it against the
anvil of East Beirut. In addition, it was transparently clear that
Syrian support for the P.L.O. in such circumstances would be
extremely limited, as would that of the U.S.S.R.

Both powers had reacted only verbally to the 1978
invasion, and few in the P.L.O. had illusions about what could
be expected of them in the future. The Soviets were careful to
make the limits of their support explicit to the P.L.O. In formal
and informal meetings, they stressed repeatedly that they could
not and would not do anything on its behalf which violated
Lebanese sovereignty, or had not been formally requested by
the legitimate Lebanese authorities.[21]

At the same time, the Soviets repeatedly affirmed to
Damascus that they were unwilling and unable to assist Syrian
forces inside Lebanon, and that any guarantees they might
extend would apply only to Syrian territory. The P.L.O. was

made aware of this. It was thus was able to factor into its calculations the cautious reluctance of both Moscow and Damascus to confront Israel and the U.S. on its behalf in such circumstances.

All of this helps to explain why the P.L.O. made its next military moves. In the four years leading up to the 1982 war, it proceeded to upgrade its forces in the south in terms of weaponry and numbers, and transformed them into something closer to a regular army. In preparation for the expected confrontation with Israel, the P.L.O. command stockpiled large quantities of equipment and supplies throughout the country, and stationed significant reserve forces in rear areas, particularly in and around Beirut.[22]

Work also commenced at this time on a chain of underground command posts in Beirut. A few came to be relatively well known and were used for routine business and even meetings with outsiders, but most were kept secret and remained unused. This process was accelerated after Israel's aerial bombing of the Fakhani district of Beirut in July 1981. These headquarters-bunkers, scattered throughout the city, were to have decisive importance during the siege of the capital.

When this buildup was completed—or rather was interrupted by the Israeli invasion—the resulting force was far from formidable insofar as Israel was concerned.[23] The heavy arms acquired were obsolete for the most part (e.g., World War II-vintage T-34 tanks and Katyusha rocket launchers). The P.L.O. was able to acquire little technically advanced equipment (which might have made a difference against Israel) such as guided surface-to-surface missiles, anti-ship missiles, or advanced radar-guided surface-to-air weapons.

Nevertheless, the effect of this development was highly visible, particularly in the cities, where the new weapons and the new formations put into the field enabled the P.L.O. to rival the ADF and more than match the LF. In some sense, this was the aim of these measures. After withdrawals of the ADF from East Beirut in 1978 and most of West Beirut in 1980, and the cementing of the Israeli–Maronite alliance, it was necessary for the P.L.O. to prepare for war on three fronts.

In and of itself this might not have been such a problem. However, it was a factor in a new series of conflicts with the Syrians, who could not accept that the P.L.O., humbled in 1976, was once again an independent force to be reckoned with throughout Lebanon. It also led to difficulties with the LNM, which chafed at the heavyhandedness with which the Palestinians, with their newfound military strength, interfered in Lebanese affairs.

Lebanese Muslims and leftists, who had fought with the P.L.O. against the Syrians in 1976, now came to feel that it was becoming just as overbearing as Syria had ever been. There was resentment at the way the P.L.O. leadership played off one Lebanese faction against the other, at the support extended to numerous small Lebanses groups, and at 'Arafat's single-handed domination of both P.L.O. and LNM through his command of the JF. At times these practices were as willful and cynical as they seemed. At others, the P.L.O. was caught between competing Lebanese allies or conflicting demands, and any option it chose made it look bad.

Following the murder of the head of the LNM, Kamal Jumblatt, in 1977, this problem was magnified by the absence of a strong leader enjoying unchallenged authority among Lebanese leftists and Muslims. Jumblatt was probably the only Lebanese figure who more than held his own with 'Arafat and the Palestinian leadership. His death, combined with the growth in military strength of the P.L.O., led to a thoroughly imbalanced relationship.

VI The Last Straw for Israel—July 1981

The P.L.O. thus found itself in an unenviable situation on the eve of the 1982 war. Long hated by the Phalangists, now in open alliance with Israel against them, it had succeeded in amassing a daunting set of new opponents. Traditional

Lebanese Muslim politicians resented the P.L.O. for its alliance with radical leftist challengers to their authority, while LNM leaders were unhappy with what they saw as P.L.O hegemony over them. Beyond the grievances of its leaders, Lebanese public opinion was affected by Phalangist propaganda (which seconded that of Israel), much of which it found believable. The net effect was to isolate the P.L.O. dangerously on the eve of its biggest battle ever.

It is worth asking at this point what the P.L.O. leadership was doing to meet this impending peril. Aside from military preparations, which we have already touched on, their efforts seemed to have focused primarily on the international level, at the expense of local and regional considerations which were perhaps even more vital.

Thus the P.L.O. was careful from the outset to cooperate with the U.N. Interim Force in Lebanon (UNIFIL), stationed in South Lebanon after the Israeli invasion of 1978. It did so even though at one stage this involved forcibly suppressing the activities of P.L.O. and Lebanese leftist groups which were opposed to the ceasefire accepted by 'Arafat and the P.L.O. leadership after that conflict.[24]

Similarly, in the wake of nearly six months of escalating cross-border hostilities launched by Israel in 1979 after the signing of the Egyptian-Israeli peace treaty,[25] the P.L.O. accepted an internationally mediated ceasefire, and enforced compliance on its various constituent groups. The result was nearly two years of relative quiet along the Lebanese-Israeli frontier, which lasted until the summer of 1981, when perhaps the most significant P.L.O. effort to appear "responsible" in the eyes of the international community took place.

The 1981 crisis began with a Syrian-Israeli confrontation in April in the Biqa' Valley. This was provoked by attempts by the LF, supported by Israel, to build a road to Zahle and thus establish themselves athwart the lines of communication of Syrian forces to the West.[26] This phase of the crisis ended after the installation of Syrian SAM-6 missiles in the Biqa', as U.S.

Presidential envoy Philip Habib's mediation in effect froze the situation on the ground rather than resolving it.

Israel then turned its attention to South Lebanon, which had already been attacked during the spring round of fighting. As part of the muscle-flexing which accompanied and followed the Israeli election campaign (and of which the Zahle crisis and the June bombing of the Iraqi nuclear reactor were part) the Israeli armed forces on July 10, 1981 launched a major new series of unprovoked attacks against P.L.O. positions, as well as refugee camps and villages in the south.[27]

The Israelis were suprised by what happened next. Instead of simply fading away as they usually did when Israel attacked, the P.L.O.'s artillery and rocket units responded in kind to the Israeli bombardments. Over thirty Israeli military bases, kibbutzes, villages, and towns were hit again and again, in spite of the most intensive Israeli efforts to destroy the guns and rocket launchers which were doing the firing.[28]

Israel then escalated, hitting the bridges connecting the south with the rest of the country. The P.L.O. not only kept up its barrage against northern Galilee, but was able to replace the bridges or devise alternate routes, keeping the flow of supplies and people moving in both directions. Infuriated, the Israelis bombed apartment buildings in the heart of the Fakhani district on July 24, 1981. The paradoxical result was a de facto P.L.O.-Israel ceasefire mediated by the U.N., the Saudi government, and Philip Habib.

The Begin government, incapable of imposing its will on the P.L.O. on the battlefield, was now in effect forced to accept it as a party to a ceasefire. This new reality was perceived by all concerned, although elaborate explanations were issued by both the U.S. and Israel to the effect that they were neither recognizing the P.L.O. nor dealing with it directly. In fact, intensive indirect Israeli–U.S.–P.L.O. negotiations were carried on through the medium of the U.N. and the Saudi government, a precedent for the 1982 war.

For the P.L.O. leadership, this was a high point. Their forces had successfully stood up to Israel militarily for nearly two weeks, they had been grudgingly recognized as a party at the negotiating table, and they were now committed to an internationally mediated ceasefire, which they observed scrupulously for nearly a year. All seemed to be for the best in the best of all possible worlds. In reality, it was the calm before the storm.

No Israeli government could be expected to tolerate such a situation for long, especially after what had happened to Galilee. Israel's policy since 1956, when Moshe Sharett left the cabinet, had been predicated on intimidating the Arabs.[29] If the puny P.L.O. did not fear the might of Israel, what of more serious opponents?

The entry of Ariel Sharon into the Begin cabinet in August 1981 settled the issue, if ever it had been in doubt. It meant that Israel would launch a full-scale war against the Palestinians at the earliest feasible opportunity, so as to prevent this new situation from becoming permanent, and perhaps to create new strategic realities in the region.[30]

And while the P.L.O.'s leaders were basking in the glow of a backhanded sort of international recognition, what of their alliances? The general positions of the USSR and Syria in case of a major Israeli offensive were known. But instead of trying to improve relations with Syria, the only Arab power with the ability to affect the situation on the ground, for better or worse, 'Arafat and the Fateh leadership were locked in a bitter dispute with it.

This conflict, which had its roots in the longstanding desire of the Syrian regime of President Hafez al-Asad to establish its control over the P.L.O., had been seriously aggravated by recent quarrels. Among other things, these had to do with the Fahd plan (a stillborn Saudi project for a Middle East settlement named for the Saudi Crown Prince, drawn up in collaboration with the P.L.O., but ignoring Damascus), and alleged Fateh backing for domestic enemies of the Ba'athist government and for opponents of the ADF in Tripoli and elsewhere in Lebanon. All the specific issues in dispute were symptomatic of a deep malaise in Palestinian–Syrian relations.[31]

The P.L.O. leadership apparently calculated that Asad was irremediably hostile, and in any case was not about to make any military or strategic sacrifices on behalf of the P.L.O. if it was attacked. They thus seem to have chosen to do as in 1978 and 1981: rely on their own resources to hang on as long as possible, while depending on Saudi mediation with the U.S. to halt the Israelis eventually. This option was based on the wishful assumption, grounded in past experience, that the U.S. would be reluctant to let Israel go all the way.

What they did not calculate was that they were dealing with a Begin-Sharon government, which was much more determined than any before it to finish off the job; that the P.L.O.'s military and diplomatic performance in July 1981 gave the Israelis all the more incentive for doing so; that the Saudis had little real leverage with the Americans; and that Washington was no longer willing or able to urge restraint on Israel.[32] Most ominous, as we have seen, was that the Palestinians had used up the last of the seemingly inexhaustible fund of Lebanese patience and forbearance which had served them in such good stead in the past.

The population of the south and the cities of the littoral had been briefly buoyed up by the creditable performance of the P.L.O. in the July 1981 fighting. They were brought back to reality when they contemplated the results of Israel's bombing of the south and of Beirut itself. The latter was a massive attack which completely destroyed several buildings and left behind hundreds of casualties, most of them Lebanese civilians. Once again, the civilian population was being made to pay the price in this unequal Israeli-Palestinian war fought on Lebanese soil.

More generally, most Lebanese were fed up with their country's intolerable situation, and were desperate for a solution. The only voice which offered a clear change was that of the Voice of Lebanon. It told them incessantly that all their problems were the fault of the Palestinians, could be resolved if the P.L.O. were disposed of, and that there now existed those willing and able to do the job.

The P.L.O. was thus in a highly vulnerable position in Lebanon when Sharon finally unleashed the much-awaited "Operation Peace for Galilee": isolated from the local population and without strong backers, its opponents must have felt that no better time could be chosen for their offensive. Events in the first half of June would appear to bear out this assessment.

Chapter 2

The Occupation
of South Lebanon
and the Siege of Beirut:
A Military Overview

I The Importance of the Military

The untold story of the 1982 war is how over a period of ten weeks, generals who had never lost a battle, and who had at their disposal a potential force of half a million men in 70 army brigades, 8000 armored vehicles, more than 550 combat aircraft and 90 naval vessels, and the best weapons in the world,[1] proved unable—using a considerable part of this force—to decisively defeat less than 15,000 men, mostly poorly armed militia, supported for less than two weeks by part of the Syrian army.

In many ways, this was the most difficult war ever waged by either of its two protagonists, as well as the longest and one of the costliest of Arab–Israeli wars. Militarily, it was unique in many ways. It was the first full-scale Palestinian–Israeli war; it was the first Arab–Israeli war involving extended military operations in urban terrain; and it was the only one not to come to a decisive conclusion. The numerous writings already devoted to military aspects of the topic attest to the interest it has already generated.[2]

Although a comprehensive assessment of this war's strategy and tactics is beyond the scope of a study of P.L.O. decisionmaking, there are two good reasons for beginning such a study with a careful look at events on the battlefield during the summer of 1982. The first has already been cited: the course of the fighting was a major element in the background against which P.L.O. decisions were taken, and at times was the decisive input in these decisions.

The second is that any account of what the P.L.O. did and why must at least touch on the military expectations and performance of a movement which was partly militarized, and described itself as dedicated to a strategy of armed struggle. This is particularly important here since, although many Israelis and some foreign military analysts have already written on the subject, relatively little attention has so far been devoted to it from the Palestinian side.

The pre-war expectations of Israel and the P.L.O. are the central element in assessing the fighting. Because it was obvious from the outset that the two sides were so unevenly matched that the Israelis could not possibly have "lost," and that the Palestinians could not possibly have "won," what must be weighed is how much better, or worse, each side's performance matched their own—and others'—expectations. Moreover, since the invasion was neither hastily planned by the Israelis, nor a surprise to the P.L.O., the extent to which the two sides foresaw correctly and planned for what was to come must also be judged.

II "Operation Peace for Galilee" in Retrospect

As its name indicates, "Operation Peace for Galilee" was supposed to remove hostile forces forever from Israel's northern borders, smash the military capabilities of the P.L.O., expel its fighters from Lebanon, and eliminate the allied Lebanese leftist and Muslim militias. At this writing, the full measure of its failure on every count is readily apparent.

P.L.O. attacks deep inside Israel and in the occupied West Bank and Gaza Strip have not been halted. In spite of over 4500 Israeli military casualties, including 655 soldiers killed, rockets have crashed into Galilee several times, Israeli warplanes have attacked alleged targets in Lebanon over twenty times since January 1984, and there remained the constant fear that Shi'ite and Druze militias in areas just north of Israeli lines would allow the return of Palestinian guerrillas. Israel must now deal with Shi'ite hostility engendered by the occupation of South Lebanon, which may last even after its withdrawal, leaving a new and intractable problem on its northern frontiers.[3]

For three years after the invasion, the only immediately apparent difference from the pre-war situation was that Israeli lines were deep inside Lebanon rather than a few miles north of the border in the Haddad zone. It was thus far easier to attack Israeli forces spread out in Lebanon than it was when it was necessary to penetrate Israel's well-guarded frontiers. Moreover, those carrying out such attacks were more likely to be Lebanese than Palestinians.

Beyond the fact that there is no peace in Galilee, there has been deep unease in Israel at the meager results of the war. Reflecting this mood, an Israeli journalist recently wrote: "Israel is ... smarting from the effects of a misadventure whose likes it has never experienced in its history and whose conclusion appears to be beyond its ken." And in the words of former Foreign Minister Abba Eban, the war has cost more Israeli lives "than all the world's terrorists had been able to inflict on Israelis in all the decades ... "[4]

However, the failure of "Operation Peace for Galilee" goes far beyond the objectives implied by the war's shrewdly chosen code name, since those who planned it had set their sights much farther afield. Of course, Galilee's demonstrated vulnerability to P.L.O. bombardment during the 1981 fighting placed the issue of the safety of the area's inhabitants foremost in the Israeli public mind, and made this a major domestic political issue.

But for Begin, his fellow ministers, and Israel's senior generals, war was necessary because of three things, only indirectly related to Galilee, which they found intolerable: (1) the P.L.O.'s exploitation of its commitment to the ceasefires— which ended cross-border fighting in March 1978, August 1979, and July 1981—allowed it to pose as a responsible political actor and demand participation in international negotiations; (2) the P.L.O.'s ability in July 1981 to defy Israel militarily, in spite of the vast military disparity between them, had enhanced its political and diplomatic stature; (3) these new realities had an effect on the West Bank and other occupied Palestinian areas the Likud government was committed to annex.

Their aim was thus not simply to drive back the P.L.O. from the border region, thereby making Galilee "safe" for its Israeli inhabitants. It was rather to destroy utterly the P.L.O., thus making the West Bank and Gaza Strip "safe" for annexation. Shattering both the P.L.O.'s military power and its claim to be a major political actor would end the danger that Israel might at some stage be forced to negotiate with it, and thus come to terms with Palestinian nationalism. "Operation Peace for Galilee" was in a very real sense a war for the future disposition of Palestine.[5]

Over and above this basic aim, the planners of the invasion had other objectives, which went far beyond Galilee or any other part of Palestine.[6] Lebanon, under Syrian influence but badly divided internally since 1976, was to be reunited under Israel's ally, Bashir Gemayel, and brought under Israeli domination. Syria, which had defied Israel during the 1981 missile crisis, was to be defeated, expelled from central Lebanon, and thereby cut down to size. In consequence, Syria's backer, the USSR, was to be pushed further out of the region, while the rest of the Arab states were to be taught an object lesson about the might of Israel.

Reviewing these far-reaching objectives today, it is obvious that, on the strategic level, Israel's war in Lebanon has been a fiasco. What will concern us most in this chapter, however, are those aspects of Israeli objectives which were apparent at the time, and which most influenced decision-making during the war. These were the tactical and operational levels: the progress of units in the field, and the overall battlefield strategic situation.

Even here, it is possible in retrospect to see major failures on the part of the Israelis, in spite of their over-whelming military superiority. These shortcomings had a significant impact on the course of the P.L.O.'s decision-making, its indirect negotiations with the U.S. and Israel, and ultimately affected negatively the latter's ability to reach its strategic objectives.

As in all of its wars, if Israel were to achieve its aims on every military and political level, the key lay in the ability of its troops in the field to win a rapid, indisputable, and psycho-logically overwhelming triumph. It was not enough for the "Israeli Defense Forces" (IDF), arguably the best, and very likely the third or fourth most powerful army in the world,[7] simply to beat the P.L.O. For both the grand strategic plan and the day-to-day operational plans to succeed, it was essential that in virtually every battle, P.L.O. forces, those of the LNM, and Syrian units in Lebanon be routed, and their men either killed, captured, or sent streaming in flight, sowing panic before them.

Because of the pressing need for speedy execution, this collapse of enemy will was an absolute prerequisite for the success of the Israeli war plan, but it did not happen. The reasons are at the root of the failure of Israel in Lebanon, both operationally and strategically. To understand why, it is necessary to go back to the beginning.

III The Four Phases of the 1982 War

From a Palestinian perspective, the 1982 war can be divided into four phases. The first, the battle of South Lebanon, lasted only from June 4 to 9. The second, involving the encirclement of Beirut, was also short, ending on June 13 with the arrival of Israeli troops at Ba'abda in the city's eastern suburbs. The third phase, which lasted from June 14 to 26, was marked by the battle for the control of the mountains overlooking the Lebanese capital. It was followed by the last phase, the siege of Beirut, which continued until the August 12 ceasefire.

The first phase of the 1982 war encompassed Israel's swift penetration of South Lebanon along multiple axes, combined with heliborne and amphibious landings at key points deep behind the front lines. The main objective in this phase was for units driving up the coast road to link up with others landed from the sea north of Sidon, thus preparing a jumping-off point for an advance toward Beirut. According to one account, "three Israeli divisional forces" were involved in this coastal push.[8] At the same time, other columns advanced through the mountains and up the Biqa' Valley in the central and eastern sectors of the front.

The initial phase took the better part of three days of ground combat. These were preceded by two days of massive "softening-up" bombardments from air, land, and sea directed at Beirut, the coastal region down to the border, and large areas of South Lebanon, beginning on June 4. (This was the day the war actually started, although the invasion was launched only at midday on June 6.) This phase ended when a linkup between Israeli armored colums advancing from the south and troops landed at the Awwali River bridgehead was effected east of Sidon, around midday on June 9.

The second phase consisted of a continuation of the drive up the coast toward Beirut, combined with another through the mountains to cut the east–west roads linking the capital to the Biqa' valley and Damascus.[9] In this stage also, the ground push was supported by seaborne and heliborne forces which cut off JF or Syrian positions which were holding up the ground advance. Simultaneously, Syrian forces in the Biqa' to the east were pushed back by tank columns advancing north up the valley, after Syrian air defences had been badly battered by the Israeli air force.

The advance was only briefly interrupted by a deceptive ceasefire, described by Israel as applying to Syrian forces only, which the IDF used to move troops up for another push, while fighting continued unabated with the P.L.O. The second phase concluded on June 13 with the arrival of Israeli troops at the Lebanese Presidential Palace at Ba'abda on the eastern outskirts of Beirut, and the consequent encirclement of the city. Israeli forces in the mountains and the Biqa' also reached positions to the south of the Beirut–Damascus highway in a number of places, not quite managing to gain control of the road itself.

Although Beirut was now surrounded and under heavy Israeli bombardment, the next phase was not an assault on the city, but rather a series of attacks culminating in a major assault on June 21 to expel Syrian and P.L.O. forces from Bhamdoun and other mountain towns along the main road to Damascus. Although Bhamdoun and 'Aley were taken, Syrian troops held on to Sofar, farther along the road in the mountains to the east. With the ceasefire five days later which marked the end of this operation, Syria was out of the war, and its forces had been pushed well back from Beirut.

The final and longest phase of the war, the seven-week siege of the P.L.O in the western sector of Beirut, now began in earnest. This involved intensive air, naval, and artillery bombardments and agressive psychological warfare directed both against the defenders of the city and its civilian population, and included calculated pressure on the morale of the besieged via the cutting off of food, water, and electricity.

Long periods of what at times resembled classical siege warfare were punctuated by heavy Israeli ground assaults. These resulted in the seizure of the airport and other areas of open terrain in the southern suburbs of the city. By war's end, the siege perimeter had been severely constricted—to about eight miles of land lines plus six more of seafront. However, the IDF never succeeded in encircling JF units, in rupturing the defending lines, or in overrunning key positions, such as the Museum and port crossing points, the Kuwaiti Embassy hill, or the city seafront from the Summerland beach resort to the port. It was on these lines that fighting ended on August 12.

To recapitulate, the decisive events which separate these four phases were the encirclement of Sidon of June 9, the isolation of West Beirut on June 13, and the capture of Bhamdoun and elimination of Syria from the war on June 26. This brief summary gives the impression of an inexorable progression of the invading forces, and an unmitigated series of defeats of the defenders. Although in one sense correct, the accuracy of this impression can be judged only in light of the extent to which the expectations and plans of the two sides were fulfilled.

IV The Plans and Expectations of the Combatants

Israel's Expectations

From our summary of the course of the four phases of the war, it may already be apparent that all did not got as Sharon and his generals had originally planned. In fact, things seem to have gone wrong from the very beginning.

In an article detailing the surprise of the Israelis at the fight put up by the Palestinians in the refugee camps along the South Lebanese coast during this first phase, Ze'ev Schiff, the respected defense editor of Ha'aretz, states: "According to the IDF campaign plan, the forces coming from the south were scheduled to link up with those landed from the sea within 24 hours."[10] The failure to do this with the required rapidity (in reality, Schiff points out, it took nearly three times as long to effect the linkup) was only the first step in the unhinging of the Israeli battle plan, but it affected crucially the timing and implementation of all the later stages of the war.

As is pointed out by Schiff (and was asserted forcefully by the P.L.O. at the time),[11] what held up the Israeli army in the coastal sector during the first phase of the war was the intensity of the resistance in the built-up areas along some of

its main axes of advance, in particular the five main Palestinian refugee camps in South Lebanon.

These were located on the eastern outskirts of Tyre and Sidon, both vital strategic nervepoints. Whenever possible, the heavily built-up camps were purposely bypassed by Israeli advance units and left to be reduced later. Unfortunately for the Israelis, while they could do this with the Tyre camps, in the case of 'Ain al-Hilweh camp near Sidon, the largest in Lebanon, this was not possible because of its location astride key routes of communication.

Earlier, in the three camps near Tyre (Rashidiyeh, Burj al-Shemali, and al-Bass) the defenders had put up a fierce fight. This was particularly the case in the former two, which were much larger than al-Bass. Schiff indicates it took a whole Israeli division (of over 10,000 men) three or four days to reduce them, during which period it suffered nearly 120 casualties. This tallies exactly with WAFA reports at the time, which indicated their fall by the fourth day of the war, although WAFA estimates of Israeli casualties were higher.[12]

Unlike the Tyre camps, 'Ain al-Hilweh could not simply be left behind as the northward advance continued. In Schiff's words, it "had to be taken to allow passage through the town northward to where Israeli forces had landed from the sea, and onward to Beirut."[13] It was here that both Palestinian and Israeli accounts agree that perhaps the most savage battle of the entire war was fought.

For days after a June 11 ceasefire had briefly halted the Israeli advance against Syrian forces far to the north, ferocious fighting continued inside 'Ain al-Hilweh. The defenders were led by Muslim *shaykhs* and spearheaded by young "*ashbal*" (tiger cubs: the name given to youthful fighters) wielding deadly RPG antitank weapons at close quarters against Israeli armor. Again and again, at nightfall they managed to retake ground lost in daylong battles marked by intense Israeli bombardment. The camp held out until June 17, becoming a tiny, isolated Stalingrad ("the Masada of the Palestinians" one Israeli called it),[14] sucking unit after unit of the IDF into grueling house-to-house combat, in which the defenders were at a natural advantage, and Israel's technological and numerical superiority were neutralized.

This vicious ten-day battle showed up a fatal flaw in the planning of Sharon and the IDF generals. They had estimated quite correctly that their forces would be able to overwhelm the semiregular units of the P.L.O. in combat in open terrain. But they had apparently not expected that many of these units would survive the initial blitzkrieg assault in the countryside and succeed in withdrawing into built-up areas, or that the lightly armed local militias and regular reserve units they joined there would fight with such élan, inflicting serious casualties on the attackers.

A second flaw was revealed by the course of the fighting in the eastern sector, in the 'Arqoub region at the southern end of the Biqa' Valley. Here, it was apparently hoped that Israeli columns could rapidly break out of what the Israelis called "Fatehland": the mountainous and constricting terrain controlled by the P.L.O. immediately north of the UNIFIL zone and south of the Syrian area of deployment, where the advance of large mechanized forces was restricted to two road axes.

The objective was as quickly as possible to get the highly mobile Israeli armor out of the narrow lower valley, where long-entrenched P.L.O. commandos awaited them, and into the broader plain to the north, where Syrian tank forces were located. Once there, the Israelis had confidence in their ability to overcome these Syrian units after destroying the air defenses which protected them.

But they apparently did not calculate on the resistance they would be offered at the southern end of the valley by P.L.O. guerrillas, enjoying the advantage of over a decade of familiarity with the terrain, and supported by well-dug-in Syrian artillery to the north. It took the better part of four days of heavy fighting for vastly superior Israeli forces to break out of the wooded, hilly, and nearly roadless terrain between their forward lines in the Haddad zone and those of the Syrians near Lake Qar'oun.[15]

In this first phase of the war, the only sector where things went more or less according to plan was the center. Here, Beaufort Castle was captured after a bloody two-day battle in which its defenders were killed to a man, but heavy casualties were suffered by assaulting units of the elite Golani brigade; Nabatiyeh was bypassed and then taken; and powerful columns were sent northwest to join the assault on Sidon, and north to enter the Shouf, where relatively little resistance was offered by Syrian and Druze forces (the P.L.O. had always been forbidden to station men in the region).

Further Israeli miscalculations appeared in succeeding phases of the war. One was the assumption that the entire length of the coast road could be swiftly seized and put to use. The IDF had extensive air- and sea-lift capabilities,[16] but complete control of this road, the best in South Lebanon, was necessary within days of the launching of the invasion: it was the only route which could sustain logistically a multi-divisional assault directed toward Beirut. The other north-south roads—narrow, winding routes which ran through the mountains to the east—would be supplying the Israeli forces facing the Syrians in these areas, and could not carry the logistical load of the coastal push as well.

This assumption was already badly damaged by the length of time it took to surround Sidon and reduce 'Ain al-Hilweh. It was shattered in the fighting between Sidon and Beirut, particularly along the stretch of road in the Damour area, and between there and Khaldeh. Here, repeated amphibious and helicopter landings behind the lines of the JF, combined with outflanking sweeps through the mountains to the east, resulted in IDF advances but failed to clear the road, which could not be used in its entirety until after the IDF reached the outskirts of Beirut.

In the end, it was necessary for the Israelis to rely on their striking success in the Shouf mountains (one of the few areas where the speed of their advance came even close to their expectations) to swing to the east around the Khaldeh-Damour region. It was by this route, rather than by the coast, that Israeli forces finally arrived at Ba'abda and succeeded in encircling Beirut on June 13, at the same time outflanking the stubborn defenders of Khaldeh.

They did so at least four or five days behind schedule, coming from a different direction than planned, and with sections of the vital coast road still unusable. Indeed, heavy fighting continued at Khaldeh until June 14, and the Damour area was not fully cleared, according to one Israeli military source, until the nineteenth day of the war. By way of contrast, an Israeli journalist was told by one officer that IDF planners had expected three days would suffice to finish off the P.L.O.[17]

The battle for Khaldeh had another important effect on the course of the war, especially on the P.L.O. It was in some ways analagous to the effect of the grueling ten-day siege of 'Ain al-Hilweh on the Israelis, symbolizing to all concerned just what the war was going to involve. The fighting at 'Ain al-Hilweh was seen and heard, if only from a distance, by the men of most fresh Israeli units traveling north toward Beirut up the coast and Shouf roads to join the fighting or to relieve other units.[18] Even those Israeli soldiers who didn't witness the fighting must have been affected by the length of time it took the vastly superior IDF, led by the crack Golani Brigade, to take the camp. This impact was undoubtedly compounded by the Golani's heavy casualties in this battle (the unit's second difficult engagement in one week, the first being at Beaufort Castle). Even though the drama of 'Ain al-Hilweh was fully covered in both the P.L.O. and the Beirut media,[19] it took place too far away to have the same impact on the besieged defenders of Beirut as it did on the Israelis.

Khaldeh, on the other hand, is on the southern outskirts of the capital, and the fighting in and around it could constantly be seen and heard throughout much of the city. Indeed, it was virtually impossible for those in Beirut to ignore it. The stubborn five-day defense of this vital strategic crossroads and the area to the south and east of it by the JF, Amal militiamen, and Syrian troops boosted morale in Beirut considerably, and provided badly needed time for preparation of the city's defense.

At this point the IDF made yet another critical mistake, in failing to launch an immediate thrust into Beirut. By doing so it would have capitalized immediately on the devastating impact on its opponents' morale of the outflanking maneuver through the mountains to the east, which had encircled Beirut and eventually forced the evacuation of Khaldeh.

Here, for the first time, Sharon and his generals opted for caution. They sat on the outskirts of the city for several days as the fighting at Khaldeh and Ouzai just to the north of it dragged on, and brought troops into East Beirut by sea to complete the siege, all the while pushing tentatively north toward 'Aley, located on the Beirut–Damascus highway. Only on June 21 did they open up a major new offensive.

Surprisingly, this was directed not at Beirut, but rather at pushing the Syrian division positioned together with P.L.O. forces in the mountainous 'Aley-Bhamdun area further away from the capital. After four days of heavy combat involving severe casualties to both sides, the Israelis seized Bhamdun along the Beirut–Damascus highway. However, the IDF failed to cut off the retreat of the Syro-Palestinian forces involved, which managed to escape encirclement and withdraw eastward virtually intact. Their survival was due largely to the grim and determined defense of Bhamdun by crack Syrian commandos, who had been ordered to hold their ground at all costs until this withdrawal was complete.

The Israeli decision to fight this costly battle instead of assaulting Beirut was fully justified in terms of orthodox strategy (although it was probably primarily a response to the absence of any decision by the Israeli Cabinet to enter Beirut). At the same time, the Khaldeh road was not yet open until after June 17, and thus there was no major overland supply route for Israeli forces in the Beirut area. In addition, the Syrian division and P.L.O. units in the mountainous 'Aley region, well supplied with artillery and easily reinforced, in theory threatened the rear and flanks of any Israeli force attacking Beirut.

Finally, there were probably not enough Israeli troops on hand for a major push into the capital.

Yet without a daring drive on Beirut, exploiting the great psychological effect of the arrival of the IDF at Ba'abda on June 13, and ignoring the many dangers, what little hope the Israelis ever had of swiftly seizing the capital and thereby achieving their initial objectives evaporated. In any explanation of the reasons for what seems curiously like a failure of nerve on the part of the normally aggressive Sharon, the senior IDF generals, and the Cabinet, the searing impact of the fighting of the first two weeks of the war, and the relatively heavy casualties already suffered by the IDF, undoubtedly take a major place.

This was the last grave mistake the Israeli generals made on the battlefield, and the last time events deviated from their plans, which were now obselete. The entire logic of their operation had been predicated on swift, cumulative success, just as the entire tactical philosophy of the IDF has always been rooted in movement, maneuver, and deep penetration. Once the last chance of a rapid advance to the gates of Beirut, and a P.L.O. collapse and surrender of the city, were gone, the IDF was in uncharted waters, both doctrinally and in terms of what they had planned for before the invasion.

In the seven succeeding weeks during which Beirut was besieged, there were progressively less coherent attempts by Israel to improvise and to bluff. During this period, the initiative eventually slipped from the hands of Sharon within the Israeli leadership, events were determined increasingly in the politico-diplomatic rather than the military sphere, and control of outcomes shifted from Israel to the United States in the larger context.

The primary reason for this complex development, which many at the time perceived but had difficulty explaining, lay in the way events on the battlefield had developed beyond the control of Sharon and the Israeli military planners from the very outset of the war.

P.L.O. Expectations

Palestinian expectations regarding an Israeli attack must naturally be looked at quite differently from those of the IDF command: whereas the latter had the advantage of being able to chose the time and place to strike, the P.L.O. could only wait and wonder where and when the blow was coming. Of course, the IDF had to revise its pre-war expectations in light of results in the field. But the Israelis should have had less need to do so than the P.L.O., because of their wide experience, their vastly superior intelligence-gathering capability, and the inestimable advantage of holding the initiative.

As regards of the pre-war period, a distinction must be made between Yasser 'Arafat's repeated public warnings that an Israeli attack was imminent, and what P.L.O. leaders and senior military commanders believed or actually did about these warnings. For at least five months before the invasion began, 'Arafat stressed publicly and privately that Israel was preparing a major attack, aimed at trapping the P.L.O. between Israel forces coming up from the south and hostile forces in East Beirut. The terms he used for this were an "accordion" or a "pincers" operation. On other occasions, he referred publicly to the possibility that the attacking forces would reach Damour, Khaldeh, or even Beirut itself.[20]

The P.L.O. leadership was in receipt of information from a variety of sources—French, Egyptian, Soviet, Lebanese, and American to name only some of them—that such an attack was being planned. At least one of these reports indicated, in the words of one of these bearers of bad tidings, that during a visit to Washington, Sharon "would unroll his maps and show anyone who would pay attention how the Israeli army planned to reach Beirut."[21]

What did 'Arafat and senior P.L.O. military commanders do about this information, which was corroborated by P.L.O. military intelligence and by observations of Israeli preparations along the frontier both in April (when an attack was planned and then cancelled), and June 1982?[22] One view, that of military analyst Yezid Sayigh, is that Israel achieved a large measure of surprise, and that many P.L.O. military commanders did not realize Israeli objectives until well into the war,[23] although he admits elsewhere that "there was some prediction and planning" by the P.L.O.[24] Overall, Sayigh gives its military commanders low marks for their preparation to meet the attack, noting that the units which did best were those which had done their own contingency planning for this eventuality, whereas others "taken completely by surprise lost all cohesion."[25] Schiff has offered a similarly negative assessment of the performance of P.L.O. regular forces and commanders.[26]

Granting the validity of some of these strictures, it must be asked how much effect preparations by commanders of a semiregular force of less than division strength could have had when they were about to be attacked by what General Chaim Herzog indicates was "a force of eight divisional groups" with absolute air and naval superiority?

Justifiable criticisms can certainly be made of the armament, training, logistics, and doctrine of P.L.O. military forces, as well of their pre-war dispositions. The responsibility for these basic shortcomings was long-standing, and should probably be divided between the P.L.O.'s political leadership and the senior military officers at the operations, sector and unit command levels. However, it has not been sufficiently appreciated by some critics that many of these dispositions were an inevitable function of the P.L.O.'s need to prepare to meet a multitude of perceived threats—local, Arab, and Israeli—at different levels of intensity. For example, the P.L.O. had to prepare to meet Israeli pinprick raids, use its miltary forces in paramilitary or police funtions in some areas, and (after the withdrawal of Syrian troops from many areas of the littoral in 1979-80), take precautions against hostile action by the LF. This naturally prevented single-minded concentration on the threat of a major Israeli attack.

But given the serious structural flaws in the organization of P.L.O. military forces, much was done in certain fields to prepare for the Israeli invasion. This included deployment of large reserve forces in the Beirut area; stockpiling of arms, fuel, food, medicines and other supplies in Beirut and elsewhere; widescale military training of Palestinian civilians and their organization on a militia basis beginning in the fall of 1981; and the building of a number of secret underground emergency military command posts in various parts of the capital.

Ultimately, better military preparations in the south might have saved a few units that were overrun by the IDF advance, and allowed a more effective and coordinated partisan war to have been waged more quickly against the IDF once it occupied the region. But excepting extensive pre-war preparation of the city of Sidon for a siege (which was politically out of the question), or breaking down semiconventional units into guerrilla formations before the war, or posting more able senior officers to commands in South Lebanon which were sure to be overrun, it is hard to see what more the P.L.O. command could have done in the way of dispositions.

As we saw in the last chapter, 'Arafat and the P.L.O. leadership can certainly be faulted for their *political* mistakes, such as incorrectly reading the angry mood of the Lebanese toward the P.L.O. on the eve of the war, alienating the Syrian regime unnecessarily, and perhaps for crying wolf too often about an imminent Israeli attack. But these are quite different from purely military failings, which were many, but largely structural or long-standing.

When Israeli troops attacked on June 6, after two days of bombardment, they benefited from an element of strategic surprise. This was the result of a certain decline of alertness on the part of some P.L.O. front-line units, after many months of awaiting an enemy attack. The July 1981 cross-border clashes, during which Israeli forces had never crossed the frontier, and a false alarm in April 1982, when heavy Israeli bombing and shelling were not followed by a ground attack, probably helped in this. At the same time, many in the P.L.O. felt a certain paradoxical relief that at last the long period of suspense was over.[27]

Tactical surprise was provided by the rapid speed with which Israeli ground forces moved forward (especially as compared with 1978); by their willingness to surround and leave behind P.L.O. strongpoints; by their massive use of air- and sealift capabilities to move forces deep behind the front lines, including armored vehicles; by the intense weight of the combined air, sea, and artillery bombardments employed; and finally by the deep penetration of their advance.

But the "Palestinian surprise" for the IDF (the words are those of Ze'ev Schiff) was that many P.L.O. units left behind or surrounded were apparently prepared for this and fought on; others cut off by Israeli heliborne or amphibious forces would turn on them and force them to withdraw (this happened at the Zahrani and Khaldeh beachheads, and in the 'Arqoub); and most often when Israeli spearheads broke through a defensive position, they would find another awaiting them farther north.[28] In sum, Schiff noted, "in this war Palestinians did not shrink from direct confrontation with IDF units."[29]

This would seem to argue for a reasonably accurate pre-war set of expectations and some preparations on the part of the P.L.O. forces in the field, if not of their most senior commanders. As a general rule, a high degree of surprise combined with adverse battlefield circumstances can normally be expected to provoke panic and flight among unprepared troops. Israeli planners were counting on their massive offensive doing this, if what several sources indicate about their projections for the rate of the advance is correct.[30] Yet it did not happen, except in a few cases.

To conclude, the P.L.O. was ill-prepared in many ways to meet the attack it knew it was coming, but this was a function of underlying flaws and weaknesses in its military organization. Its basic problem was that it was utterly mismatched in the field against a large part of the total forces (including eight of fifteen divisions) of the preeminent regional superpower. Given this imbalance, given the numbing effect of waiting for months for the inevitable attack their leaders kept telling them was coming, and given the tactical surprise the Israelis managed to achieve on a number of levels, it is surprising that P.L.O. forces fought as well as they did.

The wartime reaction and adaptation to a new situation of these same forces presents a somewhat different picture. While most units in the field appear to have reacted as well as could have been expected to the massive assault they faced, regional and large unit commands frequently failed to respond to the emerging situation, particularly in the south in the first three or four days of the war.

This was especially noticeable in the Sidon region, where the crucial Awwali landing was not dealt with effectively. This was partly because the commanding officer, Colonel Hajj Isma'il, abandoned his post on the second day of the invasion, and in consequence there was a lack of central direction in a key battle.[31] There was a similar loss of control in the Tyre area, although there the regional commander, Lieutenant Colonel 'Azmi Sghayir, fell in combat, after leading his forces in a battle in which an Israeli brigade commander was killed.

This underlines the fact that pitted against the vast superiority of the IDF, it made little difference what was done by the regional command: ultimately there was no way to maneuver large bodies of men or to move heavy weapons in the face of Israel's total command of the air and sea, and its dominance on the ground. Thus, throughout the south during the first days of the invasion, large P.L.O. units broke up, their heavy weapons destroyed or abandoned, and the men sought the cover of built-up areas or the hills. Where they were able to do this—in the Tyre and Sidon areas, and in the mountainous 'Arqoub—they effectively held up the Israeli advance.

Only when fighting reached the southern approaches to Beirut and during the siege of the city did the P.L.O. command begin to plan effectively, respond rapidly, and direct the battle so as to have an impact on the flow of events. Here, after an initial period of shock and paralysis, IDF axes of advance were foreseen, swift preparations made, reserves moved, defense lines established, and advances stopped again and again. From the initial battles at Khaldeh to the final attacks in August, when the IDF made its last attempt to breach Joint Forces lines and penetrate the city, the command and control problems which had plagued the P.L.O. military forces in the south seemed to diminish progressively.

In part this was a function of the battle becoming more static as it moved closer to the P.L.O. central leadership and military command, and further away from those of Israel. In part it derived from the uniquely favorable battlefield that the heavily built-up Beirut metropolitan area provided to a force which excelled in street fighting that was opposing another which preferred a war of maneuver in the open country. And in large measure it was a result of the time the defenders of 'Ain al-Hilweh, the other camps in the south, and Khaldeh had bought for those in Beirut to catch their breath, adjust to the reality of the vast weight of the IDF bearing down on them, and make appropriate preparations to meet it.[32]

In addition to all these givens, which the P.L.O. leadership in Beirut could do little to change, they were responsible for a number of actions which positively affected the situation. One was the appointment of a top-ranking officer, known for his courage and respected by the men in the ranks, to command the vital Khaldeh sector at the outset of the war.

Colonel 'Abdullah Siyam was a founding member of Fateh, and had been a senior officer in the Egypt-based 'Ain Jalout brigade of the Palestine Liberation Army (P.L.A.). After years of distinguished combat service in South Lebanon, he had been languishing in a minor posting, only to be propelled into what at that moment was the most important P.L.O. field command. The highest-ranking P.L.O. officer to be killed during the war, he died when his command post was overrun in the vicious battle for this intersection, but the five days the Palestinian, Syrian and Lebanese defenders of the Khaldeh/ Ouza'i area held up the Israelis amply justified his appointment, and his sacrifice.

Another such action was the redeployment in the Beirut area of units which had escaped the IDF steamroller in the south. While this may seem an obvious decision, it was not the only possible one: these forces could have remained safely in the mountains or the Biqa', where most of them first withdrew to. But impelled by their individual commanders, by orders from the P.L.O. command, or by the desire of their men to get back into the fight, these units were rushed into Beirut in spite of the impending isolation of the city, until the Beirut–Damascus road was finally cut on June 13. Smaller formations succeeded in infiltrating through the siege lines even later.

These fighters measurably stiffened the militia and regular forces already in position defending the city, bringing both their numbers and their valuable combat experience in the south to this crucial battle. In addition, several officers who managed to reach Beirut from the south were given senior commands, and played important roles during the siege. They were especially helpful in the constitution of the command, staff, and field operations headquarters of each of the eight military sectors into which the besieged city was divided, and in reinforcing the P.L.O. central operations staff.[33]

It is ironic in view of the P.L.O. decision to move as many fighters as possible into the soon-to-be-besieged city that some Israeli military analysts have faulted Sharon and the IDF for not leaving a route open for the P.L.O.'s escape. Had they done so, quite the opposite result would most probably have obtained, and the Israelis would have had to face even larger numbers of opponents inside the city.

The last phase of the war contrasts strikingly with the prewar period, when P.L.O. planning and preparation was indifferent in some areas and negligent in others, and with the early part of the war, when most of the forces in the field were rapidly overwhelmed, and organized resistance could continue only in the built-up areas and the mountainous 'Arquob. Indeed, the siege of Beirut provides many examples of accurate expectations, and of excellent preparation by the P.L.O. command and the units in the field.

Deserving of particular mention are the building of massive antitank earth barriers on virtually all main roads, and the laying of extensive minefields along the projected axes of the IDF's advance.[34] After delays in launching this work early in the war, these precautions proved their worth during Israeli attacks in July and August, when key sectors of the siege perimeter in built-up regions like the port and Museum crossing points, as well as the vulnerable seafront, proved virtually impenetrable.

Only in open areas such as the airport, the Golf Club, and the Bir Hassan region in the southern suburbs was it impossible for P.L.O. engineers to take effective measures capable of halting Israeli armor: and only here did the Israeli army succeed in advancing, from beginning to end of the siege. If anything, P.L.O. planners erred on the side of caution, preparing for a full-scale Israeli ground assault up to the last moment, although as the battle inched closer to the more heavily built-up areas of central Beirut, there were many indications that it was impossible for the IDF to storm the city without a politically unacceptable level of causalties.

On the other hand, that such caution was necessary was shown by the extraordinary measures taken to protect the P.L.O. central military command structure, the P.L.O. political leadership, and in particular its head, Yasser 'Arafat. All were targets of persistent, deadly Israeli attacks, with the Chairman's office, including its underground section, and two alternate and heavily used headquarters destroyed by Israeli air attack using precision-guided munitions (PGM) in the first weeks of the war.[35] Later on, several buildings apparently suspected of harboring members of the P.L.O. leadership were completely destroyed in air strikes.

Previously prepared substitutes for existing command posts were already staffed and manned before these attacks began, and when one was discovered (through use of radio direction-finding equipment, "traditional" espionage, or other means) and destroyed, a new one was rapidly brought into use. Except for one period of a few hours' duration, the Central Operations room was never out of radio or field telephone contact with the sector commands during the entire siege, in spite of this intense Israeli pressure on the P.L.O. command structure.

Although there were casualties among the key head-quarters staff, including duty officers, radio operators, and guards in these unremitting attacks[36] the IDF bombers never were able to hit the site where the Central Operations HQ was located, as it moved rapidly from one fully staffed bomb shelter to another. This was a direct result of meticulous preparation and acute foresight, for as the war went on it became apparent that killing the P.L.O.'s top political leadership and knocking out its military command structure was a main Israeli priority. It would very probably have been achieved had these pre-cautions not been taken long before the war.

As for expecting what might happen to the Palestinian civil population after the P.L.O. departed, its leaders were deeply fearful. They had every reason to be worried. The history of the Lebanese war was replete with massacres of defenseless civilians, most of them directed against Palestinians and Lebanese Muslims. Then, in late June, the LF were allowed by their Israeli patrons to enter the Druze areas of the Shouf, and promptly began killing unarmed civilians. This was perceived by many in Beirut as a harbinger of what could be expected in the wake of an Israeli victory, a P.L.O. withdrawal, and a Phalangist takeover.[37]

As early as June 30, 1982, a telex from 'Arafat in response to U.S. proposals for a P.L.O. withdrawal transmitted via the French was explicit in this regard: "The important subject is what are the guarantees against a massacre of Palestinians, both civilians and military, in view of what happened in Tyre and Sidon, and after what the Phalangists did yesterday to Lebanese patriots in the mountains."[38]

Securing ironclad guarantees for the safety of the Palestinian civilian population after the departure of P.L.O. military forces was a central focus of the wartime P.L.O.–U.S. negotiations. Tragically, the subject was never given sufficient importance by Philip Habib and the policymakers he represented.

Chapter 3

P.L.O. Decisions: The Military Inputs

I Communication, the Media, and Public Opinion

The men who led the P.L.O. had gone through many harrowing experiences before the Israeli invasion. Some had endured captivity or barely escaped it, all had been under fire repeatedly, and all had experienced deprivation and various forms of extreme danger. It was understood and accepted by everyone in the P.L.O. that things would never be easy. On several occasions during grim periods in the past, 'Arafat had asked rhetorically in speeches, "But when we started all this, did we invite you to a wedding, or a feast?"

However, what the P.L.O. had to face in 1982 was quite different from anything it had gone through in the past. It had witnessed apparently hopeless situations in Jordan in 1970 and 1971, and in Lebanon in the summer of 1976. But never before had it confronted the full weight of such a formidable or ruthless enemy, and never before had it seemed as if every possible factor was ranged against it, closing off all options except the most unpleasant.

Not surprisingly in view of this situation, many accounts at the time and afterward tended to lay stress on Israeli military pressure as the major influence on P.L.O. decisions.[1] Thus, assessing the exact impact of the pressure Israel was able to bring to bear on P.L.O. decisionmaking has particular importance.

This is a harder problem than it may seem, and not only because of the obvious difficulty of determining well after the event how the different phases of the war were perceived by and affected the P.L.O. leadership and rank and file. It is also necessary to clarify how information reached the leadership, how it was then disseminated to the combat units of the JF, and what effect all of this had on the general public in Beirut and beyond.

Public opinion was crucial in the calculations of the P.L.O. leadership during the war. It had been sensitive to Palestinian opinion in the past, especially that of Palestinians in Lebanon during its "Lebanese era." It became even more sensitive to it as the combat got closer and closer to Beirut, where the families of most fighters and leaders were located. Their feelings ultimately became absolutely vital to the P.L.O., for a collapse of popular morale would have had devastating results on that of the combat forces.

Lebanese opinion too became increasingly important during the war, particularly among the population of West Beirut, which was besieged along with the Palestinians. It became decisive in mid-June when it grew clear that the objective of Israel, the United States, and the Sarkis government was the expulsion of the P.L.O. and that, with one exception, no leader in West Beirut was willing to oppose that demand. Even later, when in late June Lebanese public opinion shifted somewhat toward the P.L.O., morale in the capital remained a key factor in how long the P.L.O. could hold out in its attempt to obtain more favorable conditions for its withdrawal.

Above everything else, the ebb and flow of the fighting had a direct impact on popular perceptions in Beirut. These in turn influenced how much support the Lebanese in the city gave the P.L.O., and how much military, psychological, or other pressure they and the Palestinian civilian population could withstand. All of these factors were crucial in the P.L.O.'s decisionmaking.

At the same time, it is insufficiently appreciated that the threshhold of endurance and the resistance to deprivation of ordinary Beirutis, who had been experiencing warfare almost constantly since 1975, was extremely high. They were inured to heavy fighting; used to doing without water, fuel, or electricity; well-stocked for virtually any eventuality, and experienced in finding relative safety under artillery bombardment. In sum, the people of Beirut were relatively unaffected by events which would have caused panic in the population of almost any other city. As a result, Israel could not have chosen a worse city to besiege, and the P.L.O. had an invaluable asset in its weary but war-tempered populace.

The ability of the P.L.O. to make decisions and to affect public opinion was at least in part a function of the accuracy of the information at its disposal, and of that it provided to the public. By the outbreak of the 1982 war, the P.L.O. had developed an extensive military communications network. Primarily using radio, this system stretched from units in the field to sector and regional commands, and finally to the JF Central Operations Room in Beirut. It provided a generally accurate picture of events when the situation in the field was not too fluid, and when local commands were in touch with subordinate units. When this ceased to be the case, as often happened early in the war, the information available to the leadership in Beirut grew increasingly unreliable; but when the system was functioning properly, it enabled the Operations Room to keep local and regional commands informed of events elsewhere on the battlefield, and allowed accurate communiques to be issued.

As the fighting rapidly moved closer to Beirut, and as the perimeter under control of the JF shrunk, the problem of loss of contact diminished but others arose to take its place. One was that use of radio became increasingly hazardous, as radio transmissions were easily intercepted, and could be used by the enemy to locate and destroy commandposts. The solution ultimately adopted was the use of old-fashioned field telephones within the Beirut siege perimeter. These were supplemented by field messengers when their vulnerable ground lines were damaged by shelling or bombing. Where radio had to be used, the antennas were located as far as possible from the transmitter, or the transmitter was made mobile, or transmitted in short bursts. In spite of these precautions, several radio operators were killed and many wounded in Beirut during the siege.

There were other problems. Telephone exchanges were often hit by shellfire, necessitating emergency repairs. After the IDF cut off electricity, the telephone exchanges, as well as radios, field telephones, telexes, and other communications facilities, required emergency generators. These had to be kept outdoors, and were often damaged by shrapnel. To maintain 24-hour operation of these systems, large supplies of diesel oil were required. Some of these problems were solved by good pre-war preparation, plus at times inspired improvization in the heat of combat by courageous repair crews working under indescribably difficult conditions;[2] but they were never fully banished.

Notwithstanding such communications difficulties, the P.L.O. command generally had an accurate idea of what was going on, thanks to this military communications network.[3] The most serious problems arose when radio contact with a regional command was lost, which usually meant the worst: the position was lost or the commandpost had been overrun or abandoned. This was not always the case: the commander of the Tyre district, Lt. Colonel 'Azmi Sghayir, ceased radio contact but remained in the field until he was killed much later.

That the P.L.O. command's picture of the battlefield situation was usually correct is reflected in the official communiques issued by WAFA in Beirut. When checked against Western and Israeli press accounts, they appear generally accurate in describing the military situation, and reliable in other respects, with the exception of estimates of Israeli casualties. Inflated though they often were, such estimates were at times closer to the truth than IDF's figures.[4]

The P.L.O. never released a figure on JF casualties. As for civilian casualties, in the south there was not accurate count of them; in Beirut most fell during heavy bombardments when the wounded and dead were coming in to hospitals so fast that records could not be kept; many of those killed were buried under destroyed buildings and could not be removed; others were never taken to hospitals. Figures on civilian casualties must therefore be treated as estimates.[5]

In the last analysis, the ultimate check on the P.L.O. media was that it was imperative for it to present the most truthful possible picture of the fighting, since most of the war was being fought in the Beirut citizenry's backyard. Glaring discrepancies in its reporting would only have alienated these people, whose support was absolutely vital, and eroded their confidence in the credibility of those defending the beleaguered city.

The populace had alternative sources of information. Foremost were their own eyes and ears, which could tell them a great deal as the siege tightened. They could also hear news from neighbors and friends, particularly those who served as part-time militiamen, or in the extensive civil defense services which developed during the war. These people moved around the city, and could describe combat damage and casualties, and the progress, or lack of it, of Israeli offensives.

Finally there were the non-P.L.O. media: internationally, notably Monte Carlo and BBC radio; locally, the Phalangist "Voice of Lebanon"; and "Kol Israel", which broadcast in Arabic, English, and French. The first two stations provided a valuable and much-listened-to external perspective on events, showing those under siege something of how the outside world saw their predicament, as well as the effect the long drawn-out siege was having inside Israel, in the U.S., and in Europe.

The Israeli and Phalangist radios, whose information line was obviously closely coordinated,[6] lost credibility as the war continued. This was partly because in mid-June they were central to an intensive disinformation campaign. Their news broadcasts sowed false rumors, made exaggerated claims of Israeli advances on the ground, and alleged sweeping secret P.L.O. concessions. These reports constituted the key element in a psychological offensive meant to create a wave of panic, which would stampede the P.L.O. into agreeing to leave Beirut unconditionally and in a state of complete disarray.

In the event, this apparently carefully planned campaign failed; perhaps it could only have succeeded against a background of total Israeli victory and absolute P.L.O. defeat. In consequence, the "Voice of Lebanon" and "Kol Israel" suffered a major loss of listener confidence inside the city, particularly its besieged western half.

The main Beirut papers, the leftist *al-Safir* and the centrist *al-Nahar*, on the whole bore out the tenor of JF communiques, although on occasion they flatly contradicted them. However, they told a very different (and often more accurate) story about the negotiations to end the fighting than did official P.L.O. pronouncements, which were vague, uninformative, and at times simply untrue.

Lack of credibility on this score initially harmed the P.L.O. in its efforts to deny, in mid-June, the more alarmist stories about its withdrawal that its enemies were spreading. Only in July, with the P.L.O.'s failure to precipitously pack up and leave, as it was alleged to be on the point of doing, were these rumors finally laid to rest.

II The Military in P.L.O. Decisionmaking

A. Phase 1: The Battle of South Lebanon, June 4–9

Throughout most of this brief but intense period of the war, from the first bombing attacks on June 4 until Sidon was encircled and the battle of Khaldeh began on June 9, it remained unclear to most people outside the IDF command exactly how far the invasion was meant to go. However, from the outset, it was apparent to the P.L.O. that this was something far more extensive than the limited 1978 incursion. The landing north of Sidon during the first 24 hours of the invasion confirmed that the IDF meant to go farther north than ever before, and that this was the attack which 'Arafat had been predicting for so long, and which the P.L.O. Chief of Operations, Brigadier Abu al-Walid (Sa'ad Sayel), had warned would inevitably be directed at Beirut.[7]

The speed of the advance, the massive amounts of firepower employed, and the willingness of the IDF to leave behind not just pockets of resistance, but entire cities, towns, and refugee camps, impressed all concerned with the extent of Israeli seriousness, as did the IDF's willingness to take casualties. It had been noted by many in the P.L.O. that in 1978, an Israeli decision to avoid taking the Tyre pocket had been made, apparently, to avoid heavy casualties. This time things clearly would be different.

There was, moreover, an understanding among most Palestinians that in the face of this unprecedented offensive little could be expected from the Arab states. A WAFA commentary written on June 5, after two days of bombardments—and when it was obvious that the invasion was about to begin—spoke scathingly of "the near somnolence" of the Arab regimes, concluding: "The Palestinians and their allies in Lebanon are alone in the field facing the Israeli Goliath."[8] This commentary struck a note of defiance that, like the resistance in the field, was to be maintained throughout the war, even during its darkest days.

In the face of a massive assault (the eight divisions indicated by Herzog totaled well over ten times the forces fielded by the P.L.O., with many more times the firepower),[9] and in the absence of any likely source of external aid, it is worthy of note that there was little sign during this first phase of the war that the leadership or the rank and file of the P.L.O.

were daunted. A few individuals, like Hajj Isma'il, left their posts, but they were exceptions. This was shown by the ferocious resistance of Sidon and the adjoining camps, notably 'Ain al-Hilweh, which held out until June 17 against everything the IDF could bring against it.

The reason for this apparent equanimity was twofold. On the one hand, the P.L.O. was well prepared, psychologically if not materially, for this attack, and indeed expected it. On the other, reports from the front which indicated that fierce resistance was being offered, and that the Israelis were taking heavy casualties reinforced the existing willingness to fight on. Seemingly small things like the shooting down of an A-4 Skyhawk and capture of a pilot, Captain Aharon Ihyaz, near Beaufort on June 6, or the initial failures of Israeli amphibious landings at Rashidiyeh and in the Zahrani area on the same day, had an encouraging effect out of all proportion to their actual importance, even as reverses elsewhere were being admitted.

This explains at least in part how morale held up and resistance continued even as the news grew grimmer and grimmer on June 7 and 8, with the expansion of the Awwali bridgehead and the creation of another at Zahrani (meaning the isolation of Sidon was imminent), the total encirclement of Tyre, the fall of Nabatiyeh and Beaufort castle, and rapid Israeli advances in other areas, including in the Shouf.

Partly as a rationalization, but also reflecting cold realism, the P.L.O. media by June 7 was stressing that "this is not a war of positions . . . [and] Israel has the capability to reach almost any territorial objective it desires." The limiting factors were time and the cost in Israeli lives, rather than external intervention, which was a chimera due to "Arab impotence, and to international indifference or complicity." The P.L.O.'s objective, in addition to slowing the enemy down and inflicting maximum casualties on him, was "to preserve their forces in being."[10] In a nutshell, this was the strategy followed until the end of the war.

Neither the stream of bad news from the front on June 7, including Israeli attempts to advance from the Awwali bridge-head to Jiyyeh, only 25km south of the capital, nor devastating bombing raids on the Arab University area of Beirut, appear to have shaken morale. During these raids Israeli aircraft using PGMs had scored direct hits on important P.L.O. installations, but overshadowing this was the removal, long before, of the occupants, files, and functions of the key headquarters the planes were trying to hit. All within the P.L.O., and many throughout the city, knew this within a few hours, and were encouraged by another example proving that the Israelis were less than omniscient and infallible.[11]

As the IDF came closer to encircling Sidon on June 8, and forces moving northward from the Awwali bridgehead neared Damour, Israeli columns began a rapid penetration of the Shouf, where the P.L.O. had not been allowed to station forces. The speed of this advance was deeply disturbing to the P.L.O. leadership. One June 8, Abu Jihad, Deputy Commander in Chief of P.L.O. forces, met with Druze leaders in Mukhtara to ask them to take measures to confront it, and to allow P.L.O. forces into the region. Their response was noncommittal. On the same day, a P.L.O. military spokesman recognized the seriousness of the new situation created by the impending fall of the Shouf, stating: "This indicates that the objectives of this action go well beyond the context of the Palestinian-Israeli conflict."[12]

Most worrisome to those in Beirut was that in spite of fierce P.L.O. resistance and heavy Israeli casualties throughout the south, it had yet to be proved that the IDF could be slowed down, let alone stopped. By June 9, the day Sidon was finally encircled, events close to Beirut began to preoccupy both the city's residents and the P.L.O. leadership. The Israeli spear-heads on the coast were pushing into Damour, where fierce fighting continued, and reinforcement of this major stronghold became impossible because of air and sea interdiction. More serious, amphibious landings like those successful further south threatened to initiate a leapfrogging advance to the very gates of Beirut.

The failure of one mid-day landing attempt on June 9 between Na'meh, north of Damour, and the key intersection at Khaldeh, just a few miles south of Beirut, was no reassurance.[13] Khaldeh, a prized strategic point in every earlier phase of the Lebanese conflict, was where all roads leading south from Beirut and its suburbs converged, and where several of the main routes leading east into the mountains began.

At noon on June 9, the P.L.O. Chief of Military Intelligence, Colonel Abu al-Za'im, confirmed, at a hastily called press conference, the precariousness of the military situation. He admitted that the IDF was achieving a swift penetration "intended to achieve a psychological impact," and repeated what was in effect an admission that the P.L.O. was rapidly losing ground: "We do not claim that we will fight a war of positions."[14]

At nightfall, when news came of what seemed to be another major landing—this one near the Khaldeh crossroads—the peril of the situation became clear: the capital itself was directly threatened from the south, and all forces fighting in the Ouza 'i–Khaldeh–Damour–Jiyyeh area were faced with isolation or elimination. Meanwhile, sweeping Israeli advances in the Shouf meant that West Beirut was threatened with being cut off from the southeast as well, and could soon be totally isolated.

But later that same evening, the sound of barrages of intense firing all over the southern suburbs of Beirut was preceded by astonishing good news: the menacing Khaldeh beachhead had been eliminated, and the crossroads was completely controlled by the JF. All the Israeli armored vehicles which had landed there had been either destroyed or captured in a fierce battle at the Madinat al-Zahrat School, a Shi'ite community institution, and all their occupants killed. As proof of the victory, two captured M-113 armored personnel carriers (APCs) were paraded through the southern suburbs and adjoining Palestinian camps for the rest of the night, to indescribable scenes of joy, notably the thunderous shooting in the air which had earlier been heard throughout the city.[15]

The battle of Khaldeh had begun, in a way which was to have a far-reaching effect on morale in a city which only a few days later was to besieged. For it was at Khaldeh, within sight and sound of all of Beirut, that it first became clear over a period of several days that the IDF advance could be held, or at least slowed down. The first phase of the war was over. No one watching the ecstatic popular reaction all over the city to the events of June 9 at Khaldeh would have assumed that Israel was on its way to an easy victory.

B. Phase 2: The Encirclement of Beirut, June 9-13

The five days between the commencement of the battle for Khaldeh on June 9 and the encirclement of West Beirut on June 13 saw fierce fighting along the coastal highway from Damour to Kahldeh, in the Shouf mountains, and in beleaguered Sidon. The capital was bombed daily.

But strategically, the key developments of this period took place to the east, in the Biqa' Valley. Here, beginning on June 9, Israeli planes eliminated Syria's surface-to-air missile (SAM) defenses, and then shot down 86 first-line Syrian interceptors in a few days of intense aeriel combat. The import of these events was grave. First, they confirmed unequivocally that Israel was determined to take on Syrian forces in Lebanon, even if this meant a large-scale air, land, and electronic war; in addition, they implied that the Israelis had every intention of eliminating not only the P.L.O. but also Syria from the Lebanese chessboard.

There were more immediate problems for the P.L.O. The successful attacks on the SAM missiles and the crushing blows to the Syrian air force showed that the IDF now had the total air superiority necessary for it to drive up through the Syrian armor in the Biqa' Valley, once it pushed past the last JF units still holding out in the mountainous 'Arqoub. This meant the

IDF had the option of trying to cut the Beirut–Damascus highway either in the Biqa' or in the mountains to the west, thereby driving Syrian forces away from Beirut and isolating the city. These dangers were clear to the defenders of the capital, although such grim prospects were somewhat obscured for them by the equally grave events happening before their very eyes, such as the life-or-death battle for Khaldeh, whose loss would also have led to the isolation of the city.

At the outset of the war, it was assumed among Palestinians that the Syrians would either stay out of the fighting, or that their participation would be ineffective if they were dragged in. Thus there should have been surprise neither at the passivity of Syrian forces in Lebanon during the first five days of the war nor at the swiftness with which the IDF managed to gain the upper hand once it engaged them.

But there was surprise, and even dismay, at the speed with which Syrian defenses had crumbled in the Shouf, opening up the rear of JF units fighting a desperate battle along the coast. The crushing defeat of the Syrian air defense forces provoked similar reactions. While these developments meant that for the moment the P.L.O. was no longer completely alone, and that its powerful Syrian ally had at last been drawn into the war, this had taken place under highly disadvantageous conditions which did nothing to encourage confidence in the benefits which could be derived from it.

In any case, Syria's forced entry into the war had no appreciable effect on the battlefield situation which faced the JF at this juncture. The IDF had taken on major new tasks by attacking the Syrians, but in the days which followed it redoubled its efforts along the coast, in the Shouf, and in the air over Beirut. Because of the anomalous position prevailing in the Shouf, the P.L.O. military command had, on the eve of the war, been particularly worried about the vulnerability of its position in Beirut and on the coast down to Sidon. The strategically vital Shouf region, which was off-limits to P.L.O.

forces, was defended by scattered dispositions of Syrian troops, together with the militia of the Druze Progressive Socialist Party (P.S.P.). There were not enough of the former to halt a determined Israeli offensive, while the latter could not be expected to do so single-handed, particularly in view of intensive secret pre-war Israeli blandishments to the Druze to persuade them to stay out of the conflict.[16]

Twice in the two weeks preceding the outbreak of fighting, Abu Jihad, together with Brigadier Abu al-Walid, traveled to Damascus for talks with senior Syrian military commanders. They met the Chief of Staff, Major General Hikmat Chehabi, and stressed to him that an Israeli invasion was imminent, requesting in particular immediate reinforcement of Syrian forces in Beirut and the Shouf. Chehabi stated that the Syrian assessment was that an Israeli attack was unlikely, but promised that Syria would take responsibility for the air defense of Beirut, and would reinforce its troops in Jezzin and the southern Shouf region.[17]

Unfortunately, these promises were not kept. Far from reinforcing the air defenses of Beirut, the Syrians proceeded to pull out virtually the only effective antiaircraft weapons in the Beirut area, two batteries of radar-controlled 57mm twin antiaircraft guns stationed in the vital Khaldeh-'Aramoun area. One week before the war, they also removed a total of 107 small portable heat-seeking SAM-7 missiles from the control of pro-Syrian P.L.O. groups or P.L.A. units in or around the Beirut refugee camps.[18] And when the war came, their SAM defenses and interceptors proved to be no match for the Israeli air force. The effect of all of this was perhaps more psychological than anything else: it told the P.L.O. leaders that they could count on no external assistance.

There was in any case enough close at hand to pre-occupy them: on June 10, Israeli planes raided the capital and its southern outskirts down to Na'meh five separate times, while WAFA claimed that IDF amphibious forces had made five failed attempts to land troops along the coast between Damour and Ouza'i.[19] There were six more major attacks along this vital axis over the following two days.

Although the defenders of this area held their ground in many places in spite of furious bombardments, Israeli armored columns were managing to inch up the coast road, leaving the sloping hills to the east under control of the JF. At the same time, Israeli troops moving north along mountain roads in the Shouf on June 10 attacked Kfar Matta, east of Khaldeh. Further advances here threatened to outflank these hillside positions from the high ground to the east, leaving them cut off from three sides.

By the morning of June 11 the remaining defenders of the Damour area had been effectively isolated, although fighting behind the lines was to continue for several more days, claiming the lives of many Israelis, including the highest ranking officer ever to fall in wartime, Major General Yekutiel Adam, together with another senior officer, Brigadier Sela.[20]

The "southern front" was now on the outskirts of Beirut, at Khaldeh, which continued to be subjected to daily air, ground, and amphibious attacks until after Ba'abda was taken on the 13th. Air raids on the city continued as well, but with the elimination of Syrian air defenses in the Biqa', Israeli attention seems to have shifted momentarily to that area and to the mountains. Large numbers of fresh Israeli units were now being brought into Lebanon to wage a two-front war, with many sources reporting a continuous stream of reinforcements flowing cross the border.[21] Most of these fresh troops were probably intended to face the Syrians.

At the same time, there was a perception on the part of the P.L.O. that the intensity of the fight their forces had put up in some areas of the south, the 'Arqoub, and the approaches to Beirut had had a major impact on the IDF. According to the P.L.O. media, "the Israeli military command has been stunned by the extent of the casualties inflicted on their ranks"[22]. Whether or not such reports were accurate, later Israeli accounts confirm the impression made on Israeli soldiers by the intensity of the fighting. The death of General Adam, former Deputy Chief of Staff and Director-designate of Mossad, could only have reinforced that impression.

At the same time, it had a powerful twofold effect on Palestinian and Lebanese morale. On the one hand, it gave those resisting the invasion the sense that there was an effect to their exertions, and that they were hurting an apparently invincible enemy. On the other, it gave credence to P.L.O. claims that the IDF did not control some of the areas it had occupied, and undermined the credibility of the latter's communiques.

The death of General Adam in no way diminished the seriousness of the position of the JF, as was evidenced by, among other things, the P.L.O.'s expression of eagerness to accept a cease fire on June 12. This came after an official P.L.O. denial the previous day that it had taken a stand on Israel's unilateral announcement of a ceasefire on June 11.[23] Israel, incidentally, had specified that it was a ceasefire with Syria alone. In any case, Israeli forces never ceased firing on the P.L.O., and continued their rapid advances through the Shouf and their stubborn attempts to push up the coast toward Khaldeh.

There was other evidence of the difficulty of the P.L.O.'s situation. By the morning of June 12, Israeli troops had already reached the important Qabr Shmoun crossroads, control of which meant easy access to Beirut via the Shouf from the southeast. In a two-day pitched battle at the Khaldeh intersection, the sector commander, Colonel 'Abdullah Siyam, died of a shrapnel wound in a front-line position. His forces had by then reached the end of their tether.[24]

The gravity of what was about to happen was reflected in the title of a commentary published on the same day—the last day of the war during which roads to and from Beirut stayed open. "The Battle for Beirut" made it clear that the P.L.O. expected the Israelis to attack the city. Defiant assertions like "it is not we who are besieged" (the Israelis had rather "walked into . . . a people's war of national liberation") did not mask how serious things were: for as the the article made clear, the siege of the city, the second in six years, was about to begin.[25]

According to Abu Iyyad, at this critical stage one part of the P.L.O. leadership (he would mention only Ahmed Jibril, leader of the Popular Front for the Liberation of Palestine-General Command [PFLP-GC], by name) had a failure of nerve, although the majority of the leadership had expected such a situation and showed complete equanimity.[26] And yet the confident tone of this commentary mirrored reality in one respect: its stress on the high morale of the men of the JF in the field.[27] As was attested by the Israeli troops who faced them, there seems to have been little sign of demoralization or discouragement in the demeanor of the combatants in the front lines (indeed, an Israeli spokesman stated on June 13 that IDF casualties over the preceding 48 hours—while a ceasefire with Syrian forces was in effect—had totaled 193).

The Palestinians would need all their equanimity for the upcoming phase of the war. This was the siege of Beirut, which began in an unsettling way with the triumphant entry of Israeli forces led by Sharon himself to Ba'abda, site of the Lebanese Presidential Palace, followed by a brief interlude of fighting in the mountains.

C. Phase 3: The Battle of the Mountains, June 14–26

Although their forces were less deeply engaged in combat during this phase than any other, it was perhaps the most difficult of the war for the P.L.O. leadership. Until Beirut was actually surrounded, it had been possible to focus on how little Israel had gained for all its losses since June 4, 1982. But this was not longer plausible when Israel began dictating its demands for complete and unconditional P.L.O. withdrawal from a position of great strength on the outskirts of a besieged city, echoed in this by both the U.S. and the Sarkis government, and with no sign of help on the horizon.

The new weakness of the P.L.O. position was visible in two sets of moves which betrayed nervousness and hesitation. The first set was the denials issued by P.L.O. spokesmen over the next few days of persistent reports in the media regarding alleged acceptance of what amounted to Israeli demands for surrender conveyed by U.S. envoy Philip Habib. In one case, on June 17, three different denials, one by Fateh Central Committee member Abu Iyyad, had to be issued in one day.[28] The second set of moves was the heavily publicized visits by 'Arafat, Abu Jihad, and Brigadier Abu al-Walid to front-line units, hospitals, and offices beginning on June 14, after rumors of their death, capture, or imminent flight had been spread by hostile media. During one such visit, WAFA told its readers, "Arafat urged all to ignore pernicious rumors and to confront the hostile propaganda campaign which is underway." A smiling photo of him taken on this first tour appeared on the front pages of *The New York Times* and the local press on June 15.

These visits signified the perceived need to shore up sagging morale, reassure the troops after Israel's isolation of the city, and to put to rest persistent reports that surrender was imminent.[29] Although they failed to do the latter, they seemed to have a positive effect on morale, which had reached what was probably a nadir for the whole war.

At this point, the P.L.O. was under intense pressure to leave Beirut. The U.S. and Israel were exerting that pressure diplomatically, while within Lebanon both its enemies and its Muslim and leftist allies were exerting it politically. But at a crucial stage, when Israel for the first time seemed to be on the verge of achieving its aims vis-à-vis the P.L.O., the IDF let up its pressure on the Beirut siege perimeter.[30]

Shelling of the city and its suburbs continued sporadically from June 15 to 20. It intensified markedly from the 21st until the ceasefire five days later, during which time there were four days of air raids on the city, which caused heavy casualties and great destruction. But on the ground, there was little action. Aside from a determined effort which ended the last resistance in 'Ain al-Hilweh, the IDF restricted itself to a minor advance in the direction of the Lebanese University Faculty of Sciences in Hadeth on June 16, feeble probes at Khaldeh and Shweifat on the 21st, and a failed landing attempt at three points on the sea front near the Riviera Hotel on June 25.

Meanwhile the heaviest fighting shifted to the mountains, notably the towns of 'Aley and Bhamdoun along the Beirut–Damascus road. The first Israeli attacks there after the taking of Ba'abda came on June 17 and 18, with unsuccessful attempts to advance in the direction of 'Aley. They were anticipated by the P.L.O., for a communique spoke of the commencement of "the long-awaited battle of the mountains."[31] In fact, these were exploratory attacks, followed by two days of quiet on this front.

During this comparative lull, an intense debate took place within the P.L.O. Its outlines are reflected in the differing tones of statements by two members of the Fateh leadership, Brigadier Abu al-Walid and Abu Iyyad. The words of the former were restrained, stessing the P.L.O.'s readiness to do "absolutely everything in its power to save Beirut," implying a considerable willingness to compromise on the terms of the settlement then being discussed, but concluding that the P.L.O. "may face no alternative but legitimate self defence of itself and Beirut, whatever the consequences.[32]

Abu Iyyad was much more uncompromising; he described the proposals being offered by the U.S. as "surrender terms," which he said the Palestinians "reject categorically." He stressed that "no one can disarm this revolution . . . we will never be transformed into a political party no matter what the circumstances." He claimed further that a public statement of Fateh Central Committee member Hani al-Hassan relating to the Palestinians laying down their arms as part of a political solution to the conflict had been "distorted," and later rectified by him.[33]

This brings us to a watershed in the internal P.L.O. debate, as will be seen in the study (in chapter 4) of the factors behind the decision to leave Beirut. What is relevant here is how events on the battlefield affected this debate. It seems clear from the tone of these and earlier public remarks by Abu Iyyad that as Israel delayed its long-awaited assault on Beirut, those who called for holding out so as to obtain better terms, as well as those who saw accepting discussion of the terms being offered as a delaying tactic, were greatly reinforced in their positions.

Some time during the week following Israel's arrival at Ba'abda, a potential turning point seemed to disappear. What might have developed into panic induced by the shock of this event was dissipated by the efforts of individuals at both the leadership and cadre levels, who were convinced that all was not lost, and that the P.L.O. should fight for better terms than Israel and the U.S. were offering it.

In late June, this resolve was strengthened by several things: among them were the battle of the mountains, which began in earnest on June 21; the resignation of U.S Secretary of State Alexander Haig on June 25; and an important shift in Lebanese attitudes at this time. By July, advocates of accepting the Habib terms were being savagely satirized in some P.L.O. journals as "The Withdrawal Now Movement" (a takeoff on the Peace Now Movement in Israel),[34] signifying their isolation, and the ascendancy of the more tough-minded trend.

Before this, however, the big Israeli push on 'Aley and Bhamdun was launched, with immediate positive effects on P.L.O. morale. By the end of this battle, on June 26, the Israelis had pushed the Syrian army and its Palestinian allies completely out of both towns, and with them a vast swath of the Shouf and a long stretch of the Beirut–Damascus highway.[35] Nevertheless, the Syrians were at last taking some of the pressure off Beirut, and the Israelis were taking so long to achieve their objective—sources of encouragement to the defenders of the city.

The new tone could be detected in an impromptu T.V. interview by ABC and Visnews with Yassir 'Arafat on June 20, in which the Palestinian leader affirmed that "no one will accept to lay down his arms," and that "the situation we are in now is stronger than ever." He repeatedly stressed the P.L.O.'s determination to resist, concluding: "I am here and I am staying here."[36]

As the battle in the mountains grew fiercer in the days which followed, P.L.O. confidence seems to have grown. The war's prolongation was described as a sign of Israel's weakness, as were its failure for 21 days to achieve its stated objective, and its "repeated unfulfilled threats to attack Beirut." A commentary which stressed the P.L.O.'s desire to avoid the battle of Beirut, and willingness to accept some compromise formula involving reciprocal withdrawals under international guarantees, was at the same time firm: "It must be clear to all that there is a 'red line' beyond which the P.L.O. will not go."[37]

Behind this note of defiance lay a clear belief that Israel was incapable of storming Beirut, or unwilling to suffer the casualties involved, or otherwise prevented from doing so by domestic or external restraints. This belief persisted in most P.L.O. circles inside Beirut until the end of the war.

Although the last days of the bitter fighting in Bhamdun were ones of heavy bombardment of Beirut, and intense P.L.O.-Lebanese and (indirect) P.L.O.-U.S. negotiations, there was little change in this belief, or in the P.L.O. position: the stand relayed confidentially to the U.S. via the French on June 27 was identical to that laid out in the commentary of three days earlier, just cited.[38]

In addition to the discreet encouragement the Palestinians were receiving from their new French interlocutors, there were more immediate reasons for their tough position: among these was that the IDF's mountain offensive and bombardment of Beirut had backfired politically. The result was the resignation of several key Lebanese leaders from a "National Salvation Council," meant to sanction the U.S.-

Phalangist–Israeli position on the expulsion of the P.L.O. from Lebanon.

In practice, this led to the alignment of leftist and Muslim factions closer to the P.L.O., and to a strong boost for the latter after a very strained period of relations with its Lebanese allies in the early days of the war. When all of this was followed by the resignation of Secretary Haig, apparently partly because of disputes over policy in Lebanon, it became apparent that a long and difficult process would be necessary before the P.L.O. could be brought to its knees.

D. Phase 4: Seven Weeks of Siege, June 26–August 12

The battle of Beirut was by no means the same from day to day, particularly the seven-week siege which ended the war. There were gaps of several days with relatively little fighting, long stretches without aerial bombardment, and even a few days of complete quiet. At the other extreme, there were entire days of intense bombardment, lengthy periods of continuous fighting along the front lines, and times when the bombing and shelling continued for days on end.

Throughout the war, one of the most significant indicators of the severity of the fighting was whether the Israeli air force was involved. It is notable that for the 25 days from the short-lived ceasefire, which finally came into effect on June 26, until July 21, Beirut was not once attacked from the air. This probably owed something to the intervention of Habib or the disarray in Washington after Haig's resignation. All was not peaceful, however: the IDF made a number of limited attempts to advance during this period, which also witnessed a total of ten days of artillery and naval bombardment of the city, some of it extremely intense.

Because of the length of the siege, it would be pointless to give a blow-by-blow description of how the fighting affected P.L.O. decisionmaking. However, a clear periodization of these seven weeks is possible. Following the June 26 ceasefire, there was one week, until July 4, without any significant hostilities.

Nevertheless, tension remained high in the besieged city. On July 1 and 2, Israeli planes, beginning at dawn, screamed over Beirut in mock air raids, while a psychological war of formidable proportions was waged against the P.L.O., with rumors regarding its imminent departure being spread constantly.

This war was waged against the background of an ever-present fear of car bombs, after a devastating series of explosions of boobytrapped vehicles. A sequence of public confessions by captured drivers made clear these were being utilized by the Israelis and their Phalangist allies to increase the pressure on the P.L.O. to leave.[39]

Both were doing the P.L.O. a backhanded favor in another domain at the same time as they were randomly killing people in the streets of Beirut with cars packed with high explosives. As has already been mentioned, the entry of the LF into the Druze-populated areas of the Shouf under the aegis of the IDF in late June was accompanied by outrages and massacres which had a major impact on Lebanese Muslims and leftist opinion. This was the first intimation of what an Israeli victory over the P.L.O. would mean in Lebanese terms.

The immediate result was a series of forceful statements by prominent Lebanese political figures calling for defiance toward Israel and support for the P.L.O. These included former premiers Rashid Karami and Selim al-Hoss, as well as Walid Jumblatt, Nabih Berri, and Ibrahim Qulielat, all three key militia leaders. At one point, Berri prophetically stated of his Shi'a followers: "If the Israelis stay in Lebanon, we'll become the new Palestinians."[40]

This was the first time since June 4 that such important leaders had come out openly in support of the P.L.O. It had the effect of reinforcing its stand of holding out at least for matching Israeli withdrawals and fail-safe guarantees of a settlement, backed up by the entry of reliable international forces to Beirut, before it would withdraw from the capital. This position was later summed up in an 11-point document which remained the basis of the P.L.O. negotiating position until the end of July [see appendix].

Even before the shooting started again, persistent reports were being received by the P.L.O. from a variety of sources that Israel was preparing a major assault against Beirut.[41] In view of how accurate such reports had been in the past, these were taken quite seriously by the military command, particularly those which pinpointed the starting point of the offensive as the Fourth of July weekend, when many U.S. policymakers would be out of Washington, and the handover from Haig to his successor, George Shultz, was still incomplete.

Beginning on July 4, Israel did in fact begin to increase the military pressure. For the first two days, this involved an escalating series of attacks in the southern suburbs of the city and around the airport, marked by intense artillery exchanges. The Israeli forces gained little ground in spite of several attempts to advance, and were discomfited when P.L.O.gunners effectively supported front-line units of the JF in breaking up their attacks, and their shells and rockets hit a number of Israeli artillery positions.[42]

This was followed on July 6 by intensive shelling of several areas of West Beirut, well to the north and west of the scene of the ground combat. When IDF attempts to advance were resumed the following day, they achieved little, and the shelling of residential districts of the city continued. The fighting reached a peak on July 11, when heavy and repeated Israeli assaults brought IDF lines right up to the eastern runway of the airport, as furious bombardments of West Beirut left 63 civilians dead and 211 wounded, according to Lebanese police figures.[43]

One unpleasant surprise for the Israelis during the fighting of the 11th was the return fire of JF artillery and rocket units. Directed at IDF positions in the Ba'abda and Hazmieh areas, this hit an Israeli ammunition dump whose explosion was heard throughout the city, inflicting eight casualties according to an IDF spokesman (a P.L.O. spokesman estimated Israeli casualties at 75).[44] A ceasefire intervened at this point, and held with minor breaks for 10 days.

It is interesting to gauge the effect of these eight days of combat on the P.L.O.'s outlook and negotiating position. Whereas before this pressure was applied, the P.L.O. line was firm and uncompromising, with Abu Iyyad claiming, "We will not surrender," and 'Arafat telling a French paper the P.L.O. was not yet prepared to leave Beirut,[45] there was little apparent change after the fighting died down. On July 17 Abu Iyyad stressed again that there would be no climbdown from the minimum position laid out in the P.L.O.'s 11-point negotiating position.[46]

In contrast with mid- and late June, when the tone of the P.L.O. media was strident, reflecting the intense stress the Palestinians were under, the eight days of Israeli attacks in early July seem to have had little effect on their mood. A WAFA report had spoken on July 5 of the new assault marking "the first phase of what promises to be a long battle of Beirut,"[47] but in the midst of the fighting, the agency carried statements by both Brigadier Abu al-Walid and Abu Iyyad stressing that there was no change in the P.L.O. position, with the former emphasizing that the city had been turned into a fortified stronghold, and that the effect of the siege on the Joint Forces was minimal.[48]

On the last day of this round of combat, a WAFA commentary drew up a sober balance sheet of the war after five weeks, betraying neither any particular despair, nor any excessive confidence ("the Joint Forces [never] ... claimed that they were able to stop the Israeli army single-handedly").[49] On the same day, 'Arafat drew David and Goliath parallels between the P.L.O. and Israel, and blasted the silence and impotence of the Arab regimes.[50] His focus on the latter rather than Israel betrayed what was and continued to be a primary concern of the P.L.O. leadership.

A sarcastic WAFA commentary after the ceasefire finally came into effect, entitled "Israel's Losses after 5 Weeks of War," ridiculed Israeli Chief of Staff General Eytan's claim that there was only one P.L.O. gun left in Beirut, citing Western news agency reports that P.L.O. artillery and rocket fire had scored direct hits on IDF positions and had forced the withdrawal of Israeli tanks from exposed areas of Shweifat the previous day.[51] The clear message of this commentary—that Israel was fighting a war of attrition which it was far from winning—was repeated a few days later in a similar piece which spoke of the war not only as Israel's Vietnam, but also as her Verdun.[52]

Nothing said publicly by the P.L.O. during this round of fighting or in the ten days which followed indicated that Israel's military pressure had achieved anything, an impression which is amply confirmed by the confidential diplomatic exchanges going on at this time, discussed in chapter 4, which show little change in the P.L.O.'s stand.

In fact, by mid-July the attention of the P.L.O. leadership was turning increasingly to what would be done in Washington by an Arab League delegation composed of Saudi and Syrian Foreign Ministers Prince Sa'ud al-Faisal and 'Abd al-Halim Khaddam, and Fateh Central Committee member Khaled al-Hassan, It was here that they looked for the emergence of something new, whether positive or negative, rather than on the battlefield, where Israel had done little over the preceding 25 days to make them believe it could impose its own will single-handed.

That belief was about to be tested, for on July 21 Israeli attacks recommenced with an attempt to advance on the airport. It marked the beginning of an almost continuous escalation of violence which continued until the war's final ceasefire on August 12. This 22-day period witnessed 16 days of Israeli bombing, as well as the two largest Israeli ground operations of the entire siege.

In deducing the effect of these three weeks of attacks on P.L.O. perceptions and decisionmaking, it is necessary to realize that by the last half of July, there was only one decision left for the P.L.O. to take: whether to accept the generally unsatisfactory terms being offered by Habib, or to continue to hold out further in the hope that some external factor would change the situation in their favor and thereby allow accept- ance of their own terms: the "11 points."[53]

Although both plans entailed the withdrawal of the P.L.O.'s forces and leadership from Beirut, the 11 points featured a number of highly significant additional provisions. These included prior arrival of international forces with a firm and explicit mandate, reliable international guarantees for the safety of civilians in West Beirut, and matching IDF with- drawals (both at an initial and final stage of a P.L.O. with- drawal), as well as the P.L.O.'s continued political presence in Beirut, and a limited military presence elsewhere in Lebanon.

The key point to keep in mind when assessing the effect of what the IDF was doing during this final apocalyptic period of the war is that the P.L.O. dropped its own plan as a basis for negotiations before the end of July. It had definitely done so, and had begun to negotiate on the basis of the terms offered by Habib, well before August 1, when the two major ground assaults and the most massive bombing raids began.

Equally important, as we shall see in the next chapter, it seems to have been the utter failure of Arab efforts during July to change the U.S. position—worse, tacit Arab acceptance of that position—which brought the P.L.O. to decide that there was little point in holding out further. At this point, acceptance of the Habib plan became an unpleasant but inevitable choice.

As to what the P.L.O. perceived the IDF to be doing at this stage, it was seen not so much as pushing it to leave Beirut, or do so under certain conditions, as trying to circumvent the entire negotiating process so as to crush the P.L.O.—psycho- logically if not physically—and thereby make a negotiated settlement redundant. While perhaps not totally accurate, such a perception does not seem far-fetched in light of the grandiose Israeli objectives discussed earlier, and Israel's frustration at not having achieved them.

Although they had little effect on the negotiations, or on the outcome of the conflict (except in terms of losses in lives and property), these three weeks of Israeli attacks deserve special mention here, for at least three reasons. The first is that during this period there were two serious Israeli attempts to make significant ground advances, which met with limited success. The second is the intensity of the Israeli bombing of Beirut, which surpassed that in any period of the war. The third is that this round of fighting was marked by determined Israeli attempts to kill P.L.O. leaders via aerial bombardment of densely inhabited buildings.

After a day of limited probing attacks toward the airport, the final weeks of the war opened with five consecutive days of bombing raids on south-central Beirut, the Palestinian refugee camps, and the southern suburbs, coupled with shelling of areas of the city further north and even more full of people.

The next day, July 27, was one of unparalleled ferocity, with 36 air attacks during one two-hour period. Its high point was an air strike which devastated three densely populated apartment buildings in the Raouche area at the westernmost tip of the city, leaving over 350 casualties, virtually without exception civilians.[54] According to rumors in Beirut at the time, the target was an apartment used by a P.L.O. leader, but no one was killed, nor was evidence ever adduced that anyone had been in the area or frequented it.

The IDF tactic of trying to kill P.L.O. leaders was not unexpected, and had been the subject of repeated warnings from foreign sources. A Central Operations situation report issued two days before this attack warned of "either special or extensive regular military operations in Beirut against institutions, individuals, or leaders, or against specific areas. This is confirmed by all reports received, and has always to be considered as priority in our planning."[55]

In a postwar interview, Abu Iyyad, the head of the P.L.O. security services, revealed that seven Israeli agents of a group of 24 (all of them Arabs) had been captured by P.L.O. counterintelligence in July and August. They had confessed that their mission, which began in January 1982, was to discover the meeting places, offices, and residences of the leadership, as well as military targets, so as to pinpoint them for air attack. Ironically, he pointed out, ten of these agents were killed in air strikes they themselves called in on presumed targets, victims of the callousness of their bosses, or of pilot error.[56]

The Raouche bombing appears to have made little impression on P.L.O. leaders, as is clear from Central Operations situation reports during this period. Far from stressing the effect of Israeli bombing, they focused on "the paralysis of Arab action"; "this Arab slave market"; and the seven Arab foreign ministers meeting at Jedda "at their leisure, as if no Arab capital were being besieged," and asked "Don't the Arabs worry about the fate of their capitals in the near future . . . ?" which give an indication of the P.L.O.'s preoccupations.[57] A bitter WAFA commentary on July 30, the day the results of the Jedda meeting became known, stated that the U.S. was "twisting the arms of virtually every Arab state."[58] Clearly, nothing could be expected of the Arabs, and U.S. pressure and Israel's attacks would continue unabated.

As if to underscore this, the next day there were two hours of fierce air attacks on heavily populated residential areas along the Corniche al-Mazra'a, in the heart of the West Beirut, and in neighboring districts, as well as the southern suburbs and the Palestinians refugee camps. Artillery simultaneously pounded the entire city from dawn until just after 9 P.M.[59]

The worst was yet to come: this was especially ironic in view of the P.L.O. leadership's acceptance in principle of the Habib plan. While it is impossible to date the decision precisely—memories are hazy, the negotiations were highly confidential, and many key agreements were apparently oral (and certainly do not exist in any of the archives consulted)—it can definitely be placed before August 1.

Negotiations on the new basis had proceeded so far by that point that a Central Operations situation report of August 1 notes that the P.L.O. had already presented a working paper for withdrawal, including a timetable, which was to have been the subject of a P.L.O.–Lebanese military meeting at which U.S. and Lebanese responses to it were to be discussed.[60] The meeting had to be postponed due to Israel's escalation.

From this point on, and in spite of a number of obstacles which arose during the course of negotiation, an agreement had been reached in all but name, and only the details of the accord finally announced on August 18 still had to be worked out.[61] But twelve more days of bitter fighting had to pass before a lasting ceasefire was imposed.

Because these had little or no effect on P.L.O. decision-making or on the solution finally arrived it, they can be reviewed briefly. The three high points of these last twelve days were the airport attack of August 1, the major ground assault of August 4, and the nine hours of air raids involving over 220 sorties with which the fighting ended on August 12.

The August 1 attack was covered by more than 200 sorties by Israeli planes, and involved attempts to push up the coast from Khaldeh, as well as a seaborne assault against the Summerland Beach, both of which failed. The main thrust of the assault was directed against the airport, which was lost by the JF after a 15-hour battle.

This new defeat was the occasion for another attack on the passivity of the Arab regimes by Abu Iyyad who, in the first such critique to refer to specific states, said that if they were serious in their claims to support the P.L.O., Saudi Arabia should cut off oil to the U.S. and Syria throw its full military weight into the battle.[62] It was perhaps not coincidental that these were the two countries which had sent their foreign ministers to Washington, and had later jointly presided over the seven-party Jedda meeting.

At the same time, a WAFA commentary claimed that politically the battle marked "perhaps the most spectacular failure Israel has suffered since the war began." This was the case since the attack had failed to intimidate the P.L.O., and at the same time resulted in a Security Council resolution condemning Israel, thus removing settlement efforts from friendly U.S. hands, even if only temporarily.[63]

The IDF offensive of August 4 was even more intensive. It involved an attempt to push into West Beirut at five points. Israeli troops pushing off from the newly captured airport achieved success on the southern axis of advance, reaching a Lebanese Army barracks only a few hundred meters from Shatila camp. They were finally halted before the Kuwaiti Embassy, which they could not take in spite of repeated attacks backed by heavy air strikes. On the other four axes of advance, the port, Tayyouneh, the Museum, and Summerland Beach, the IDF could not advance at all, suffering relatively heavy losses (in the neighborhood of 100 according to both sides[64].

Although the siege perimeter was tightened in the south by the advance to the Kuwaiti Embassy, the IDF's failure to break through along all four axes of attack located in built-up areas—the southern advances having been along the last remaining area of open ground on the front lines—seems to have had more of an impact on the defenders than the loss of a few hundred meters of ground.

This was the opinion of many P.L.O. military officers at the time. It was mirrored in a WAFA report, which stressed that the IDF's sole advance of the day was a few hundred meters in "the open terrain between the airport road and Ouza'i." In a later interview, however, 'Arafat himself noted that after Israeli forces reached the Kuwaiti Embassy they were in rifle range of Corniche al-Mazra'a, the Fakhani area, and Shatila, a situation which had to be taken seriously. On the other hand, Abu Iyyad stated that after a visit to forward P.L.O. positions at the Kuwaiti Embassy following the battle, he had been impressed by how little progress the IDF had made.[65]

The IDF was now up against the unbroken chain of multistory concrete buildings which formed the battlements of fortress Beirut, having taken all the flat clear terrain where its armor could maneuver freely and its planes see their targets. Perhaps for this reason, the attack of August 4 was the last major Israeli ground offensive (although three limited attacks were launched at the Museum on August 9, 11, and 12, all unsuccessful).

The IDF thereafter restricted itself to concentrated air and artillery bombardment, including both indiscriminate barrages and pinpoint attacks like the bombing raid on August 6, which completely flattened a nine-story building in the Sanaye' district killing perhaps 200 people ('Arafat had reportedly been seen there just before the attack[66]). The combat phase of the war ended with the intense day-long bombing raids of August 12. The 220 sorties flown on this last day of punishment of Beirut inflicted over 500 casualties.[67]

Strange as it may seem, there appeared to be little despair in P.L.O. ranks after it was all over. A commentary on the last day of the bombing even struck a cautiously optimistic note: Israel had shown it could destroy Beirut and starve its inhabitants if it wanted to, but 10 hours of nonstop bombing were proof that it had not yet succeeded in its aims. In spite of "the cowardice and treachery of the Arab world . . . Israel has not prevailed," the commentary continued. Indeed, after 70 days of war, Beirut was still resisting, which meant to the Palestinians that in spite of their superiority, "the Israelis . . . are not invincible."[68]

Striking the same note, Abu Iyyad stated just after the bombing stopped that the only possible explanation for the raids was to mask Israel's "failure to confront the Joint Forces on the ground," and to "raise the morale of their soldiers who have been forced to fall back in attack after attack on our positions."[69] At the same time, a Central Operations situation report pointed out that three IDF attempts to advance while Beirut was being turned into an "inferno" by the bombing had been foiled with heavy casualties, and that attacks were still being launched by the JF behind enemy lines. It concluded with Koranic verse warning against sadness, "for God is with us."[70]

If the P.L.O. had been beaten after 70 days of fighting, its leader's statements and the tone of its media certainly did not show it. That the combat phases of the war had ended with the P.L.O. battered but still dug in behind its fortified positions in Beirut and with the vastly superior Israeli army still besieging the city, prevented from storming it for whatever reasons, apparently meant more to the defenders of Beirut than the fact that they had lost and would be forced to evacuate the city.

In an unequal contest, they had fought longer than had all the Arab armies put together in all their wars with Israel, doing better than anyone could have expected. But, as an August 9 editorial August concluded, "In the end, the only thing which we were unable to affect was the immobility, the paralysis, the frozen will of the Arab world."[71] Speaking much later, 'Arafat reflected that because the P.L.O. had fared better against Israel than the Arab regimes, they could not allow it to leave Beirut with even a symbolic victory, and thus extended no help whatsoever.[72] This, and their demonstrated ability to stand up to Israel under the right conditions, were the main lessons the Palestinian fighters carried away from Beirut with them.

Chapter 4

June 1982:
The Decision
To Leave Beirut

I Beirut, the Palestinians, and the P.L.O.

During the 1970s, Beirut came to be a second home (if only a temporary one) for many Palestinians. Among them were P.L.O. combatants, cadres, and leaders who had been obliged to move to Lebanon after the P.L.O.'s expulsion from Jordan in 1970–71 and had established or begun their families there. In this cosmopolitan city they joined those of their countrymen who had first arrived in Lebanon in 1948–49 as refugees, as well as political exiles from all over the region who had made Beirut their home.

There were many other Palestinians in Beirut, who were there by choice. Over the years, members of the growing Palestinian bourgeoisie[1] were drawn to the city's free political and economic environment. Many managed to obtain Lebanese citizenship. The Lebanese capital also attracted thousands of young Palestinians from the occupied territories, Jordan, and the Gulf, who came to study at the American University, Beirut University College, the Lebanese University, or the Arab University of Beirut. Most went home after a few years, but many stayed after their education was completed or after leaving university.

While all these institutions had large numbers of Palestinian students, the Arab University had a mainly Palestinian student body. It was located near the Fakhani quarter where most P.L.O. offices were found, and adjoined the sprawling Sabra and Shatila refugee camps. For Palestinians in the years 1971–82 this roughly one-square-mile area in the center of Beirut was the closest thing they had had to a political, intellectual, financial, administrative, and spiritual capital since 1948.

This was true even of many Palestinians who had never seen Beirut. For those suffering the daily humiliation of the Israeli occupation, as well as for others subjected to varying levels of intolerance in the Arab host countries, the P.L.O.'s presence in Beirut meant a great deal.

On the one hand, it was a powerful symbol of Palestinian existence, autonomy, and peoplehood. On the other, in a concrete sense it was their court of last resort, their administrative center and the guarantor of their status. Instances of the P.L.O. in Beirut dealt with serious disputes between Palestinians, and with requests for economic aid, scholarships, and payment of medical expenses, as well as complaints about bad treatment by Arab governments.

The P.L.O. structure briefly discussed in chapter 2 was carrying out functions many of which had never before been performed on a national level. Neither at the height of their pre-1948 national movement nor in the two decades which followed the 1948 defeat had the Palestinians managed to develop modern integrated national institutions.[2] This the P.L.O. had done, and it was something of which Palestinians were justifiably proud. It was also realized by Israel's leaders, who were deadly foes of anything which reinforced Palestinian nationalism.

Palestinians in Lebanon were acutely aware that their powerful Israeli enemies were bent on ending the P.L.O.'s presence in Lebanon. Nevertheless, the idea that it might be forced to leave Beirut would have seemed fantastic to most of them on the eve of the 1982 war. It also seemed highly unlikely to many Lebanese.

Many factors contributed to this sense of the permanence of the P.L.O. ministate in Lebanon, and to a disbelief that the objectives of their opponents could be realized. Among them were memories of a recent string of failed attempts to dislodge them; the seeming solidity of P.L.O. structures; the extent to which individual Palestinians had settled in Beirut; and the degree to which the P.L.O. had become integrated into the conflict-torn Lebanese political map.

However, all of these apparent certainties crumbled in mid-June, with the IDF at the gates of Beirut and the world's greatest superpower insistently seconding the demands of Israel, President Sarkis, and the Lebanese right that the P.L.O. leave Beirut forthwith. As a result, the P.L.O. leadership faced one of the toughest, most painful decisions in its history.

We have already seen what an unenviable situation the P.L.O. was in as it faced these demands. By this point it had long since lost the support of the vast majority of Lebanese. Moreover, in the wake of its defeat in the south, the rapid advance of the Israelis through the Shouf, and the isolation of Beirut, the P.L.O.'s military position contained no glimmer of hope. Morale at every level reflected these harsh givens.

How did its leaders take the decision confronting them? What were the dynamics of the interaction between them? Who played the key roles, and when were the essential decisions taken? These questions may never be answered definitively. However, what follows offers responses based on the archival record of what was written and said at the time publicly and privately, and on the recollections of participants in these events.

II The P.L.O. Leadership

A handful of men were involved in the P.L.O.'s decision to withdraw from Beirut. To understand this decision, and why it was accepted by the P.L.O. rank and file, it is necessary to describe the individuals concerned, and the context within which they functioned.

The formal structures of the P.L.O. were rarely the forums for crisis decisions, and most P.L.O. decisions had to be made in times of crisis. However, in "normal" circumstances, the P.L.O. Executive Committee, Central Council, and National Council all played specified roles in taking decisions, in promulgating them, or in giving them legitimacy.[3] This was particularly the case for the Palestinian National Council (PNC). This body, made up largely of elected representatives, served as the equivalent of a legislature, meeting annually (when possible), approving the budget, reviewing the actions of the Executive Committee, and passing on major changes of course, such as acceptance of a West Bank/Gaza Strip state as the P.L.O.'s provisional objective in 1974.

While the 60-member Central Council was little more than an advisory sounding board, the Executive Committee was supposed to be more than that. It was certainly not a cipher. The Executive Committee performed several important functions, including approving all major spending decisions, and defining the parameters of the P.L.O.'s policy toward the Arab regimes and the course of its international diplomacy.

The Executive Committee was nevertheless highly unsuited to crisis decisionmaking. With its composition determined at each session of the PNC by bargaining between different groups, and its members based in different Arab states and sometimes representing their interests inside the Palestinian polity, it reflected many of the least attractive aspects of the consensus politics which characterized the P.L.O. Far from being the seat of real executive power, in practice it resembled nothing more than an unwieldy and weak coalition government with little control over vital matters.

Real power was located in the top ranks of Fateh and the other groups which made up the P.L.O. Among them, the *primus inter pares* was unquestionably Yasser 'Arafat (Abu 'Ammar), affectionately known to all in Fateh as *al-khityar* (the old man). Identified in the mid-1960s only as the spokesman of the Fateh leadership, he was now Chairman of the P.L.O. Executive Committee and Commander in Chief of all P.L.O. military forces. As one of fourteen members of the Fateh Central Committee (whose Secretary, Abu Lutf [Farouq al-Qaddoumi], was also P.L.O. Foreign Minister), 'Arafat dominated that body.

'Arafat's preeminence inside the Fateh leadership was by no means absolute. Opposition within the Central Committee often forced him to back down from positions he had staked out, and he had constantly to consult with its members. His closest ally on the Committee was usually Abu Jihad (Khalil al-Wazir), Deputy Commander in Chief of P.L.O. forces, while the part of the loyal opposition was often played by Abu Iyyad (Salah Khalaf), chief of the P.L.O. security apparatus, normally allied with Abu Lutf. Both Abu Jihad and Abu Iyyad also had important Fateh responsibilities in addition to their P.L.O. titles, the former with relation to Fateh military forces and the occupied territories, and the latter regarding security and intelligence matters.

This foursome had provided the core leadership of Fateh for decades (together with others who had died along the way). In spite of differences which at times arose among them, they had a relationship with one another which was extremely durable, and were linked by strong bonds of mutual affection and respect going back to their common background in the Gaza Strip, Egypt, and Kuwait in the early 1950s.[4]

Other early leaders of Fateh beyond this core played significant roles. Among them were Abu Sa'id (Khaled al-

Hassan), based in Kuwait,[5] and Abu Mazin (Mahmoud 'Abbas) and Abu Maher (Muhammad Ghunaym), both based in Damascus. However, they were usually not in Beirut, which meant that their input into daily decisionmaking was less regular and less frequent than that of others

In addition to these older men, who had been active in Palestinian politics since the early 1950s, and who by 1982 were in their early and mid-fifties, there was a somewhat younger second generation of leaders, who were not among the founding fathers of Fateh. Three of them require special mention, either because of their wartime prominence, or their importance in terms of the internal political balance of the leadership.

Brigadier Abu al-Walid (Sa'ad Sayel), the P.L.O. Chief of Military Operations, was to play a key role in 1982, both in directing the fighting and in the negotiations. Like the Deputy Chief of Operations, Colonel Abu Musa (Sa'id Musa Maragha) and many other officers in the top Fateh military leadership, he had been a Jordanian regular army officer until 1970. His stature had grown since the mid-1970s, a fact recognized when he was elected to the Fateh Central Committee in 1980. It was to grow further during the siege of Beirut. His postwar assassination was a severe blow to Fateh.

Hani al-Hassan, like his older brother Khaled, was identified with the conservative, "pragmatic" wing of Fateh. He was one of the main P.L.O. negotiators during the siege, playing the same role of senior envoy he had previously performed in Iran after the revolution and elsewhere in the region. With the formal title of Political Advisor to 'Arafat, he had a narrow organizational base inside Fateh, and was often chosen to carry out delicate missions and to stake out positions which could later be abandoned.

Nimr Saleh (Abu Saleh) was on the other side of the political spectrum. The outspoken, impulsive leading figure of Fateh's "radical" faction, he tended to lean toward Syria and the Soviet Union. In ill health and severly hampered politically by the death in October 1981 of Majid Abu Sharar, his far shrewder, more intelligent, and more respected ally inside the Central Committee, Abu Saleh was often in a minority of one. In spite of being a member of the Central Committee group supposed to supervise the Fateh military forces, his role during the war was limited. After the war he became a leader of the insurrection against 'Arafat.

On an entirely different level were the heads of the Popular Front for the Liberation of Palestine (PFLP) and the Democratic Front for the Liberation of Palestine (DFLP), which together with Fateh had been the main independent political forces in the Palestinian arena for over a decade. Dr. George Habash and Nayef Hawatmeh both had longstanding relationships with 'Arafat and the core Fateh leaders. Habash had once been a serious rival to the P.L.O. Chairman for leadership of the entire Palestinian national movement, but had seen his own group decline in the 1970s. The PFLP had formed the nucleus of the "Rejection Front," dedicated to opposing the 1974 decision to accept the idea of a West Bank/Gaza Strip state, but which disintegrated after the 1975–76 war. The DFLP, a 1969 offshoot of the PFLP, had originally championed the idea of a West Bank/Gaza Strip Palestinian state, and remained loosely allied to Fateh from the early 1970s onward.

Ironically, in view of the recurring tension between the political positions of the PFLP and Fateh, and the closeness between those of the latter and the DFLP, personal relations between Habash and most members of the Fateh core leadership were generally closer than those enjoyed by Hawatmeh. However, by 1982 it could be said that a certain level of confidence and mutual trust existed between the leaderships of Fatah and both groups. This was particularly true of those individuals located in Beirut, and proved important when the time came for taking and implementing hard wartime decisions.

III The First Week of War

When the war broke out, chance dictated where individual P.L.O. leaders were located. 'Arafat, in Saudi Arabia when the bombing of Beirut and the south started on Friday, June 4, was able to return on Saturday, the day before the invasion began. Abu Lutf stayed abroad and traveled to New York for meetings of the U.N. Security Council. Habash and Hawatmeh's deputies, Abu 'Ali Mustafa and Yasser 'Abed Rabbo, were not in Beirut (the latter left the city on the night of June 11–12 to take command of the Souq al-Gharb sector in the mountains), and thus both leaders acted without the influence of these younger and often more dynamic men. In the end, seven of fourteen Fateh Central Committee members found themselves in the Lebanese capital during the siege, as well as five of eight DFLP Political Bureau members, the majority of the PFLP leadership, and only five of fifteen P.L.O. Executive Committee members.

Initially, the P.L.O.'s diplomatic activity focused on obtaining U.N. action to halt the Israeli advance.[6] In retrospect this may seem like an exercise in futility, but it did not appear to be so at the time. Past experience taught that most of Israel's wars had been ended within a matter of days by an international consensus operating through the United Nations. This was true of the 1956, 1967, and 1973 conflicts, which were halted in this fashion in five, six, and eighteen days respectively, as well as of Israel's 1978 invasion of South Lebanon, and the 1981 cross-border fighting, both of which lasted for a matter of days (seven and nine respectively).

When confronted with a major Israeli escalation in the past, the P.L.O. almost routinely requested the Arab states, the Soviet Union, the European Community, and the nonaligned and Islamic blocs at the United Nations to put pressure on the United States, each in its own way. The "moderate" Arab states headed by Saudi Arabia would be asked to use their presumed influence in Washington to press for U.S. action to restrain Israel, while America's European allies often made similar moves, simultaneously backing nonaligned and Arab initiatives at the U.N. to stop the fighting. The USSR could be counted on to support such a course, and to threaten unspecified consequences should U.N. action not suffice.

The expectation in June 1982 that something similar would eventually take place, and that the P.L.O. had only to hold out until then, ultimately proved incorrect, but it was not totally unfounded. It was reinforced by the passage of Security Council resolution 509 late on June 6, the first day of the invasion, with the U.S. voting in favor. This demanded that "Israel withdraw all its military forces forthwith and unconditionally withdraw to the internationally recognized boundaries of Lebanon," and an immediate halt to hostilities.

Had such a resolution been enforced, the previous pattern would have been repeated, and Israel's invasion would have been brought to an abrupt halt. For this to happen, however, hard decisions would have been necessary in Washington. That the Reagan administration was not willing to take them in 1982 was demonstrated when Israel continued its advance, and when the tone of U.S. pronouncements changed perceptibly. (On June 13 Haig told a TV interviewer that the U.S. did not demand an immediate Israeli withdrawal from Lebanon, while by June 21 a State Department spokesman declared that S.C. 509 was no longer relevant.)

The first signal of this change was a U.S. veto on June 8 of a Security Council draft resolution which would have condemned Israel for noncompliance with S.C. 509, and which stated that sanctions against it would be considered if it did not halt its invasion within six hours. All Security Council members except the United States were in favor of this draft. But from this point on, the U.N. was virtually paralyzed by an American refusal to consider any serious measures against Israel.

The administration was clearly divided internally on what to do, and apparently suffered from mixed signals while the President and Secretary Haig were in Europe in early June.[7] It finally decided to support Israel unreservedly, in the apparent hope of utilizing Israel's invasion of Lebanon to achieve U.S. regional objectives vis-à-vis the P.L.O., Syria, and the USSR, and in the process to transform the Lebanese internal situation.

This position did not change during the war. In a sense, it remained unaltered until the withdrawal of U.S. Marines from Beirut in February 1984. Haig's description of the war as providing "a historic opportunity to deal with the problem of Lebanon," and creating "a fresh opportunity to complete the Camp David peace process" (or Kissinger's, "it opens up extraordinary opportunities for a dynamic American diplomacy throughout the Middle East")[8] not only reflected their hard-line views, but summed up as well the basic attitude toward the situation emerging from Israel's invasion of most leading members of the Reagan Administration, including the President and Haig's successor, George Shultz.

The P.L.O. initially hoped that the new, tougher U.S. position which first emerged on June 8 could be reversed. This illusion was encouraged by telephone contacts with the Saudi leadership, and in meetings in New York and Paris between P.L.O. representatives and Saudi Foreign Minister Prince Sa'ud al-Faisal. Telexes on June 11 reported in almost identical terms what the Saudi minister told Abu Lutf in New York and P.L.O. Paris representative Ibrahim al-Souss about his contacts in Washington, Paris, and Bonn.[9]

The essential point which emerges from Sa'ud al-Faisal's account of his talks with American officials is that they tried to convince him of U.S. good faith, at a time when the United States was in fact preventing implementation of S.C 509 at the U.N., thereby enabling Israel to continue its advance. The President, for example, told the Saudi diplomat that the U.S. knew in advance of the Israeli operation, but not that it would be on this scale. Reagan assured him that the U.S. was embarrassed by the invasion, stressed that the cancellation of a planned visit by Haig to Israel was a sign of displeasure, and "promised to use leverage on Israel for complete withdrawal" from Lebanon.[10]

At this stage, on June 11, Israel did in fact announce a ceasefire with Syrian forces after the bulk of operations against them had been completed, but it pointedly excluded the P.L.O. from its provisions. This ceasefire was most likely related to U.S. intercession, influenced by Arab and U.N. moves and a Soviet démarche. Soon afterward, however, the Israelis again violated the ceasefire they had proclaimed. When they reached and surrounded Beirut on June 13, and proclaimed harsh conditions for their withdrawal—amounting to unconditional surrender by the P.L.O.—the U.S. now firmly aligned its position with Israel's.

From this point on, the P.L.O. had to contend not only with the full weight of Israel, but also with that of the U.S. This was quickly perceived by the P.L.O.: telexes from Beirut spoke often of "the American-Israeli position."[11] The Organization's leaders quickly realized that they would have to drastically revise many of their assumptions about how long Israel would be allowed to carry out a major offensive military operation. This time, the U.S. was not going to step in to stop the IDF.[12]

The frustration of the P.L.O. leadership at the inability of the U.N. to obtain a binding ceasefire, or to station its truce observers on the spot (U.S. obstruction in the Security Council prevented this) reached a peak on June 13, the day the Israelis reached Ba'abda. Hours before that, 'Arafat had ordered that a detailed breakdown of Israeli ceasefire violations, based on radio messages received by Central Operations, be sent to New York. His hope was that after one week of uninterrupted fighting between Israel and the P.L.O., this would aid in obtaining decisive U.N. action to halt the advance of the IDF.[13]

It failed to do so, and 'Arafat's angry reaction to the paralysis in New York emerges from a peremptory telex sent later the same day to Abu Lutf and Zuhdi Tarazi, the P.L.O.'s U.N. representative. It read: "There is a waste of time . . . the enemy succeeded this morning in the face of the absence of observers in occupying the Khaldeh triangle . . . We asked of you since yesterday [sic] to move truce supervisors, but it appears the delay is intentional so as to give Israel the opportunity to complete its task." The message ended harshly: "There is no point to the exchange of telexes only. We demand action . . . we demand steps on the ground.[14]

No such action was forthcoming. Indeed, because of persistent obstruction of such action by the U.S. and Israel, U.N. observers were not deployed in Beirut until mid-August, after fighting ceased. In the absence of effective U.N. action to impose or supervise an effective ceasefire, the P.L.O. leadership encircled in Beirut with the bulk of its military forces, and with little hope of any external relief, had to decide under enormous pressure how to respond to the Israeli demand of June 13 for the P.L.O. to lay down its arms and withdraw from Beirut.

IV The Internal P.L.O. Debate
Over Withdrawal

There rapidly emerged two distinct schools of thought within the leadership on how to deal with the P.L.O's grim situation. The first, identified with Hani al-Hassan, saw no alternative to withdrawing P.L.O. military forces from Beirut, but wanted three things in exchange: a political gain as a quid pro quo for withdrawal, a morale victory resulting from prolonged resistance, and the retention of a P.L.O. political and military presence in Lebanon as one element in a formula to protect Palestinian civilians in Lebanon.[15]

The desired results of this approach included some form of U.S. recognition of, and direct contact with, the P.L.O.— which of course was never achieved. Some argued that this approach was linked to the transformation of the P.L.O. into a purely political body, which would attempt to gain its ends diplomatically rather than forcibly.

Support for this position within the ranks of the P.L.O. went up and down in the feverish days of mid-June. By early July, its partisans had been discredited, and were scornfully described by their opponents as "The Withdrawal Now Movement," a takeoff on the Israeli "Peace Now Movement." But in the crucial days after June 13, some P.L.O. leaders saw no realistic alternative to acceptance of Israel's demands. As an initial result of the intense internal debate within the leadership, the partisans of the first approach received a green light to explore what could be obtained, although this did not stop their opponents from criticizing this policy bitterly in private and in public.[16]

The semipublic way in which the P.L.O. internal debate was carried out at this stage caused great confusion, both within the movement and for foreign observers. This was true particularly when the propositions being discussed by Hani al-Hassan first became known. Opponents of this approach fought it in the P.L.O. media, in on- and off-the-record discussions with local and foreign journalists, as well as in internal P.L.O. councils. At the beginning they had an uphill fight because of the number and influence of those who supported the idea of negotiating a withdrawal.

The composition of this group was surprisingly disparate, including a number of individuals who were not normally political bedfellows, and some of whom had reached the point of "collapse" according to Abu Iyyad.[17] Besides Hani al-Hassan, there was the PFLP spokesman, Bassam Abu Sharif, who spoke often to journalists at the Commodore Hotel about how desperate the P.L.O.'s situation was, affirming that immediate withdrawal was the only way out; Ahmed Jibril, the bombastic leader of the pro-Syrian PFLP General Command (PFLP-GC), whose normally hearty appetite for fighting the Israelis seemed to wane after Beirut was surrounded; the leaders of two minor radical factions, Dr. Samir Ghosheh of the Popular Struggle Front (PSF) and Abu al-'Abbas of the Palestine Liberation Front (PLF); and a number of Fateh leaders, among them Abu al-Hol (Hayel 'Abd al-Hamid), and Brigadier Abu al-Walid.

The position of Brigadier Abu al-Walid among this group requires elaboration. Having long argued that if the Israelis launched a major military operation their only alternative was to make Beirut their objective, he realized that this was happening as soon as he heard the first report of the Awwali landing on the first night of the invasion.[18] He was thus not surprised by the IDF's arrival at Ba'abda, unlike some other P.L.O. and LNM leaders. Throughout the war, he maintained his equanamity. Even while arguing that the logic of the military situation dictated P.L.O. acceptance of the demand for its withdrawal, he was constantly supervising day-to-day military operations, as well as the feverish building of fortifications and sowing of mines which were to make the defense of Beirut possible for the last eight weeks of the siege.

The attitude of the P.L.O.'s senior commander was probably rooted in his traditional military background. An engineering officer who had reached the rank of colonel in the Jordanian army, Brigadier Abu al-Walid had received advanced staff training in the United States (at the same time as Mordechai Gur, IDF Chief of Staff during the 1978 invasion). He argued in mid-June that Beirut was militarily indefensible (the term used in Arabic was "saqita 'askariyan"). From the standpoint of classical military principles, this was a reasonable claim, especially in light of the hopeless odds, the complete isolation of the city, and the IDF's position in the heights overlooking it. Brigadier al-Walid modified this view only in late June, after completion of P.L.O. defensive preparations and the appearance of a strong Israeli reluctance to storm the city. Until then, he sided with those who said withdrawal was inevitable.

The opposing group argued that the matter could not be looked at in classical military terms. It too was composed of disparate elements, many of them individuals who agreed on little else, including Fateh leaders Abu Iyyad, Abu Saleh, Sakhr Abu Nizar, the Secretary of the Fateh Revolutionary Council, and Colonel Abu Musa, as well as Dr. George Habash and Abu Maher al-Yamani of the PFLP, Nayef Hawatmeh of the DFLP, and Talal Naji of the PFLP-GC. They stressed that the situation was not hopeless, that the war was far from over, and that the Palestinian and Lebanese defenders of Beirut had a good chance to hold out for better terms.

The military men in this second group argued forcefully that Beirut, its southern suburbs, and the adjoining refugee camps were nearly ideal for the type of warfare the Joint Forces were best suited for, and atrociously inappropriate for what the Israelis were comfortable with. The intensity and length of the fighting in Sidon and 'Ain al-Hilweh, as well as in Damour and Khaldeh (all far smaller and more easily assaulted than Beirut), were used to buttress their argument. Moreover, they claimed, a reluctance to enter the city had already been evinced by many quarters in the Israeli military and government, and it would be foolish for the P.L.O. to throw away an opportunity to take advantage of this.

There were differences among those holding this position. A few, like Colonel Abu Khaled al-'Amleh, later a prominent leader of the Fateh rebellion, argued that Beirut and the adjoining camps were practically impregnable. They held, moreover, that as a matter of principle the P.L.O. should not withdraw from the city under any circumstances, and should hold out against the Israeli demands indefinitely, whatever the consequences.

But the majority of the second group (which ultimately became the core of a majority within the leadership as a whole), saw things differently. While sharing the slender hope that the P.L.O. might be able to drag out the siege, wear down the Israelis, and thereby ultimately avoid withdrawal altogether, they perceived that this was not likely. In their view, negotiations were an open-ended tactic. The objective was to obtain the best that could realistically be expected from the situation. While differing from the maximalists who refused any compromise, a gulf separated them from the minimalists, who were fully reconciled to accepting some version of the U.S.-Israeli terms, but hoped to obtain specific political compensation in return. This difference was summed up in the words of Abu Iyyad: "Negotiations were a tactic for some in the leadership, and a strategy for others."[19]

In the immediate aftermath of the collapse of the Shouf followed by arrival of the Israelis at Ba'abda, the second point of view was almost inaudible inside the P.L.O. This was partly because of the drastic effect of these events on most Lebanese, who were unprepared for the Israeli invasion and stunned by it. During the first weeks of the war, "we were in a state of shock," said Walid Jumblatt soon afterward.[20]

Already seriously alienated from the P.L.O., many Lebanese took the seemingly unstoppable Israeli advance as the occasion for an outpouring of hostile feeling against the Palestinians. This naturally took different forms. In the south, many Shi'a welcomed the Israelis, assuming that their arrival meant the end of the state of war which had lasted for a decade, during which time the southerners had paid the heaviest price. There was unrestrained jubilation in Maronite circles at the prospect that Israel would eliminate the Palestinians, and thereby clear the way for a new order in Lebanon, of which they would be the natural beneficiaries. Even among the Sunni urban population, closest in many ways to the Palestinians, there was some expectation of positive results from the new state of affairs.

Thus at a critical moment of decision in mid-June, P.L.O. leaders found themselves almost completely deprived of any Lebanese support. It was not surprising that confronted with the might of Israel and the insistent support for it of the United States, many Lebanese should feel that they had no alternative except to go along with what seemed like a *fait accompli* imposed by the U.S. and Israel. The deep involvement of the U.S. in the shaping of events was symbolized by the ubiquitous presence of Philip Habib, who spent most of his time during the weeks that followed either in meetings at the Presidental Palace in Ba'abda or directing the negotiations from his headquarters at the U.S. Ambassador's residence in nearby Yarzé.

The Council of National Salvation, whose formation was called for by President Sarkis on June 14, was generally understood to be intended as a vehicle for a unanimous Lebanese front in dealing with the P.L.O. on the basis of the Israeli demands of June 13 and the nearly identical position of the United States. The reservations regarding it of Walid Jumblatt and Nabih Berri did not conceal the fact that in practical terms the P.L.O. had no organized Lebanese backing. In the immediate aftermath of the occupation of Ba'abda, even the P.L.O.'s allies in the LNM advised them that they had no alternative but withdrawal.[21] Some of its parties, Jumblatt acidly said at the time, had become "virtually Phalangist."[22]

It is important to reiterate that while some Lebanese public attitutes, such as Maronite hostility to the P.L.O. or the antagonism toward the commando presence of the bulk of the southern Shi'a population, were stable, others fluctuated violently. Thus, less than two weeks after the occupation of Ba'abda led to the coalescence of what seemed to be a broad anti-P.L.O. front, the outlook of many Lebanese was reversed. This was the effect of new factors like Israeli-Phalangist cooperation in occupied areas, fears of what this might portend in the wake of a P.L.O. withdrawal, the renewal of IDF attacks on Syrian forces in the mountains, and a higher estimation of the ability of the P.L.O. to hold out in Beirut.

As we saw in the last chapter, the turning point in this shift in Lebanese attitudes came during the last week of June. Even before that, however, the balance within the Palestinian leadership had shifted. As a result, a unified position had finally emerged, embodying elements of the outlooks put forward by both sides in the internal P.L.O. debate. This became clear during negotiations via the mediation of France, which began in the second half of June. The final decision was formally embodied in a brief handwritten memo delivered by Yasser 'Arafat to Premier Shafiq Wazzan on July 2, promising that the P.L.O. leadership would leave Beirut.

The text, never published—and reported in distorted terms in the press at the time—was deliberately vague, and referred only to the P.L.O.'s acceptance in principle of the movement of its headquarters from Beirut. Vague though it was, this was the first firm, formal, written commitment by the P.L.O. regarding withdrawal. Wazzan claimed at the time that he had no intention of delivering it to anyone, but that it was an assurance to the Lebanese about the P.L.O.'s intention to do everything possible to spare Beirut. This is consistent with the

way the P.L.O. described the pledge, which, at a meeting at
Saeb Salam's home the same day, was delivered also to the
traditional Sunni and Shi'a politicians of the Islamic Grouping
and the Front for Preservation of the South.[23] It remains for us
to go back and describe how such a commitment was agreed on
unanimously by the P.L.O. leadership in the final two weeks of
June.

V The Decision is Taken

The catalyst for the P.L.O.'s decision was the fierce internal
debate that arose following the leaking to the press of the terms
being discussed by Hani al-Hassan with intermediaries for
Israel and the United States. They caused a stir not only in
Beirut, but also among supporters of the P.L.O. abroad.[24] The
furor was all the greater since many of the points being
discussed were distorted or taken out of context in the local
and foreign media. On top of this, as previously noted, a variety
of hostile actors were simultaneously trying to create panic in
West Beirut by exaggerating the P.L.O.'s concessions and
describing its capitulation as imminent.

What seems to have caused the first reaction against the
approach ascribed in the press to Hani al-Hassan was the
sudden realization by many Palestinians of how harsh the
Israeli terms were, and shock at the fact that acceptance of
them meant leaving Beirut. They differed in their reaction from
a few members of the P.L.O. leadership who advocated this
approach and seemed to regard the prospect of leaving Beirut
with relative equanimity. This was probably because these
individuals aspired to shift the focus of P.L.O. activities
elsewhere, had no personal political base in Lebanon, or were
uninvolved in P.L.O. military affairs.

The reaction to this line, when it came, took the form of
pressure on the leadership to deny press reports of the terms
the P.L.O. was allegedly willing to accept. Specifically, there
was intense pressure for a disavowal of statements attributed

to Hani al-Hassan regarding transformation of the P.L.O. from a military into a political movement, calling for a dialogue with the United States, and accepting the inevitability of leaving Beirut. This pressure reached a peak on June 17, the day when four P.L.O. denials of press reports on this subject appeared, two specifically refuting propositions attributed to Hani al-Hassan.

On the same day, a confidential memo was sent to 'Arafat by a senior P.L.O. official criticizing remarks made by Hani al-Hassan to Western journalists on several occasions. In some of the things he said, the memo stated, al-Hassan not only was contradicting the public P.L.O. line on the question of withdrawal, but also was severely undermining morale and public confidence in the P.L.O. leadership, and severely weakening the P.L.O.'s negotiating position, as exaggerated or distorted versions of his remarks were published in the foreign media and had wide circulation in Beirut.[25] Similar complaints were being voiced throughout the P.L.O., and made their way to the ears of 'Arafat and his fellow leaders, sometimes in a forceful manner.

Particularly sensitive in this regard was the issue of the P.L.O.'s laying down its arms, a condition then being firmly demanded by Israel, and which al-Hassan had been reported by U.P.I. on June 16 as having accepted. It was imperative for the leadership to draw the line here, because of the devastating effect such a rumor, if believed, would have had on the forces in the front lines. Not surprisingly, this was the key point in three of these four denials issued over a period of 24 hours. One said the P.L.O. was not "prepared to negotiate regarding its arms" (this and other issues relating to Palestinian-Lebanese relations could be discussed only "after the withdrawal of the occupation forces," it cited al-Hassan as having said to U.P.I.). Another denial quoted Abu Iyyad as having said that the Palestinians "will not throw down their arms," and that al-Hassan's words had been "distorted and falsified." In a third, a military spokesman declared: "nobody can disarm the Joint Forces."[26]

Perhaps responding to this internal pressure, on the same evening, June 17, 'Arafat took one of his toughest public stands since the beginning of the war, in a message "to the Arab, Lebanese and Palestinian masses . . . and to all the fighters in the field." In it he savagely attacked Arab hesitation, cowardice, and timidity. The battle of Beirut, he stated, had not yet begun, and added: "We are ready for this battle, which will be the Karbala of this age . . . and the Stalingrad of the Arabs . . . "[27] It was probably not a coincidence that conciliatory public statements and off-the-record interviews with foreign journalists by Hani al-Hassan ceased for a time.

In fact, an important decision had been taken by the P.L.O. leadership. The initial exploratory negotiations they had authorized, and in which al-Hassan had taken a leading role, had revealed Israeli and American conditions which were unacceptably harsh. The strong negative reaction from the base and from middle-level cadres reinforced the position of those in the leadership who had been skeptical all along about the course initially followed. At the same time, the state of near-panic which had seized a few P.L.O. leaders subsided, as the battlefield situation stabilized in the somewhat calmer atmosphere after June 13.

In consequence of all these factors, during the third week of June the P.L.O. stand crystallized around making a commitment in principle to withdraw, while categorically refusing the original Israeli-U.S. terms. This was linked to acceptance of French good offices, offered formally by Francis Gutman, Secretary-General of the French Foreign Ministry. This took place during meetings on June 15, 16, and 17 in East Beirut at which Hani al-Hassan first put forward the proposals noted in the preceding section of this chapter. The objective in using this French channel in addition to existing Lebanese ones was to attempt to get better terms than were being offered on the theory that sympathetic go-betweens in Paris were better than hostile ones in Ba'abda, with Habib and the Israelis at their elbow.

It was 'Arafat who finally decided the issue. He had been under intense pressure since June 11, when disagreement arose within the P.L.O. leadership over acceptance of a ceasefire.[28] His initial inclination had been to play for time while hoping for new factors to arise and for the situation to improve. But given the weak stand during the first days of the war of their Lebanese Muslim and leftist allies—whose support was essential for any sort of resistance—he and most other P.L.O. leaders had initially seen no alternative but to make some sort of commitment to withdraw.[29]

The French offer of meditation of June 15 constituted just the sort of new factor 'Arafat had been awaiting. It made itself felt over the next two weeks as the P.L.O. was taking its decision to offer a vague commitment in principle to withdraw. This was ultimately done via the memo delivered to Wazzan on July 2 after approval by the entire P.L.O. leadership.[30]

The extensive telex correspondence with the French government via the P.L.O. office in Paris which began at this point makes it possible to watch the evolution of the P.L.O. position, and of the role of 'Arafat in particular. This is possible because, in the absence of his "Foreign Minister," Abu Lutf, nearly all these telexes were drafted by 'Arafat or contain extensive corrections in his hand on the Arabic originals.[31]

The P.L.O. leader was naturally gratified by France's new role, and repeatedly expressed this to the French.[32] There was good reason for his gratitude. Once Hani al-Hassan had made the P.L.O.'s June 15 proposal to Gutman to consider ending its armed presence in Beirut and preserve only a political presence there in exchange for a political quid pro quo, France considered that it had received a green light to explore alternatives to the harsh terms of Israel and the U.S.[33] It was to do this in a determined manner.

Four days later, after meeting French Foreign Minister Claude Cheysson at the United Nations, Abu Lutf met with French Premier Pierre Mauroy and again with Cheysson in

Paris, the first official meetings on such a high level. The French position as outlined to Abu Lutf was clear: unequivocal condemnation of Israel's invasion, an immediate ceasefire and unconditional Israeli withdrawal, noninterference in Lebanese domestic affairs and P.L.O.-Lebanese negotiations to regulate the former's status in that country, a link between solving the Lebanese crisis and the Palestine problem, and self-determination of the Palestinian people with their own state on the West Bank and Gaza Strip.[34]

The position conveyed to Abu Lutf by Mauroy and Cheysson was the basis of French policy for the next six weeks of the war. This policy only changed then because at the end of July the P.L.O. finally abandoned its efforts to get a better deal than Habib had been offering. In the meantime, the French showed perseverence in the face of often brusque attempts by Israel and the U.S. to discourage their initiative. They were deeply convinced that what both powers were trying to do was misguided in the long run. In the end, France agreed to join the American-inspired Multi-National Force (MNF) only because of a P.L.O. request, tied to a desire to preserve some of their traditional influence in Lebanon.

The first active move made by French diplomacy was the introduction of a draft resolution before the Security Council on June 25. This would have provided for an initial disengagement of forces (a key P.L.O. demand), with the IDF pulling back 10 km from Beirut and P.L.O. forces retiring to the refugee camps, with U.N. observers, the Lebanese armed forces, and possibly a U.N. military force being interposed between the two sides. The U.S., rightly perceiving this as part of what Secretary Haig would later call "attempts to relieve the P.L.O.'s dilemma,"[35] on June 26 vetoed the resolution, which was supported by the other fourteen Council members. By this time, however, the Secretary had resigned, an event resulting in part from the problems for U.S. policy resulting from the invasion, but one which also had an important impact on the course of the war.

VI Haig, the P.L.O., and the Role of France

As the war in Lebanon entered its third week, the American
Secretary of State was in his final days in office, aware of his
precarious position within the administration, and apparently
trying desperately to score a last-minute diplomatic success.
This perhaps explains why his published account of events at
the end of June diverges in some respects from the story which
emerges from the P.L.O.-French diplomatic correspondence, as
well from that given by most other sources.

Haig claims in his memoirs that the French, although
"anxious to appear as friends of the P.L.O., were offering
valuable support for our position on P.L.O. withdrawal." He
states specifically that on June 24 the French "agreed that the
P.L.O. must disarm," and "would convey this view to the
P.L.O."[36] However, his detailed account of events on June 25,
the day his resignation was announced by the President, omits
a peremptory message to the P.L.O. sent via the French which
is highly revealing of the French position. In an urgent telex to
'Arafat dated 25 June, Ibrahim Souss wrote:

> I have just been notified by the French authorities that the
> American Secretary of State, Haig, has asked the French
> government to transmit to the P.L.O. leadership: "Specific
> American thoughts on what steps the P.L.O. in Beirut would
> have to take with the Lebanese government in order to assure a
> peaceful resolution of the problem in and around Beirut:
>
> 1. All Palestinian fighters in West Beirut and the camps to the
> south of the city will hand over all arms to the Lebanese armed
> forces and turn these areas over to the control of the Lebanese
> armed forces and the Government of Lebanon
> 2. The leadership of the P.L.O. and such others as may chose to
> join them will depart Lebanon under safe conduct guaranteed,
> monitored and assisted if requested by outside observers.
>
> Immediately after the agreement to these points is given steps
> will be taken to ensure that Israeli forces will adjust their lines

so that the foregoing steps will not be seen to be carried out
under threat of Israeli guns"

Had the French message conveyed by Ibrahim Souss stopped
at this point, Haig's claims regarding France's position might
have stood some chance of substantiation. But Souss added a
further passage, containing the first of many French commen-
taries on the U.S. messages they were asked by Washington to
transmit:

> The authorities conveyed to me their entire disapproval of the
> American terms which in their opinion are completely alignated
> [sic] on those of the Israeli government. Furthermore as the
> Americans have asked them to transmit to the P.L.O. those
> terms "in the most severe manner" they have asked me to make
> very clear to you that France is in no way associated directly or
> indirectly with this American position.[37]

Aside from the urgency which must have motivated Haig, what
is most remarkable in this communication is the extraordinary
presumptuousness of its author. It is reminiscent of nothing so
much as the Foreign Minister of a great power at the height of
the age of imperialism dictating terms to a much weaker state.
Haig's request that these terms be conveyed "in the most
severe manner" recalls the kind of diplomacy symbolized by
the instructions of British Foreign Secretary Sir Edward Grey
to his Ambassador to the Ottoman Empire in 1910 that a 10-
page dispatch making onerous demands on its recipients be
read in full to both the Ottoman Foreign Minister and Grand
Vizier.[38] Sir Edward, however, did not specify the tone to be
used by his envoy.

The impression that Haig was in a hurry and cared little
for the feelings of those he dealt with is confirmed by other
sources. In the words of a French official closely involved in
the negotiations, Haig had telephone conversations with
Cheysson on this issue which were "out of this world" (the
word used was *sidérant*). All that was necessary for a
resolution of the crisis, Haig had said, was to crush the P.L.O.
He refused to listen to what his French interlocutors were

saying in response—that this would only put the P.L.O. under Arab control, make the Palestinians into desperate terrorists, and remove the only spokesman for the Palestinian cause.[39] This same inattention, combined with a tendency to hear only what is desired, is apparent from even a casual comparison between the account of events in Haig's memoirs and French communications with the P.L.O., as can be seen in the dispatch cited above.

Whatever reaction the outgoing American Secretary of State may have expected from the P.L.O. to his ultimatum (and his memoirs makes it appear that again and again he had the impression that he nearly single-handedly had 'Arafat on the point of surrender), it was ruined by the impact of his resignation, announced at about the same time the French message of June 25 was received. Not surprisingly, there was jubilation in Beirut at the news, and a sense that the P.L.O. had surmounted a major crisis. One official in the Chairman's office privy to the negotiations recalled later: "I felt as if we had won the war that night."[40]

The pronounced shifting of Lebanese sympathies, at least those of its traditional allies, in the P.L.O.'s favor at around this time had a further bracing impact on the morale of those besieged. This was reinforced by the analysis of the situation by senior French officials in a meeting with Souss in Paris the next morning, after the effect of Haig's resignation had sunk in. Pointing to divisions in Israel and within the American administration (of which the P.L.O. had its own abundant evidence from independent sources[41]), the French saw that the situation had shifted somewhat, that an Israeli assault on West Beirut, "while still possible," was less likely, and that there was now some pressure on Israel to withdraw.

Their central point was to reassure the P.L.O. that "The American request for disarming the Palestinian forces has met with total French rejection. Any such step, according to France, should necessarily be linked to a global approach to the Palestinian and Lebanese problems," which meant movement toward Palestinian self-determination. Moreover, the French added, the U.S. proposal provided no guarantees for the Palestinians.[42]

All this relatively good news did not induce euphoria in 'Arafat and his colleagues. The Palestinian leader responded cautiously to the American ultimatum of the 25th, essentially agreeing with the negative reaction of the French, and leaving it to them to convey his response to Washington, saying "We accept what you agree on with the U.S. administration." He added, "We thank the French government for this stand and this attention. Our people will never forget it."[43]

In response to a French request for a more detailed P.L.O. answer to the U.S. message, 'Arafat on June 27 specified terms which, formulated later into an 11-point position paper, were to be the core of the P.L.O. stand for over a month. These called for a neutralization of Beirut and a disengagement of forces, with a joint Lebanese-U.N. force under international supervision interposed between the combatants. A first stage was to include a P.L.O. withdrawal to the camps and an Israeli withdrawal of five miles from its positions around Beirut. Finally, they called for "agreement on some formula for Palestinian presence in Lebanon which would include . . . the kind of weaponry, and its size, all in accord with Lebanese sovereignty." 'Arafat concluded that with regard to a P.L.O. political presence and that of Palestinians resident in Lebanon "there is no disagreement with the Lebanese government."[44]

Not surprisingly, the American response to these P.L.O. terms was negative. It was conveyed to Abu Lutf during a meeting on June 28 in Tunis with a senior French emissary. The U.S. Under Secretary of State, Lawrence Eagleburger, had told the French Ambassador in Washington that the U.S. considered this proposal "under the circumstances to be unrealistic, essentially because according to the U.S.A. the P.L.O. does not provide firm commitments, and therefore [it] cannot be considered the basis for serious negotiation."

The French stated that they had responded that the P.L.O. proposals were "serious, realistic and acceptable." They pledged to continue their talks with the U.S., but for the first time raised an issue which was to become a refrain during the remainder of the negotiations. This was Eagleburger's claim that in negotiations with Habib in Beirut via Lebanese intermediaries, the P.L.O. had put forward significantly different terms from those transmitted by Paris. He made specific reference to its reported willingness, expressed to Sa'eb Salam, to hand over weapons to the Lebanese army and leave either by road or sea.

The French shrewdly added that they "estimate there has been some distortion of information as relayed to them through American channels."[45] In fact, there was probably also a delay in the transmission of information to the State Department via the tortuous Lebanese channels described in the first chapter. Thus the terms Eagleburger mentioned were very likely those mooted by Hani al-Hassan as much as ten days earlier, but since superseded by the position embodied in the negotiations via the French.

'Arafat responded immediately to the U.S. claims, denying that anything had been said about handing over weapons, and stressing the demand for a P.L.O. military presence in Lebanon along the lines of that in other Arab countries. He added that a disengagement of forces was imperative to create a proper atmosphere for negotiation. Regarding the issue of the P.L.O. leadership remaining in Beirut, he said that the P.L.O. had expressed a "readiness to understand the Lebanese point of view." (This meant in effect accepting the demand for its departure, which he, Abu Jihad, and al-Hassan had by this point already done verbally in repeated meetings with Lebanese interlocutors.) 'Arafat finally reminded Souss: "You must understand that the American position stems from annoyance at the French move because they want to be the only ones dealing with this crisis."[46]

American annoyance showed itself over the next few days of feverish negotiation. The next day, June 29, the French informed the P.L.O. that they had been told by Washington that negotiations via the Lebanese and Saudis had brought the P.L.O. to the point of accepting a departure from Beirut without its weapons. Souss went on:

> The Americans have suggested to the French not to interfere in the Lebanese crisis insisting that the P.L.O. is not taking the French role seriously and therefore does not keep France regularly and accurately informed about developments in negotiations. The Americans have insinuated to the French that the P.L.O. is transmitting to them false information about the real P.L.O. position. The authorities here have requested clarification . . . due to the fact that the Americans have told them that the P.L.O. is playing a double-faced game.[47]

Remarkably, the same day the State Department twice used the French channel to transmit its counterproposals to the earlier conditions set forth by the P.L.O., while stressing that Habib had been asked to transmit the same terms via Lebanese intermediaries. These contained little that was new. What was interesting about them is that they were sent via the French just after the latter had been told "not to interfere," and that the French bluntly described them to Souss as "not serious," adding "they cannot see how the P.L.O. could accept them." Souss added: "The French appear to be very perplexed by the confusing propositions coming out of the American admini-stration."[48]

'Arafat responded immediately to these messages, and to the American insinuations about P.L.O. bad faith, referring to "the psychological war and the various fabricated lies being circulated," and adding, "These are all part of the on-going battle." He sarcastically added that "The U.S. State Depart-ment seems to be unaware even of Israeli statements," noting that Begin the day previously had offered to allow the P.L.O. to leave with its personal weapons, a concession not included in Eagleburger's first set of terms. He affirmed further: "We have informed Philip Habib that we will not repeat not hand over our weapons to anyone."

In this and a later message the same day to the French,

'Arafat stressed an issue he was to come back to again and again: "The important point is what are the guarantees against a massacre of Palestinians, both civilians and military, in view of what happened in Tyre and Sidon, and what the Phalangisists did yesterday to Lebanese patriots in the mountains?"[49] This was a question which until the end never received a satisfactory answer.

VII The Importance of the June Decision

The welter of confusing proposals and counterproposals just surveyed has perhaps obscured several important things that happened in the last two weeks of June. The P.L.O. contemplated and then drew back from accepting in their entirety the terms of its enemies. The French offered their mediation directly to the P.L.O., and then were brought into the negotiations by the Americans. The U.S. thereupon tried to undermine French confidence in P.L.O. good faith, but this maneuver failed. The P.L.O. put forward, via the French, proposals which were to form the core of their negotiating position until the end of July. And in saying that they were ready "to understand the Lebanese point of view" on the issue of the leadership's departure from Beirut, the P.L.O. made an important concession, which was later to be formalized in the signed note delivered to Wazzan by 'Arafat on July 2.

This was a major decision. It meant that the leadership of the P.L.O. had accepted in principle the idea of evacuation from Beirut. As the following six weeks of siege were to show, this by no means meant that a final agreement had been reached. Indeed, many in the P.L.O. had made this decision with the greatest reluctance, and still harbored the hope that it would somehow be possible to avoid meeting the American-Israeli terms in full. But 'Arafat had made a formal written commitment to Wazzan which was the fruit of intense internal deliberations, and the result of an extremely unfavorable military situation. Nearly everyone in the leadership recognized that this meant that in one way or another the P.L.O., or most of it, would have to leave Beirut.

What remained was the negotiation of the terms for the departure. These matters were regarded as minor details by Habib and the United States, which repeatedly expressed irritation at the way the P.L.O. stubbornly insisted on obtaining satisfaction regarding each specific point. The Americans and the Israelis suspected that the Palestinians were holding firm to their terms simply to drag out the negotiations and postpone the inevitable, to both of which the P.L.O. was certainly not averse.

However, to the P.L.O. these were far from minor matters or insignificant details. Issues like P.L.O. retention of its weapons, an IDF withdrawal a few miles from Beirut and a disengagement of forces before any P.L.O. withdrawal, the arrival beforehand of U.N. forces, and clear, binding international guarantees not only of the evacuation, but also for the civilians remaining behind, were vital matters. They were particularly important in view of the well-known propensity of the IDF for violating ceasefire agreements, and the intensity of the Begin government's commitment to annihilating the P.L.O. 'Arafat summed up this concern as follows: "To us, international guarantees are basic to any agreement between us and others, especially in view of the tragedies in the occupied areas [of Lebanon]."[50]

Although many of the grave consequences 'Arafat and others feared were to ensue because Israel and the United States ultimately refused to entertain most P.L.O. demands— both those just mentioned relating to the situation on the ground and the broader political ones relating to a regional settlement—it is remarkable that the P.L.O. was in a position to put forward any conditions at all at the end of June.

That they could do so while virtually unsupported by either friends or allies, and while facing the full might of the U.S. and Israel, was a testament to the fighting capabilities of the Palestinian, Lebanese, and Syrian forces which had held the IDF at arm's length, while inflicting enough casualties to give Israel serious pause before it contemplated storming Beirut. It was also a tribute to the cohesion and negotiating skills of the P.L.O.'s leaders. In an exceedingly grave situation, these men had surmounted grave differences, had held together as a group, and by means of a sometimes confused decision-making process had finally fashioned a compromise negotiating position satisfactory to all concerned within the leadership.

Their cohesion and their nerve were to be further tested in the six weeks of war which remained. Difficult, sometimes distasteful decisions had to be taken by these men during this period, as the siege perimeter was tightened and they themselves became targets of repeated Israeli attempts at assassination by aerial bombardment. Foremost among these decisions was accepting the Habib plan with its grossly inadequate safeguards for their people who were to be left behind in Beirut, a plan they had been fighting against since June 15. But in spite of everything, according to the memories of the participants and the documents produced at the time, none of this was as trying as what they had already gone through in June.

Chapter 5

July 1982:
The Decision To Accept
the Habib Plan

I Beirut Under Siege

As July began, the P.L.O. could turn its attention from the internal front in Beirut for the first time since the beginning of the war. This was because the P.L.O.'s pledge to leave the city embodied in 'Arafat's July 2 memo had convinced its traditional Muslim leaders of the P.L.O.'s desire to do anything within reason to spare Beirut from further harm. Moreover, the growing anxiety of many Lebanese about the local imbalance of power which would result from a Palestinian evacuation meant that Lebanese pressure on the P.L.O. to leave was replaced by support for its efforts to hold out for better terms and firmer guarantees from Israel and the U.S.

From late June on there had been a constant improvement in relations between the P.L.O. and its erstwhile allies, as Lebanese leaders from Wazzan and Salam to Jumblatt and Berri accepted that the P.L.O. was truly willing to leave under certain specific conditions and guarantees. They realized, and began to declare publicly, that the delay in obtaining a settlement, and the resulting punishment of Beirut and its population, were the gratuitous result of the stubbornness of Israel, backed by the U.S., in holding to its demands for virtually complete P.L.O. capitulation.[1]

If the P.L.O. was a guerrilla fish out of water before the 1982 war, its isolation had never been so painfully exposed as during the first two weeks of that conflict. Yet things could have been worse. Palestinian leaders at one point early in the siege were expecting public Lebanese expressions of discontent in Beirut. After the war, one of them pointed out that it was fortunate that there were no demonstrations by Lebanese in West Beirut demanding the P.L.O.'s departure, adding that such manifestations would have been a terrible embarrassment.[2] This did not happen for many reasons, one of them the P.L.O.'s rapid acquiescence to the legitimate concern of the people of West Beirut that their city not be destroyed needlessly.

But the P.L.O. had to have more than passive, grudging support from the populace of Beirut for its defense of the city. It was necessary for it to meet their needs for food, shelter, and medical care, to establish security and prevent the occupation of empty homes or the looting of businesses, and to organize services like ambulance stations to meet the demands imposed by the fighting and by Israel's blockade of water, food, and electricity.

Together with the shared experience of suffering deprivation and surviving under the harshest conditions, such civil defense efforts helped establish a sense of a common destiny among the besieged. From any account of a population under siege, whether that of Leningrad during World War II or Jerusalem during the 1948 war,[3] one can see how a siege can lead to cohesiveness among the beleaguered population. All of this was crucial to the P.L.O.'s strategy of continuing to fight in the hope of obtaining better terms. The passionate outpouring of emotion from ordinary Beirutis, and from their leaders, when the P.L.O. left in August showed that something had indeed changed from the bleak days of mid-June.

Another factor in this newfound fellow-feeling was the growing anger with Israel among Beirutis as the siege dragged on. In the years before the war, the Lebanese had tended to forget their traditional hostility to Israel as a result of growing friction with the Palestinians and Syrians. But as the war went into a second and then a third month, and as Israel made clear its intention of staying through the winter, many Lebanese, especially those in Beirut and the south, began to awaken to the fact that their country now had a major problem with Israel independent of that of the Palestinians. They also realized that the siege of Beirut was partly a function of the desire of Israel and the United States to rearrange the Lebanese order in favor of their clients.

The indiscriminate nature of the Israeli bombardment of the city intensified these effects. It was all well and good for Israeli propaganda to claim that only military targets were being hit. Occasionally this was true, as on most occasions when PGM's (precision-guided munitions) were used (which, because of their expense, was infrequently). However, the areas most heavily hit were the city seafront, the southern suburbs, and the adjacent refugee camps—all of which in effect became front-line areas and much of whose population fled. Here, saturation artillery bombardment and the destruction of entire buildings by aerial bombing took place. It could be tenuously justified by the proximity of military positions, although heavy civilian casualties were sometimes caused in these sectors.

But in other areas—the heavily populated central districts of the city where Israeli bombing and shelling caused most of the civilian casualties—there was no such military pretext. Indeed, the claim that P.L.O. weapons were cold-bloodedly sited near civilians for protection is a gross canard.[4] Such a ploy would never have occurred to P.L.O. commanders because in their ample experience Israel had never in the past shown any compunction about hitting civilian areas, irrespective of whether military targets were nearby. More to the point, most P.L.O., Syrian, and LNM forces and weapons were necessarily stationed in the front lines, where they were badly needed to hold off a vastly superior foe.

The back cover of D. Bavly and E. Salpeter, *Fire in Beirut: Israel's War in Lebanon with the P.L.O.*[5] is a perfect example of the falseness of the claims of Israeli and other apologists for the IDF, most of whom had no idea what was actually going on in West Beirut. The dust jacket shows a section of the Ramlet al-Baida beachfront, including numerous weapons and military emplacements (mainly Syrian: shown is the barracks which was the headquarters of the Syrian 85th brigade), with a caption reading: "Aerial photo of West Beirut, taken in July 1982, showing P.L.O. heavy weapons placed in close proximity to embassies, hotels, churches, mosques, and residential buildings."

Unmentioned is the fact that the entire Beirut seafront, including the area shown, was part of the siege perimeter. It was constantly shelled and repeatedly bombed, which drove away most of its population, and was the target of three Israeli landing attempts between June 25 and August 4. All were in close proximity to Ramlet al-Baida. This area was crucial to the IDF plan for the penetration of West Beirut that was foiled in early August, when a linkup between seaborne forces to be landed in the vicinity and others driving west along Corniche al-Mazr'a from the museum was planned. In view of the strategic importance of the area, it would have been surprising if weapons were not emplaced there.

The main reason the P.L.O. did not, indeed could not, site military emplacements in heavily populated areas during the siege is simple: Lebanese and Palestinian civilians were highly sensitive to the presence of potential targets near inhabited residential areas, for they knew the might of Israel, and could see what it was capable of. They therefore protested violently (and usually successfully) to the P.L.O. when they felt that its dispositions were threatening to bring Israeli attacks down on their heads.

An example was the reaction of the people of the Jeanne d'Arc quarter in Ras Beirut when toward the end of the war the

P.L.O. radio station, the "Voice of Palestine," placed its mobile transmitter there. It had to be moved away again because of neighborhood protests.[6] As the siege perimeter tightened, and as the P.L.O. was slowly driven back from the largely Palestinian southern suburbs into the central and northern parts of the city, finding sites for sensitive communications and command facilities became a major problem. In July, when 'Arafat himself became a target, his staff had great difficulty finding safe quarters for him which did not endanger innocent civilians.[7]

However, everyone in Beirut, including foreign journalists and the few diplomats who remained, knew perfectly well that most civilian casualties were inflicted in areas with no legitimate military targets nearby. It was common knowledge in West Beirut that many of the bombardments, especially by naval and ground artillery, were indiscriminate, random, and arbitrary, hitting whole regions at a time rather than specific targets. There can be no other explanation for the repeated shelling of every hospital in West Beirut, most embassies and hotels, and whole residential quarters without the slightest strategic importance. As a result of these attacks, the PRCS was forced to relocate its hospitals repeatedly.[8]

II The Franco-Egyptian Draft Resolution

While the leaders of the P.L.O. had the dubious satisfaction of knowing that most of the half million or so people left in West Beirut shared their feelings about the Israelis, and accepted the sincerity of their willingness to leave and thereby spare the city if their minimum conditions were met, none of this solved the basic problem of how to change the balance of forces so as to bring Israel and the U.S. to accept their terms. This dilemma was to preoccupy them until the end of the war.

The P.L.O. explored two main avenues in an attempt to improve its position during July. The first was via a project for a Franco-Egyptian draft resolution in the Security Council (which was never formally presented to the Council). This would have linked the Lebanese crisis and the Palestine question, and would have embodied mutual and simultaneous recognition between the P.L.O. and Israel, thus bypassing the U.S. insistence on prior P.L.O. recognition of Israel as a condition for a U.S.-P.L.O. dialogue. Although stillborn because of the unbending opposition of the U.S. (which wanted the P.L.O. eliminated rather than rehabilitated), this draft resolution was central to P.L.O., French, and Egyptian diplomatic efforts until near the end of July.

The second was an attempt to use the visit to Washington of an Arab League delegation including the Saudi and Syrian Foreign Ministers, Prince Sa'ud al-Faisal and 'Abd al-Halim Khaddam and Fateh Central Committee member Khaled al-Hassan to strike some sort of direct deal with the United States. This would have involved the U.S. opening a dialogue in return for some P.L.O. move toward recognition of Israel. The second approach was equally fruitless, and indeed ultimately resulted in the two Arab powers' tacit acquiescence to the terms being put forth by Habib without any satisfaction of the P.L.O.'s requirements.

In spite of this barren outcome, these two episodes reveal how far the P.L.O. leadership was willing to go in the direction of an overall regional settlement, what concessions it was and was not willing to make under extreme duress, and why in the end it finally gave in and accepted the terms which Habib had been trying to force on the P.L.O., essentially unchanged,[9] since the middle of June.

The French government first transmitted to the P.L.O. what it called a preliminary outline of a draft for submission at the U.N. Security Council on July 2.[10] This was revised again and again, but its basic ideas stayed the same until the end. It included provisions which had been featured in the French draft vetoed on June 26, such as an immediate ceasefire, mutual preliminary Israeli and P.L.O. withdrawals (the Israelis to a distance of five miles from Beirut, the P.L.O. to within the camps), and a separation of forces to be policed by Lebanese and U.N. troops. However, in addition to a call for a total, rapid withdrawal from Lebanon of Israeli forces, and of all non-Lebanese forces except those authorized to remain by the "legitimate and representative" Lebanese authorities, the draft laid down the basic elements of a lasting Lebanese and regional settlement.

It specified that the crisis was to be settled on the basis of security for all states and justice for all the area's peoples. It also confirmed the sovereignty, territorial integrity, independence, and unity of Lebanon, and the restoration of central government control over all its territory; the right to existence and security of all states in the region in conformity with Security Council resolution 242; and the legitimate rights of the Palestinian people, including their right to self-determination, and the P.L.O.'s involvement in the negotiations for a settlement.

The resolution was notable in a number of respects, aside from elements like mutual preliminary withdrawals which had led to the imposition of a U.S. veto on the French draft resolution of June 25. One was the specification that it was up to "legitimate and representative" Lebanese authorities to decide which foreign forces were to remain and which to depart. The implication was clear that the Sarkis regime, operating in an area occupied by Israel, and dominated at this point by Bashir Gemayel and the Maronite right wing, was neither fully legitimate nor representative.[11]

Among other features of the resolution were its explicit linkage of security for all states in the region (the terminology of S.C. 242) to justice for all its peoples, an unmistakable reference to the Palestinians; the reference to the principles of S.C. 242 and to the resolution itself, of significance in a draft strongly supported by the P.L.O. as a basis for a regional settlement; the mention of legitimate Palestinian rights including self-determination; and the inclusion of the P.L.O. in negotiations based on the French argument that "to be engaged, the Palestinian people must be represented in the negotiation, and thus the P.L.O. should be a party."

It was to be expected that these features would be anathema to a U.S. administration which accepted fully Israel's rationale for its invasion, was helping it to achieve its aims, and was irremediably hostile to the P.L.O. The implication that the government in Ba'abda was illegitimate and unrepresentative was naturally unwelcome to the U.S., as was placing justice for the Palestinians on a par with Israel's security.

More fearsome still was the possibility that via the Franco-Egyptian resolution the P.L.O. might obtain a revised version of S.C. 242 which met its own objections and which it could therefore accept. This would have meant that the Palestinians would at last have met the conditions set down in Kissinger's secret 1975 memorandum of understanding with Israel for a U.S.-P.L.O. dialogue. It can be seen how embarrassing such a prospect would have been for the U.S. at a time when it was working to eradicate what Kissinger, in June 1982, called the "mirage" that "the key to Middle East peace is to be found in a P.L.O.-Israeli negotiation based on various formulae to 'moderate' the P.L.O."[12]

Neither the P.L.O. nor the French had any illusions as to the tenacity of American opposition to the resolution. Both sides understood clearly that the approach it embodied directly contradicted everything that Washington had done almost since the war began, and that it posed a serious threat to American policy because it was virtually the only alternative approach to Habib's for solving the Lebanese crisis. However, both were determined to push ahead with it in the hope that American determination would be worn down by the P.L.O.'s resistance.

After the French draft had been placed before the Security Council, Souss reported that both officials of the French Foreign Ministry and advisors to President Mitterrand were convinced that "it is totally unreasonable to ask the P.L.O. to make concessions in Lebanon without giving it substantial political gains." Given this view, they not surprisingly found that "The USA has still a completely negative attitude." Souss added that "the American argument is that at a moment when nearly all Arab states consider that the P.L.O. 'has already disappeared from the international scene' it seems incomprehensible that France is opening up new horizons to the Palestinians."

The Americans were not the only ones to have the impression that the Arab states had given up on the P.L.O. The same telex relates a French description of Arab attitudes as "totally 'passive and marked by impotence,'" and the impression that "Arab envoys to Washington and New York are very much influenced by American pressures."[13] The effect of this timid Arab stand was stressed in another message from Souss the same day: "The USA considers that it has no use for the P.L.O. (according to the terms used by the French) in its global strategy in the region and in this attitude the US feels encouraged by relative passivity on the side of the Arab countries."[14] Arab passivity was often replaced by something worse: active complicity with the U.S. in putting pressure on the P.L.O. and undermining the French role.

An example of this arose a few days later, at a time when the U.S. was engaged in trying to stampede the P.L.O. into evacuating Beirut unconditionally during the very last days of Haig's tenure at the State Department. In the outgoing Secretary's own words, "It was essential to maintain the momentum. Above all the P.L.O. must be moved out quickly."[15] Unfortunately, his haste, and his reliance on the Saudi interpretation of what was happening in Beirut,[16] seem to have led Haig to fail to pay close attention to the actual position of the P.L.O. or to the stand of his French ally.

Unlike the French, who were skeptical of what was coming out of Washington, the Saudis seem to have been very much impressed by the arguments of Haig and his successors. Thus, on July 8, at the height of a wave of reports that the P.L.O. had accepted the Habib terms, the French related to Souss that their ambassador in Saudi Arabia had been called in by Sa'ud al-Faisal and informed of Saudi "preoccupation and anxiety" because the French were not willing to join an

American-organized force to supervise the imminent evacuation of the P.L.O. from Beirut. The Prince insisted to the
envoy that a French force must participate.

The French were unmoved by this Saudi pressure,
asking Souss to tell 'Arafat that they considered "that all this
information enters into the cadre of the intoxication campaign
being waged by Israel and the United States." They issued a
statement the same day stressing that preconditions for sending
a disengagement force to Beirut included a Lebanese government request, P.L.O. agreement, agreement of all parties, and a
clear definition of its mandate.[17]

Refusing to be rushed by the Americans, the French
would calmly ask the P.L.O. each time whether one of the
many reports they had heard from Washington that a final
agreement had been reached was true. Upon being repeatedly
assured by 'Arafat that these assertions were false, they
proceeded to ignore requests from Washington that they drop
their planned draft resolution and immediately fall into line
with U.S. plans by agreeing to provide a force to help U.S.
Marines oversee the P.L.O.'s departure.

These French queries and P.L.O. denials regarding
exaggerated U.S. claims of the imminence of an agreement
eventually came to seem almost ludicrous to both the French
and the P.L.O. 'Arafat's first denial came in a telex dated July
2; it was followed by two new French inquiries on July 3, two
P.L.O. denials the same day, three queries on July 8, and two
P.L.O. denials the same day. The last embodied the 11-point
summary of the P.L.O. stand, which was to remain the basis of
its position until the end of July, and was later transmitted to all
P.L.O. offices.[18]

By the end of this dizzying sequence, on July 8, French
officials had the distinct impression that the Americans were
confused; they told Souss the Americans had "fallen prey to
their own campaign of intoxication."[19] A day later, the French
told the P.L.O. envoy "that there is a lot of American double,
triple, and quadruple play." Souss added in his telex, "Altogether, the feeling is that there is a lot of American maneu-

vering to gain time, maybe according to them with the complicity of many parties." Specifically, the French suspected the Syrians and the Saudis of collaborating with the U.S. Much of this activity, they felt, was aimed at derailing the Franco-Egyptian draft in the Security Council, which Paris was intent on pushing ahead with.[20]

The French were reassured by 'Arafat's transmission to them of the 11 points, which they were told had been given widespread distribution. At a meeting on July 9, Cheysson told Souss that "The French Government has taken into consideration the 11 points ... and will deploy all efforts on the international scene on this basis." Souss further told 'Arafat that the French would continue to try to push through the Security Council draft as rapidly as possible, "according to your wish,"[21] although in later meetings French officials expressed some skepticism as to the outcome because of intense U.S. pressure on all delegations in the Council, and even on Egypt, co-sponsor of the resolution.[22]

This pressure was being applied in spite of what the French described to Souss as "the absence of the capacity to take clear political decisions on the American side" following the ousting of Alexander Haig and before George Shultz took over. Under Secretary Lawrence Eagleburger did not have the authority to make decisions, the French added, while they perceived the President to be "totally out of the picture." (Haig's description of Reagan in his memoirs is not dissimilar.) He was said to be acting on the advice of White House advisors "who are considered by the French to be amateurs." Apparently, however, Eagleburger and the U.S. Ambassador to the U.N., Jeane Kirkpatrick, were not hampered by this vacuum at the top in their intensive and successful efforts to "avoid the Security Council" as the main forum for treatment of the crisis.[23]

After a full meeting of the Palestinian leadership discussed the latest messages from Paris, a telex was sent to Souss on July 11 to inform the French that after careful deliberation at the highest level, the P.L.O. fully endorsed the line being followed by the Mitterand government, particularly its emphasis on U.N. sponsorship for the international disengagement force.[24] This was specified because both parties hoped to prevent what eventually transpired, a resolution mediated solely by the United States, and its resulting domination of the international force sent to Beirut.

It is perhaps coincidental that this message and the last copies of the 11 points were sent to P.L.O. offices abroad on July 11, a date which in the words of the definitive Israeli account of the war "would become a watershed in the conduct of the siege." On that day a meeting was held in Ariel Sharon's office in Tel Aviv at which "a critical discussion of the issues took place." Possibly in response to intelligence intercepts of this unequivocal indication from the P.L.O. leadership that it was holding firm to its stand, Sharon was impatient. He told his assembled generals that the southern part of Beirut, including the Palestinian refugee camps located there, "must be cleaned out, utterly destroyed." He concluded: "We are not waiting any longer. I want an attack next week!"[25]

In fact, Israeli attacks had been going on throughout the preceding week, climaxing with heavy fighting on the 11th. This was followed by a 10-day lull, after which the fresh attack ordered by the Israeli Defense Minister was launched exactly as he ordered, in the middle of the following week. There was thus not much time for the P.L.O. to obtain what it wanted before Sharon resumed his efforts to force complete capitulation on his foes with more military pressure, if need be steamrolling the efforts of Habib.

It was argued earlier that this pressure was not decisive in the P.L.O.'s decision to accept the Habib terms. This can be proven only after an examination of the effect of the Sa'ud al-Faisal/Khaddam/Khaled al-Hassan mission in Washington in the following section. But it can be partially confirmed via the assessments of the situation transmitted confidentially to the P.L.O. by a number of French defense analysts, including a senior officer and strategic thinker who was advising Cheysson

on the Lebanese crisis, a former head of the Institut d'Études
Stratégiques, General George Buis.

These tended to reinforce the P.L.O. leadership's perception of its situation vis-à-vis Israel, and encouraged them in
the course they were following. The French analysts argued
that "Israel is heading towards a strategic defeat... [which
would] nullify its series of tactical victories achieved at the
start of the war." This assessment grew out of the calculation
that Israel would lose strategically whether it attacked Beirut
or not. In the latter case, it would simply have fallen short of its
objectives, and the ultimate result would be the fall of the
Begin government.

If it tried to attack Beirut, however, Israel would have
other problems. The first was that although it had the
capability to coordinate its air, land, and sea forces for such an
operation, and military leaders capable of taking the necessary
decisions, "it now lacks (for the first time in its history) the
capacity to take a political decision of this calibre." This was a
reference to the acute political differences which beset the
Israeli polity and the Begin cabinet over the question of an
attack on Beirut. It was probably a correct estimation, if
accounts of dissension within the Israeli cabinet and suspicion
of Sharon by his fellow-ministers are correct.[26]

On an entirely different level, an attack would lead to
other problems. These would include "intolerable" losses, the
inefficiency of Israeli air, land, and sea forces operating on an
urban battlefield, and the "tremendous" dissuasive effect of
"the presence of the international press and the mobilization of
international public opinion." All of this led the French
defense experts to the conclusion that "the P.L.O. cannot now
be defeated except by intense diplomatic pressures,"[27] a
perceptive point apparently realized in Washington, if not by
Sharon and his generals. The Americans were soon to exploit
this, finding the P.L.O.'s Achilles' heel in their Arab brethren.

The estimation that a failure to attack Beirut meant a

strategic defeat for the Israelis was based on the strong belief
by these French analysts that Israel's objective from the
beginning was "the total defeat of the P.L.O., both militarily
and politically." This in turn required that the strategic
objective be Beirut, "the only serious objective for Israel."
Souss added in one of his telexes reporting these views: "Again
and again I heard the same remark from various personalities:
'Beirut was the Israeli objective. There could not be any other
objective for them.'"[28] This view is seconded in the definitive
Israeli account of the war, which confirms that Sharon had no
other objective than Beirut from the outset, although he took
pains to conceal it.[29]

The French perceived Sharon's desire to finish the war
quickly, as well as the "technical" and political reasons why
this did not happen. One of the technical problems was the
failure to assign the IDF "a precise and accurate objective
task," which Beirut manifestly was not—a criticism later
echoed in Israel. Another problem was that after a certain
period of time, as the French correctly observed, bombardments are no longer effective and kill only civilians, "definitely
not the military objectives assigned." Among the political
problems was that the P.L.O. was not only a military force, but
also, in the words of these analysts, "is first and foremost a
tremendous political force in the Middle East." Souss concluded another of his telexes: "General Buis is convinced that
the 'operation' camouflaged by Israel as 'Peace for Galilee' will
be reduced by any historian to 'a series of secondary tactical
successes and a very serious strategic defeat, the first Israel has
known'. And again I quote him: 'But what a defeat.'"[30]

While such a view seems fully justified in retrospect, it
may have seemed hard for the leaders of the P.L.O., besieged in
Beirut, and with little prospect of relief, to accept it fully. But
this advice, and the unstinting diplomatic support offered by
France, helped to reinforce their newfound equanimity in the
period beginning in late June. At the same time, the French
doggedly continued throughout July to try to convince
Washington to offer the P.L.O. a political quid pro quo in

exchange for its withdrawal from Beirut, and to accept some of the conditions in its 11 points, while simultaneously warning the P.L.O. when they got word of impending Israeli military operations.[31]

In the course of these exchanges, the French repeatedly had occasion to ask about the latest exaggerated U.S. reports on the progress of the negotiations over the Habib plan. In his reply to one of these queries, 'Arafat on July 14 told Souss to pass on some details of the negotiations with Habib, so as to show Paris exactly where things stood. 'Arafat reported Wazzan as having said that Habib was disturbed by what he perceived to be an Israeli game, of which he was the target. What was meant, presumably, was that the U.S. envoy felt he was being used by Tel Aviv to achieve its ends.

The Israelis, according to Habib, were initially unwilling to withdraw one inch, or to have foreign forces arrive in Beirut before a total P.L.O. withdrawal, but he had obtained a modification of their position on these points. In fact, if the Israelis ever made these concessions, they went back on them, for they were to resist both until well into August. According to Wazzan, Habib "affirmed complete guarantees and full responsibility for the safety of the departure and the safety of those Palestinians who stay."

The same message informed the French that in spite of both Israeli "concessions" and this guarantee, on the evening of July 13, the P.L.O. had informed Habib via Sa'eb Salam of its rejection of his latest terms and its insistence on the P.L.O. plan.[32] It is an indication of the level of confidence between the two sides that this was one of the few times that the P.L.O. needed to inform the French fully of the exact tenor of its negotiations with Habib, in spite of repeated incorrect reports about them, which the French eventually came to believe were purposely floated by American diplomats to sow suspicion between Paris and the P.L.O.

This was stated explicitly to Souss by a French official who had just returned from Moscow in late July and who told him: "The Americans have been giving the Soviet Union false

and distorted information about France's position.''[33] Such
"intoxication" campaigns, which the French declared Habib
had also engaged in on trips to Rome and London late in July,[34]
did not discourage them. In discussions with Souss on July 24
they stressed "The necessity of insisting always that the
problem is not technical but political: the Americans . . . want
the problem to be reduced to a technical one, that of the
evacuation of Palestinians forces and the French are insisting
that the . . . whole problem is political, i.e. the Palestinian
question.''

He continued that the officials he spoke with were "very
convinced" that a solution must "adopt the formula presented
by the Chairman of 'a political plus against any possibility of a
military minus.' " To Paris, this meant that "any practical
measures which would have an effect on the military capacity
of the PLO in Lebanon should be obligatorily compensated by
concrete political steps towards Palestinian aspirations.''[35]

France was deeply committed to this course, as was
shown by President Mitterrand's reception of an Arab League
Foreign Ministers' delegation, including Abu Lutf, on July 15.
The group was told that the P.L.O. forces in Beirut had shown
themselves to be courageous and steadfast, and to be prepared
to die to defend the city. Mitterrand stated that he regretted that
the Arabs hadn't recognized Israel, and that the Palestinians
had chosen military means to achieve their ends, but he added
that he understood Israel had driven them to it by refusing
political solutions, and understood the P.L.O.'s choices. The
P.L.O., Mitterrand concluded, must be a basic party in all
future negotiations.[36]

This supportive French position did not change the facts
on the ground, however. Although the P.L.O. appreciated
France's efforts, these were clearly not enough to break the
deadlock and bring about a shift in its favor. From mid-July on,
the Palestinian leadership began to look to the Arab states, and
specifically to the trip to Washington of the two Arab Foreign
Ministers and Khaled al-Hassan, as a possible avenue for
gaining a favorable resolution of the crisis. When this failed, it

became clear that the P.L.O.'s only alternatives (assuming it could avoid total defeat) were to keep fighting in the hope that attrition would compel Israel and the U.S. to accept some of its own terms, or for it to accept Habib's.

When Paris realized that the P.L.O. was on the point of doing the latter at the end of July, Gutman asked Souss to warn 'Arafat against the "trap" of a U.S.-sponsored evacuation agreement.[37] But it was already too late. The Arab states, notably the two which together constituted the key regional axis, Syria and Saudi Arabia, had added their weight to that of Israel, the United States, and their Lebanese clients in putting pressure on the P.L.O. At this point, all factions of the P.L.O. leadership saw no viable option but to accept the Habib offer, before Sharon imposed his own solution by force of arms. How this happened is the subject of the next section, the last episode in the story of how the decision to leave Beirut was taken.

III The Arab "Brethren" and the War in Lebanon

In terms of the depth of heartfelt anger for their role in the war, those most resented by the P.L.O. and the Lebanese and Palestinian civilians besieged in West Beirut were not the Israelis, nor their American patrons, nor those Lebanese who supported them. They were rather the Arab regimes because of their universally perceived complicity in what was happening.

Some expressions of these feelings by the official P.L.O. media—normally very discreet where the Arab regimes are concerned—have been noted previously. But what was printed was no more than a pale reflection of what was said and felt during the siege, a point noted at the time by many foreign journalists in Beirut. In the words of Selim Nassib, covering the P.L.O. evacuation on August 22: "The Arabs. They are the main target for the anger of those who are leaving and those who stay behind. The anger is not directed against Israel. Israel is the enemy, and has behaved as such. It is on their self-styled 'brothers' that the anger of Beirutis is focused."[38]

This was not simply a popular perception. It was one shared by the P.L.O. leadership, who felt a bitterness identical to that of their followers for the pitiful performance of the Arab states in failing to come to their aid throughout one of the longest Arab-Israeli wars. Indeed, according to a P.L.O. calculation made on the last day of the fighting, its 70 days of continuous combat made the 1982 conflict the longest of all (if the truces during the 1948–49 war are taken into account), and nearly as long as the combined total of less than 90 days of fighting during the 1948, 1956, 1967, and 1973 wars.[39]

However the focus of the P.L.O.'s bitterness was not Arab passivity but something worse: tacit complicity and even collaboration with the foes of the P.L.O. Strong though such sentiments may seem, they were heartfelt. In a postwar interview, 'Arafat described the position taken by most Arab regimes as more than a coincidence:

> We did better than all the Arabs in this war. They therefore couldn't let us win. In the past, against the French, the Italians, the British, there was Arab solidarity, especially as in time the Arabs won. But this wasn't the case with the Israelis in this war, after they had all been beaten by them. So we were alone. Not just the Syrians; all of them intentionally left us on our own.[40]

This feeling started early on in the war. It began when the conservative Arab states failed to put any meaningful pressure on the United States to moderate its all-out support for Israel. It was reinforced when Syria failed to believe it would be a target of Israel's offensive, then accepted a ceasefire on June 11, and finally withdrew from the war on June 25 after its forces had been driven out of 'Aley and Bhamdoun. To some extent, all of this was expected and even accepted: in the past these same states had not done much more. What was new during July was the active and highly unsupportive role played in particular by Saudi Arabia and Syria during and after the Arab League Foreign Ministers' visit to Washington, culminating in the Jedda meeting of seven Foreign Ministers of July 28–29.

The P.L.O. did not confine its complaints about the policies of the Arab states to its media or to diplomatic exchanges with the French. 'Arafat and his colleagues were equally blunt in their communications with these Arab governments. Commenting on complaints by the Egyptians in the first part of July that he was not sufficiently appreciative of their efforts and those of Saudi Arabia, and indeed was ignoring them, 'Arafat replied in a top secret message to Egypt (one of the first via the newly opened channels of communication between the P.L.O. and the Mubarak government) during a heavy bout of fighting on July 11:

> It is absolutely not true that we have closed the Cairo–Riyad road . . . However, there is Arab inaction, including in the two capitals. In spite of the intensity of enemy military activity around Beirut, where the inferno has reached a dangerous stage, this inaction continues . . . How can we be silent in the face of Arab silence regarding death and destruction in Beirut? Will no one in the Arab world be moved by this death and destruction?[41]

The P.L.O.'s main problems with the Arab states, however, were not with Egypt. This country, only just beginning to emerge from the isolation in the Arab world to which Sadat had condemned it, was eager to win its way back into Arab favor via backing for the beleaguered P.L.O. Egypt was thus generally supportive of the P.L.O., if only weakly so, and with much wavering due to intense pressure by the Untied States and Israel. Although it refused to abrogate its peace treaty with Israel or even to break diplomatic relations with that country during the war, Egypt's backing of the projected Franco-Egyptian resolution was significant. Egyptian diplomats stated to a P.L.O. envoy at the U.N that this document was specifically meant to put on record Egypt's departure from those provisions of the Camp David framework and the peace treaty with Israel that related to West Bank autonomy.[42]

The greatest difficulties for the P.L.O. were with Saudi Arabia and Syria. We have already seen how extraordinarily responsive the former was to U.S. suggestions and advice, even when these were opposed by the P.L.O. This was obviously a grave handicap given that Saudi Arabia was necessarily one of the main avenues of Palestinian–American communication. The problem of its failing to stand up to the United States on behalf of the P.L.O. was to be compounded when Sa'ud al-Faisal returned to Washington in July.

Syria posed a more serious problem. Ostensibly aligned with the Soviet Union rather than the United States, aggressively radical and Arab nationalist in its public posturing, and hegemonic in its attitude toward its smaller and weaker neighbors, the Syrian regime was not particularly well disposed toward the P.L.O. leadership or its explicit aspirations for an independent policy.[43] The personality clash between Hafiz al-Asad and Yasser 'Arafat was a further complication.

Like most other Arab states, Syria had seemed perfectly willing to see the P.L.O. defeated in Lebanon at an early stage of the war, when the foolish illusion still prevailed that Israeli objectives were limited to dealing with the P.L.O. But the indifference of these regimes turned to concern when Israel's intentions toward Lebanon and Syria became apparent. This concern grew when the P.L.O. appeared to have withstood the initial Israeli blow and managed to hold out in Beirut, thus embarrassing the Arab regimes by juxtaposition of its resistance with their inaction, and even seemed as if it might achieve a minor victory via the Franco-Egyptian initiative.

Syria, especially, tried to cover up for its defeat on the ground and in the air with a media blitz to convince its own citizens that the Syrian army and air force had done all the fighting in Lebanon. The more successful the P.L.O. was in dragging out the siege, the worse the Asad regime looked; and any prospect of a P.L.O. victory, or even a mere avoidance of defeat, meant a major blow to Syria's prestige, and its hope to remain the dominant Arab power in the Fertile Crescent-greater Syria region.

The Syrian attitude toward the diplomatic strategy being pursued by the P.L.O. emerged clearly in the first part of July. Not surprisingly, it was entirely negative. The only original thing about it was the logic in which this stand was couched. The kernel of the Syrian argument was that it was a grave mistake to link the question of the Israeli occupation of Lebanon with the broader Middle East crisis, as was done in the Franco-Egyptian draft resolution. This, the Syrians argued, was because such an approach risked perpetuating the former without solving the latter, since at this time the balance of forces between Israel and the Arabs (for which read Syria) was negative.

At a meeting at the Foreign Ministry in Damascus on July 11, the same day the Syrians were informed of the P.L.O.'s 11 points, 'Abd al-Halim Khaddam told Abu Maher that the French draft resolution was a bad proposal for all these reasons. Although Abu Maher pointed out that there were differences between the text the Syrians had and the one he had been supplied with, the Syrian Foreign Minister was adamant. Khaddam added that the Syrians had asked the Soviets to veto the resolution should it come up for a vote.[44] The Quai d'Orsay was aware of this obstacle, and though repeated French-Soviet and French-Syrian contacts were devoted to clarifying the resolution and meeting Syrian objections, French diplomacy had some success in Moscow but little in Damascus.[45]

Foreign Minister Khaddam repeated the same arguments at another meeting with Abu Maher on July 13, at which the main topic of discussion was whether Syria would accept the P.L.O. leadership and forces evacuated from Beirut. Khaddam said his country's official position was to accept the former but not the latter.[46] This was fine with the P.L.O., since they were in no hurry to leave Beirut, and still had hopes that they could get better terms for their eventual evacuation. This was one of the few occasions during the entire war when Syrian and P.L.O. objectives coincided, although their motives were far from the same.

'Arafat was naturally unhappy with Syria's position on the French draft, and tried hard to meet its objections. These were apparently rooted in fears that if an Israeli withdrawal from Lebanon, which Syria considered it vital to obtain, were linked to that of the P.L.O. from Beirut, it might never take place, given the Palestinians' obvious aversion to leaving the Lebanese capital. This at least was what the Americans were informing the Syrians, according to the estimate of the French. They told Souss on July 13 that they were sure that U.S. Special Envoy Habib's assistant, Ambassador Morris Draper, had helped to convince Damascus to oppose the Franco-Egyptian draft during a visit there on July 9–10.[47] In a message sent to Abu Maher for the Syrians, 'Arafat replied to Khaddam's arguments against the resolution, pointing out that it included provisions for a ceasefire, disengagement, and a total Israeli withdrawal from Lebanon.[48] These points should have overcome Syrian objections, but did not.

A final meeting in Damascus for P.L.O.-Syrian coordination before Khaddam's departure for Washington brought this out clearly. Abu Maher reported the Syrian minister as saying bluntly that he was "opposed to relating the withdrawal from Lebanon with the Palestinian cause, because that is a dangerous thing, and we have to give priority to Israeli withdrawal from Lebanon." What should be done in Washington, Khaddam said, would be to discuss the Palestine question "in general" and to ask the U.S. to recognize the P.L.O. and Palestinain rights. He refused to discuss the matter of a solution to the Arab-Israeli dispute in Washington "in view of the current balance of forces." Pressed further, Khaddam in effect cut off the discussion by saying he was "not entitled by the leadership to enter into negotiations with the U.S. over broader questions.[49]

However reasonable Khaddam's position may have seemed, it effectively sabotaged the P.L.O. strategy of trying to get a broader political quid pro quo in exchange for a withdrawal from Beirut. This meant that the two Arab ministers would in effect confine themselves to vague generalities about a settlement of the Arab-Israeli dispute and an Israeli withdrawal from Lebanon on the one hand, and what would be no more than a discussion of the mechanics of getting the Palestinians out of Beirut on the other. This amounted exactly to the circumscription of the discussion to technical details which the French had repeatedly warned the U.S. was trying to achieve, and which they and the P.L.O. had been trying to avoid.

The Saudis meanwhile maintained their position of sowing doubt as to P.L.O. commitment to the Franco-Egyptian draft, insinuating that the P.L.O. was on the point of reaching an agreement with the U.S. through Saudi good offices and via the intermediary of their political ally in Beirut, Sa'eb Salam. This provoked 'Arafat to send a firm message to Souss and Zuhdi, affirming "We asked Saud al-Faisal before he left for the U.S. to support the French initiative. We are with it, with our amendments (the 11 points), which we insist on. The crux of the resolution is the rights of the Palestinian people . . . and we insist on French participation . . . [while] the U.S. wants to act alone."[50]

At the same time, the Syrian position continued to be one of unremitting opposition to the entire approach followed by the P.L.O. This was probably as much because Egypt was a co-sponsor of the resolution which was the vehicle for this approach, as because a P.L.O. victory via the resolution would be a defeat for Asad in the ruthless zero-sum game of inter-Arab politics. The Saudis, meanwhile, timid as ever, were reluctant to stand up to the United States on this issue. They too were jealous of the Egyptians, and were probably loath to see Yasser 'Arafat and his battle-hardened commandos emerge into the Arab world after the inferno of Beirut with a political victory largely of their own making.

Since the P.L.O. had to suffer the frustration of using an intermediary to communicate with the United States, the visit of the two ministers was vital if a breakthrough were to be achieved in Washington. But it was doomed to failure given the lukewarm support of both Syria and Saudi Arabia for the

P.L.O. position, combined with the unbending hostility of the Reagan administration. In the circumstances, the failed visit became the straw that broke the camel's back as far as the P.L.O. was concerned, and finally forced its leaders to acquiesce in the Habib plan they had resisted for so long, but which their Arab "brethren" accepted with almost indecent alacrity in Washington.

IV The Arab League
Delegation in Washington

A key figure in much of what occurred—and what did not occur—during the visit of the Arab League delegation to Washington was Khaled al-Hassan. In many ways, he played as crucial a role in the negotiations in the U.S. capital as had his younger brother Hani in those which took place in Beirut.

The Arab League Foreign Ministers had originally decided to send delegations including a P.L.O. representative to the capitals of all permanent members of the U.N. Security Council. Abu Lutf's meeting with President Mitterrand on July 15 had come in the context of one of these visits, while similar delegations traveled to Peking, London, and Moscow. Khaled al-Hassan was thus a full member of the Arab League delegation as far as its members and sponsors were concerned, but not in the eyes of the government it was dealing with.

His anomalous position did not prevent al-Hassan from showing great activity. While it is difficult to reconstruct all of his moves (much communication took place by telephone, and some has not been clearly recalled by the participants), it is clear from the evidence in the P.L.O. archives that he began his efforts to break the logjam in the negotiations even before Khaddam and Saudi Foreign Minister Sa'ud al-Faisal arrived in the United States on Sunday July 18 for meetings the following week with President Reagan and members of his administration.

Khaled al-Hassan proposed to 'Arafat in a confidential telex from New York on the 17th that the resolution of the crisis required the Chairman himself to restate publicly the P.L.O.'s position. The idea at this stage was relatively simple:

> What is required is a clear statement from you concerning the French initiative, even if this were linked to a condition— American recognition of PLO and dialogue and non-use of veto on the French initiative—or our acceptance of the initiative with some slight amendments that have been sent to PLO representative at the UN, and subject to affirmative vote by the USA.[51]

Al-Hassan affirmed optimistically that "On the whole, situation in our favour if we act prudently as stated above." The same telex expressed concern that in the negotiation process in Beirut "some facts are lost in the process of transmittal between mediators," and suggested that a check be made on what Habib was being given and what was received in Washington, and also on the proposals being made by the U.S. envoy. He concluded, "On this matter I sensed some preoccupation here."

In his next message to 'Arafat from Washington two days later, Khaled al-Hassan maintained his positive tone, and his insistence that a personal initiative from the P.L.O. leader was necessary if his mission to the U.S. was to make headway. He reported Sa'ud al-Faisal's "successful" meeting with the Senate Foreign Relations Committee, and that the Prince's information as to the favorable situation in Washington coincided with his own. Al-Hassan added that in view of "the change to our benefit both in the Congress and the White House," it was possible to win the battle for Beirut as well as the Palestinian struggle for self-determination "if we know how to take advantage of the momentum and if we know how to direct it."

As a member of the Fateh Central Committee and a founder of the movement, Khaled al-Hassan could allow

himself to be forceful in urging a course of action on 'Arafat.
He thus told him, "Now we are at a point where we have to
make policy and not diplomacy," adding, "the usual Arab
approach of 'wait-and-see' should be avoided." To continue a
reactive policy, he went on, would be a "fatal mistake." All of
this led up to a major new proposal for action by the Chairman,
which al-Hassan stated was needed "very urgently," specifically within the following 14 hours (i.e., before the two Arab
ministers saw Reagan).

The proposed statement, of which a draft was submitted, was to be issued by 'Arafat personally and stressed that
the P.L.O. had "no objection to 242 regarding the full withdrawal of the Israelis from all the territories occupied in the
1967 war," which would be "acceptable to us if the right to
self-determination of the Palestinian people is connected with
it." The statement also called for the opening of a dialogue
with the U.S. and for face-to-face negotiations with Habib.[52]

The difference between this suggestion and that made
two days earlier is noticeable. Originally, all al-Hassan was
calling for was a public restatement by 'Arafat of P.L.O.
support for the Franco-Egyptian resolution, with its balanced
combination of a repetition of the principles of 242 with an
affirmation of the Palestinian right to self-determination. The
provision in al-Hassan's first proposal to 'Arafat that the U.S.
vote for the draft would in effect have meant supplanting 242
with a new text more acceptable to the P.L.O. But now, after
meeting the Saudi Foreign Minister, Khaled al-Hassan was
advocating something entirely new and far less favorable. This
was an open acceptance of 242 by the P.L.O., conditional only
on its linkage (in an unspecified fashion) to the principle of
Palestinian self-determination.

Not surprisingly, there was intense skepticism in Beirut
about this new proposal. A participant described a meeting of
the P.L.O. leadership to consider al-Hassan's suggestion on the
night of July 19, the eve of a meeting Sa'ud al-Faisal and
Khaddam were to have with Reagan. At one point, after being
urged by a Fateh Central Committee member to respond

positively to al-Hassan's message, 'Arafat turned to a colleague, saying: "You see what they are trying to get me to accept? If I go out on a limb like this what guarantee do I have that we will get anything at all in return? You see what kind of pressure I am under? I will not do it."[53]

At 3:30 A.M. Beirut time, after extensive deliberation, an unconvinced 'Arafat carried the day. A telex was sent to al-Hassan pointing out that there seemed to be no guarantee that P.L.O. acceptance of 242 would be linked to a binding process whereby the Palestinians' right to self-determination could be achieved. The key phrase used in the telex (a literal translation from the Arabic) was that the proposal left Palestinian self-determination as "a fish in the water," with absolutely no assurance that it could be landed.[54]

Al-Hassan responded immediately, declaring that those who had suggested the proposal to him were sure that there would be a positive response. He added that the proposed statement could initially be in the form of a nonbinding offer rather than an ironclad commitment. Al-Hassan perhaps revealed the quarter which influenced this proposal when he stressed that Sa'ud al-Faisal concurred in thinking this was a wise idea, and that the Prince expected a positive response after seeing the new Secretary of State, George Shultz, on the morning of the 20th.[55]

Before those in Beirut had a chance to respond, however, al-Hassan sent another telex asking them to delay action on both of his messages until further notice, which he expected to be able to give them the following day. After the war, the Fateh leader explained his change of advice by saying that he was getting contradictory suggestions from different quarters in Washington, with Sa'ud al-Faisal and others proposing the P.L.O. accept 242, and semiofficial U.S. contacts discouraging P.L.O. concessions. Al-Hassan indicated that certain moves by the U.S. toward the P.L.O. were hinted at during these semiofficial contacts, but then the idea was dropped for unknown reasons.[56]

None of this was known at the time in Beirut, where July

20 came and went with no word, and 'Arafat sent a telex to Washington saying he was "awaiting together with brothers" al-Hassan's current opinion on his earlier proposals.[57] They were also anxiously awaiting the results of the meeting with Reagan and Shultz that day, but inexplicably recevied no report on it from their envoy either on 20th or the next day. On the 21st, 'Arafat sent al-Hassan two urgent telexes demanding written clarification of what he had apparently reported in summary form by telephone. The P.L.O. leader's irritation was evident:

> Until now we have not received anything regarding the discussion except what you said on the phone to Abu Jihad. I want something documented and official so as to move in light of it. Please insist that Prince Saud knows that so as to act in light of it in our moves and discussion with the Lebanese and Habib. We cannot move in light of a telephone conversation.[58]

'Arafat and the P.L.O. leadership had to wait until the following day to receive a report on what had occurred in Washington from al-Hassan, and they got it only via the P.L.O. New York office, which fulfilled an urgent request to repeat the text of a highly confidential message sent originally (and inexplicably) to Abu Lutf in Damascus rather than to Beirut.[59]

In his telex, which contained a detailed report of all his activities in Washington, Khaled al-Hassan noted that he had met Sa'ud al-Faisal on Monday the 18th and had given him a copy of the P.L.O.'s 11 points, and that he met him again after the Prince and Khaddam met with Shultz on the 19th, and once more after the two ministers' encounter with the President and Shultz on the 20th.

According to al-Hassan's account, based on what he was told by Sa'ud al-Faisal, during the initial meeting with the two Arab ministers Shultz restricted himself to insisting on the withdrawal of Palestinian forces from Lebanon, while his interlocutors stressed the necessity for linkage between a settlement of the Beirut issue and a comprehensive settlement of the Palestine question.

The later meeting with Reagan and Shultz, Khaled al-Hassan reported, had resulted in an agreement on a number of points. These included a ceasefire; the presence of an international (U.N.-sponsored) or multinational force to disengage the opposing forces; a regrouping of P.L.O. forces and simultaneous Israeli withdrawal from around Beirut and from the P.L.O.'s routes of withdrawal (this was the first and only time any mention was found in any source that the U.S. had accepted such a condition); a redeployment of P.L.O. forces in Tripoli or the Biqa' Valley, or both, until an Arab League decision on their final disposition; Syria would host the P.L.O.'s leadership, its administrative staff, and 1000–1500 of its troops, in addition to the P.L.A. brigades originally from Syria; other aspects of Palestinian–Lebanese relations were to be agreed upon between the parties.

The message concluded with a brief account of perhaps the most crucial points discussed:

> The American side expressed its commitment to Israeli withdrawal from Lebanon in accordance with resolution 509 but did not indicate any guarantee or time-table. The American side accepts linkage of Beirut issue and Palestinian question, and did not indicate time or form of settlement, but said this will be soon. Formula[tion] of strategy for this purpose is underway.[60]

In light of the disappointing nature of what was being offered by the United States, it can perhaps be seen why the proposal on 242 was not raised again by al-Hassan, why it took him so long to respond to 'Arafat or to report on these meetings, and why when he finally did so it was via a telex to Abu Lutf in Damascus. For 'Arafat had been completely correct in his skeptical initial reaction to the proposal regarding 242. According to al-Hassan's account of the meeting, there was to be no U.S. quid pro quo, and no guarantee of a favorable U.S. response, not only regarding Palestinian self-determination, but even on the far less sensitive matter of an Israeli withdrawal from Lebanon.

The Sa'ud al-Faisal/Khaddam/Khaled al-Hassan mission

had been a total failure as far as P.L.O. interests were concerned. However, the full depth of this failure is apparent only when this account of the meeting between Reagan and the Arab ministers is compared with another, considerably fuller, version. This was published after the war in a Paris Arabic-language magazine, Kul al-'Arab, and later reprinted in the Beirut daily al-Safir. According to a reliable source, this text originated with a senior Saudi diplomat in Washington, and constitutes a complete and accurate transcript of the meeting.[61]

A number of important points emerge from it. The first is Ronald Reagan's single-minded insistence on eliminating the P.L.O. from Beirut, and on seeing it as the exclusive cause of the war and source of the troubles of Lebanon which preceded it. Characteristically, the President ignored the historical record. The obsessive stubbornness of the President on these points was the rock on which the optimism of Khaled al-Hassan and Sa'ud al-Faisal was to founder. It is as clear from this transcript as it is from Haig's memoirs or the speeches of Jeane Kirkpatrick in the Security Council during the war that there was never any realistic hope of changing the United States' intransigent stand toward the P.L.O. Any other view was wishful thinking.

More important, it is striking that at no stage during the lengthy meeting did either Arab minister even mention the P.L.O.'s 11-point plan, or the concept of a political quid pro quo in exchange for its withdrawal from Beirut. The closest they came was Sa'ud al-Faisal's attempt to obtain assurances that the Palestinians would eventually return to their homeland "because those people are homeless, Mr. President, and there must be a resolution of their problem." This humanitarian approach had no more effect than that of Khaddam, who after conveying Asad's "warmest greetings" to Reagan, launched into a lengthy disquisition on the history of the conflict and other matters. He devoted most of his presentation to stressing Syrian security concerns regarding Israel's withdrawal from Lebanon and the future situation of that country.

In fact, regarding the central question of the siege of

Beirut, both ministers implicitly accepted the U.S. approach, which divested the issue of all its political implications, narrowing it down to the bare technical problem of when the P.L.O. was to leave and where to. More than two thirds of the discussion was devoted to this subject. While Sa'ud al-Faisal focused on a compromise solution involving an intial move to Tripoli and the Biqa', Khaddam's main concern was to avoid "moving the problem to Syria." He expressed his government's fear that the Palestinians would become "foci of terror in the Arab world . . . creating a very serious security problem" for the entire region as a result of their fourth exodus in 30 years, not to speak of "the security problem for Syria this would constitute."

Not only did the two ministers fail to resist the American approach to the problem, which Reagan bluntly made clear was fully aligned with Israel's ("The reason the Israelis gave [for their invasion] is getting the P.L.O. out and we will do everything in our power to make that happen, . . . " the President said). Having refrained from defending the P.L.O.'s stated position, they could not even secure the basic elements which concerned the security interests of their two countries. These included a binding American commitment to ensure an Israeli withdrawal, which Reagan and Shultz would not give; American support for an interim P.L.O. withdrawal to other parts of Lebanon, which was not forthcoming; and some acceptance by the Americans that a solution to the problem involved going further than simply shipping Palestinians from Beirut into another exile: to the end, neither Reagan nor Schultz would address this issue.

In fact, Khaled al-Hassan's report appears flawed in at least two ways in light of this full transcript. On the one hand, many of the principles he was told had been "agreed" with the Americans had simply been put forward by the Arab side and discussed, but neither accepted nor openly rejected by the U.S. In fact, there was no agreement on points like a P.L.O. move to Tripoli and the Biqa', or an Israeli withdrawal from around Beirut.

On the other hand, much was missing from Khaled al-

Hassan's report, including points important only because they showed the narrow limits of what was possible with the U.S. administration, such as Reagan's insistence (before a roomful of people who knew better) that the P.L.O. had always initiated cross-border exchanges before the war; or his statement that the Palestinians in West Beirut were "terrorists responsible for acts of terror all over the world, . . . [and] an obstacle in the path of the peace we all want." Other missing points were substantive ones, such as the major divergence between the actual line taken by the two ministers and that of the P.L.O., or the failure of the U.S. to address any of the central concerns of either the P.L.O. or the Arab ministers.

Worst of all, the P.L.O. was to get the impression from al-Hassan's delayed report (and presumably from the Saudis) that some sort of agreement had been worked out between the Arab ministers and the United States,[62] when in fact that was not at all the case. A careful reading of what Reagan and Shultz actually said shows that all they wanted from the Arab side was support for the stand the U.S. had held firmly since the war began. Specifically, they wanted Saudi help in putting pressure on the Palestinians, and Syrian acquiescence to hosting the P.L.O. after its evacuation from Beirut. This they obtained, without giving anything in return.

It remained for the French, once again, to put events into the proper perspective. They told Ibrahim Souss a few days after the Washington meeting that:

> Their information is [that] one of the reasons behind the lack of any expediency [sic] on the part of the Americans to deal with any "Palestinian gesture of overture" is that both Reagan and Shultz found Faisal and Khaddam "cool" and "rather not in a hurry to deal with the Palestinian issue as a global political question", thus opening horizons for the solution of the Lebanese crisis.[63]

This was an accurate assessment. Aside from what amounted to an undermining of the stated position of the P.L.O. (and the incidental complication of Palestinian–French relations caused by the incorrect impression of the P.L.O. attitude to the French envoys in New York and Washington)[64], the visit led only to informal Arab acquiescence to the U.S. approach. This was to be finally consecrated at the Jedda Arab League conference on July 29. It was not a result any of the members of the delegation could be proud of.

V The Denouement: Jedda and Afterwards

Little more needs to be said regarding P.L.O. wartime decisions. By the end of July, the Arab states—or at least the leading powers among them—had adopted the view of the United States, Israel, and the Sarkis government that all the issues raised by the war could be addressed by solving the technical problem of the P.L.O.'s evacuation from Beirut. In a certain sense the decision had thus been made for the P.L.O. by its "brethren."

The Jedda conference adopted a six-point plan: (1) a ceasefire; (2) the P.L.O. to move its forces from Beirut under Lebanese government guarantees for their safety and for the security of the camps; (3) the siege of Beirut was to be lifted with the partial withdrawal of Israeli forces; (4) the Lebanese government was to ensure the security and safety of the citizens of the city of Beirut and its suburbs, including the Palestinian camps; (5) an international force was to participate in the entire operation; (6) the Arab states would help Lebanon obtain implementation of Security Council resolution 508 and 509 in their entirety.[65]

There are strong grounds for assuming that these six points, drafted largely by Sa'ud al-Faisal and Khaddam, were based on the mistaken belief that the U.S. had agreed to the points raised in Washington by the two ministers.[66] Such an impression is reinforced by the inclusion of matters such as the lifting of the siege of Beirut, a partial Israeli withdrawal, and the implementation of SC 509, which called for a complete, immediate, and unconditional Israeli withdrawal from

Lebanon. Mention of them in a document issued by an inter-Arab meeting would have been meaningless had U.S. assent to them not been obtained.

However, when the fog of Arab diplomacy had dissipated, it was apparent that nothing at all had been agreed in Washington or settled in Jedda. Thus, at the end of July the P.L.O. leadership in Beirut found itself under intense Israeli military pressure, and confronting the task of coming to terms with the Americans without the slightest assistance from the Arab "brethren." The latter had indeed made their task all the harder. In the harsh circumstances, this meant that the P.L.O. had little alternative but to accept the hated Habib plan.

This bitter pill was finally swallowed in the last three days of July, although the exact date is hard to pinpoint. The intensive bombardment of Beirut from air, land, and sea, and the attacks on P.L.O. headquarters and meeting places all over the city, made it harder and harder for the Palestinain leadership to meet, while even consultation was often difficult because of communications difficulties. By the end of July, however, the P.L.O. had already presented Habib and the Lebanese government with a working paper including a timetable for withdrawal.[67] This is the first concrete indication that it had accepted the approach that had been pushed by Philip Habib since mid-June.

The fact that the leadership had reached this point was not widely known within the P.L.O. There was surprise when the Jedda communique was published, and distress when the daily operations reports in late July provided more and more detail on the advanced stage of the negotiations. But as the Israeli attacks reached a new intensity in the first twelve days of August, it became clear to everyone in Beirut that there was no alternative to evacuation. The gallant attempt to hold out and explore every possible avenue for obtaining better terms than Habib's was over, and the decision of their leaders was quickly accepted by all within the movement.

Even the minority opposed to a withdrawal, led by Abu Saleh, at this point accepted the inevitable. At a July 21 meeting of the P.L.O. leadership, Abu Saleh had urged making a last appeal to the Soviets and to Syria. 'Arafat thereupon stalked out of the meeting in disgust, refusing to associate himself with the proposal because of his certainty that nothing could be expected of either power. The two messages were then drafted and dispatched.

The Soviet response was rapid: there was nothing the USSR could do, since it could act only via Syria, and this was not possible. Asad did not reply directly: apparently embarrassed by a direct appeal in which the P.L.O. told him they would hold out in Beirut if he told them to do so, he let it be known on August 10, via the director of the Office of the President, that he would not respond. Well before this, nearly everyone in the P.L.O. had reconciled himself to leaving: but after August 10, the P.L.O. decision was unanimous.[68]

It remained only to ensure that Israel would not prevent the safe departure of the P.L.O. forces, and that adequate guarantees could be obtained for the safety of those who remained behind, a subject which had preoccupied the P.L.O. leadership from the first. In the infernal atmosphere of the incessant Israeli attacks of the first twelve days of August, this was not an easy task. However, properly speaking, no further important P.L.O. decisions were required. The last stage of the negotiations is therefore part of another story, that of broken promises and trust betrayed which forms the ugly background to the Israeli occupation of Beirut and the Sabra and Shatila massacres.

Chapter 6

Wartime Decisions
and Their Consequences

I The Results of the P.L.O.'s Decisions

Once the P.L.O. finally decided to accept Habib's terms at the end of July the consequences of this decision began to take shape. Strictly speaking, these are not part of the story of P.L.O. decisionmaking during the 1982 war: once the Palestinians had made their decision, events left their hands and took their own course. But because of the great importance for the Palestinians and the P.L.O. of some of the consequences which ensued, they must at least be touched on.

These consequences included negotiations with Philip Habib to secure U.S. guarantees for the safety of the Palestinian civilian population after the withdrawal of P.L.O. forces from Beirut; the intense Israeli military pressure applied throughout the last few weeks of the negotiations; the conclusion of the U.S.-Israeli-P.L.O.-Lebanese agreement and the evacuation of P.L.O. and Syrian forces from Beirut; and finally the flagrant violations of these accords which followed soon afterward. Most notable among these violations were the Israeli army's invasion of Beirut after the assassination of

Lebanese President-elect Bashir Gemayel, and the subsequent Sabra/Shatila massacres of September 16–18.

For Palestinians who remained in Lebanon, and for those who departed with the P.L.O. evacuation, the momentous events of the preceding months were overshadowed by the massacres, the betrayal of the assurances for the safety of the Palestinian civilian population made by Habib, Israel, and the Phalangists, and the failure of the P.L.O. leadership to secure the guarantees for which it had held out so long. It is impossible to deal fully with these important topics here, for together they constitute the beginning of what is in effect another narrative: that of the Palestinians and the P.L.O. after the 1982 war. A brief discussion of them will nevertheless serve both as an epilogue to this account of wartime decision-making, and as an introduction to the story of the uncertain world which faces the Palestinian people in the wake of the war—a story which remains to be told.

II U.S. Guarantees for the Safety of Palestinian Civilians

From an early stage in their negotiations with the United States, P.L.O. negotiators were preoccupied with securing firm guarantees for the security of the Palestinian and Lebanese civilians in Beirut who would be left at the mercy of the Israeli army and its Lebanese allies after a P.L.O. evacuation. Concern about this problem was heightened by the harsh behavior of Israeli forces toward Palestinian civilians in occupied South Lebanon, and by the massacres of Druze civilians in the Shouf in late June by the LF after the IDF facilitated their entry into the region. This preoccupation eventually became a central focus of the concerns of the P.L.O. leadership.

Although the P.L.O.'s 11-point plan of early July was seen as no more than a negotiating ploy to stave off inevitable concessions to Israel and the United States, its terms were inspired largely by a desire to secure ironclad guarantees for the safety of the P.L.O. civilian population in the context of a full or partial P.L.O. evacuation. Among the provisions designed to achieve this end were those calling for Israeli withdrawal five miles from Beirut, for international guarantees for the safety of the Palestinian camps, and for the establishment of a U.N.-controlled (rather than U.S.-dominated) buffer force between the two sides. In the end, the balance of forces between the P.L.O. and Israel, and the stubborn resistance of the U.S. to any scheme which did not give it a central role, doomed this proposal. But P.L.O. leaders and Palestinians in Beirut felt strongly that this approach would have provided far more solid guarantees for their safety than the one being proposed by the U.S.

Even before they finally reconciled themselves to the fact that their own 11-point plan was unrealizable, the P.L.O. leadership set about obtaining clear and unequivocal guarantees from Philip Habib. This was an exceedingly difficult task for many reasons. One was that the U.S. envoy was being asked to guarantee not the behavior of his own country, but rather that of its most independent-minded ally, Israel, and of the Phalangist-dominated Lebanese Forces. Neither had a reputation for responsiveness to the pleas of Americans or others for good behavior when the well-being of Palestinian civilians was at stake.

In the minds of those on the Palestinian side throughout these negotiations was the specter of Tal al-Za'tar. There, after a three-month siege, and in spite of the collapse of the camp's defenses and the presence on the scene of representatives of the International Red Cross, the Lebanese right-wing militias had perpetrated a large-scale massacre on August 12, 1976. Many hundreds of people had been killed after the fall of the camp, nearly all of them noncombatants.[1] In view of this tragic history, what the Palestinians feared was that after the departure of P.L.O. forces the IDF would allow these same militias to finish in the refugee camps of Beirut in 1982 what they had started at Tal al-Za'atar and other Palestinian camps in 1976.

After repeated, insistent P.L.O. requests, Habib eventually expressed his government's willingness in principle to provide the required guarantees regarding the safety of the camp population. However, as late as August 2, the P.L.O. transmitted to Paris the draft of a 13-point plan received from Habib which failed to clarify the nature of these guarantees. By its terms, rather than having clearly specified responsibilities for the protection of Palestinian camps the projected multinational forces [MNF] were to perform "such duties as were assigned by the Lebanese government," and were to arrive only after the P.L.O. evacuation had begun, leaving a period of dangerous vulnerability to Israeli moves before their arrival.[2]

Finally, in answer to a Palestinian proposal dated August 3, which insisted on definite U.S. guarantees as part of any evacuation accord, Habib responded positively. The text of the U.S. message, the first documentary evidence which could be found explicitly offering such guarantees, reads: "Regarding U.S. Government guarantees as regards security for the departing Palestinian forces along with the security of the camps. Comment: We will provide these guarantees." The P.L.O. was clearly satisfied, responding immediately: "We record the importance of the U.S. provision of guarantees . . . ensuring the safety of Palestinian camps."[3]

Even after this major hurdle had been cleared, a variety of other important details remained to be worked out between the U.S., Israel, and the P.L.O. Among them was the issue of when the MNF was to arrive, a serious matter in view of the P.L.O.'s fear that the Israelis might try to exploit any gap between the commencement of a P.L.O. departure and an MNF arrival to finish off their enemies. The principle of MNF arrival simultaneously with the commencement of the P.L.O.'s departure was finally accepted by the U.S. on August 4. This same day witnessed the last major Israeli attempt to advance, combined with intense bombardments of West Beirut. Because of the fierceness of the Israeli attacks, communications between East and West Beirut were repeatedly interrupted. As a result, both Brigadier Qureitem, the main Lebanese military intermediary between the P.L.O. and Habib, and former Premier Sa'eb Salam had difficulties in relaying important proposals to the U.S. side, and reported this to the P.L.O.[4]

Nevertheless, by August 4 agreement had been reached on the points of contention. This was summed up in a U.S. memo of that date to the P.L.O. which stated: "We appear to be in agreement on U.S. assurances about the safety of . . . the camps . . . Points of Agreement [include] U.S. guarantees governing the safe passage of the departing Palestinian forces as well as the Palestinian camps." A later memo added: "We also reaffirm the assurances of the United States as regards safety and security . . . for the camps in Beirut."[5] The final text of the agreement, finalized on August 11 (and only slightly modified in its final published form of an exchange of notes between the Lebanese and U.S. governments on August 18 and 20) put the U.S. security guarantees for the camps as follows:

> Law-abiding Palestinian non-combatants remaining in Beirut, including the families of those who have departed, will be authorized to live in peace and security. The Lebanese and U.S. governments will provide appropriate security guarantees . . . The U.S. will provide its guarantees on the basis of assurances received from the government of Israel and from the leaders of certain Lebanese groups with which it has been in contact.[6]

III The Effect of Israeli Military Pressure

Guarantees for the camps had been the main thing the P.L.O. was seeking after a certain point in the negotiations. Once they had been received, and once the other matters at issue (such as the arrival date for the MNF) had been settled, nothing stood in the way of the finalization of the accord on P.L.O. evacuation, an end to the siege, and a peaceful resolution of the crisis— nothing, that is, except the apparent desire of Sharon and the IDF to prevent a negotiated evacuation of P.L.O. forces from taking place at all.

Such concerns about Sharon's intentions were not confined to Palestinians, who had every reason to be suspicious of him. They were shared by many observers at the time, including Habib himself. He declared in a postwar interview that it was his belief that Sharon always wanted to enter West Beirut, planning to avoid a politically unacceptable level of IDF casualties by using Phalangist military forces in the assault if they could be persuaded to go along.[7]

Habib added: "Sharon wanted to get the P.L.O. fighting men. He would love to have gotten them, and he had a pretty broad definition of fighting men, including the political cadre." Habib stated that he strongly believed that Sharon would have aborted the evacuation agreement had he been able to. This he would have done via his usual tactic for disrupting the negotiations, as described by the U.S. negotiator: "Sharon didn't want a ceasefire. He would find a reason to move, the other side would fire, and shooting would start again."[8]

These repeated Israeli escalations, whether intended to interrupt the negotiations or not, were described as an obstacle to his efforts by Habib: "I did not feel the shelling and bombing were helpful. The P.L.O. had made its decision [by late July in his estimation], and it was not necessary."[9] Although the P.L.O. was convinced that, on many occasions, Israeli military pressure was used by Habib as a lever to extract concessions, according to the U.S. envoy himself this was not always the case. Speaking more than two years after the event, Habib stated that it had been his belief that Sharon had some sort of understanding with Haig over Lebanon. He added that until the former Secretary's departure from the State Department, he found it exceedingly hard to move Washington to restrain Israel or to support his own efforts.[10] Perhaps not coincidentally, Haig's departure from his post toward the end of the first week of July marked the beginning of a period of relative restraint on the part of the Israelis, who did not use their air force for several weeks, and made no attempts to advance on the ground until the last ten days of July.

It was toward the end of this latter period, when Habib

argued that the P.L.O. had finally come around to accepting the basic outlines of the U.S. plan (a conclusion which is supported by most of the evidence presented in the preceding pages) that he felt his efforts were most obstructed by Sharon's obstinate desire to win an absolute victory over the Palestinians. The impression left by Habib's remarks is that Washington was incapable of stopping Sharon, even after the departure of his ally Haig, without the direct intervention of the President with Begin.[11] This did not take place until August 12, at the end of a three-week crescendo of Israeli escalation, and following a day of nonstop aerial bombardment of West Beirut.

In terms of stated U.S. and Israeli objectives, the suffering inflicted on the city and its inhabitants in the course of this application of Israeli pressure against the P.L.O. was totally unnecessary, since these objectives had been met once the P.L.O. accepted the Habib plan in late July. This is the inescapable conclusion from the remarks of Habib himself, and was apparent to many observers at the time. Not surprisingly, the Israelis then and their defenders since have argued that far from obstructing Habib's efforts, the IDF was supporting them with its military pressure.[12] As is clear from Habib's own words, this self-serving argument is baseless.

According to Hani al-Hassan, quite the contrary was true: far from rendering the Palestinians more amenable to U.S. or Israeli terms, military pressure markedly increased their unwillingness to compromise. He affirmed further that it became a conscious policy of the P.L.O. negotiators to withhold concessions when they were under heavy Israeli attack (he cited as examples June 25 or July 4, when previous P.L.O. concessions were withdrawn). Conversely, the P.L.O. would moderate its demands in periods of calm, such as during the relative lull which followed the failure of the Israelis to advance at the airport and the Museum in early July (at which point al-Hassan says the P.L.O. purposely reduced its terms from 26 points down to 11).[13]

While this may be an exaggeration, it noteworthy that when asked for the main reason the P.L.O. accepted the Habib

plan at the end of July, virtually every P.L.O. leader interviewed stressed that it was the absence of hope for better
terms, the lack of "horizons" in the words of Abu Lutf, which
played the key role.[14] Although Yasser 'Arafat confirmed that
the P.L.O. was sensitive to Israeli military pressure, he referred
specifically to the IDF advance to the edge of Shatila camp on
August 4, by which time the P.L.O. had already accepted the
Habib plan.[15] By way of contrast, the same battle was cited as
an example of how little effect Israeli advances had on P.L.O.
morale by Abu Iyyad, who stated that Israeli military pressure
was less important in P.L.O. decisionmaking than the
Lebanese, Arab, and international situations.[16]

IV The Habib Plan is Implemented

In spite of intensive IDF military pressure during the last
weeks of negotiation, and notwithstanding Washington's reluctance to stand up to Sharon and the Israelis, agreement
between the different parties was finally reached on August 11.
After a few more days of minor modifications of the terms, it
was published on August 20, and its implementation began on
the following day with the arrival of the initial French
contingents of the MNF, and the departure of the first units of
the P.L.O. by sea. The evacuation was completed on September 1,
two days ahead of schedule.

A variety of problems arose during the evacuation, as
the Israelis quibbled over points in the agreement, and
repeatedly held up the movement of P.L.O. forces from Beirut
until they could obtain satisfaction. Even earlier, however,
serious misgivings about provisions of the agreement began to
be voiced, particularly with regard to the crucial question of
guarantees for the safety of the Palestinian civilian population
to be left behind after the evacuation.

One of the first such expressions of concern came from
the French, who during the latter phases of the negotiations
had played a less prominent role than in the earlier stages, but

who had always considered this a question of the utmost importance. Upon receiving the text of the draft agreement from the P.L.O., they asked regarding the issue of guarantees for Palestinian civilians: "How can what is mentioned here be guaranteed? . . . It is imperative that the U.S. alone obtain all guarantees and assurances from Israel and the Phalangists. France is going to insist on this point with the Americans."[17] The P.L.O. fully shared this French concern. 'Arafat responded to the message from Paris the next day, at the height of the Israeli bombardment of Beirut: "The P.L.O. insists that France shoulder its real official and moral responsibility in this regard."[18]

In fact, as a result of the agreement the P.L.O. had already acquiesced in, there was little France could do, beyond exhorting the United States to be faithful to its promises. For thanks largely to the diligence and single-mindedness of Habib, the final agreement was an American one, the final guarantees were American, and the forces introduced to Lebanon to implement it were American-dominated. The proof of this was to come when the United States decided unilaterally on the precipitate withdrawal of its forces from Beirut, largely for domestic political reasons, obliging the forces of France, Italy, and Britain to withdraw immediately thereafter.

What had taken place was exactly what the French and the P.L.O. had warned against and tried to avoid throughout the first six weeks of the negotiations. The U.S. had succeeded in confining the definition of the conflict, and the negotiations to end it, to the technical question of a P.L.O. withdrawal from Beirut. This was seen in Washington as virtually the sole task of the MNF,[19] and once this evacuation had taken place, U.S. troops were almost immediately removed. Thus, instead of there being a truly international force stationed on the spot with a clear and irrevocable mandate to protect the camps and prevent Israeli violations of the agreement, once the MNF withdrew there was nothing standing in the way of Sharon and his implacable desire to enter Beirut.

After the withdrawal of the MNF, only two things in

theory restrained the IDF from entering Beirut and allowing the barbarities against the camp population which virtually everyone in Lebanon fully expected if Israel's Phalangist allies were allowed to have their way. These were the written word of the United States of America to an organization it did not recognize (never delivered formally, but rather embodied in an exchange of letters with the government of Lebanon), and the manifestly uncertain will of the Reagan administration to keep the promises made by its envoy.

In the event, both paper promises and American will were to prove insufficient following the killing of Bashir Gemayel. Unaffected by the existence of these commitments, and even before the President-elect's body had been found, the IDF began preparing to enter the city, and Israeli generals began discussions with their Phalangist allies over the entry of the Lebanese Forces into the now-defenseless refugee camps.

V. The Massacres

Asked whether the U.S. had failed to keep its word to the P.L.O., and whether Israel had violated the commitments it had made to the United States when it entered West Beirut, Philip Habib later answered, "Of course."[20] A White House statement of September 16 affirmed that Israel's entry into West Beirut was "contrary to the assurances given to us," while a statement by the President two days later demanded an immediate Israeli withdrawal.[21] But by then it was too late for the victims butchered in Sabra and Shatila from the evening of Thursday September 16 until the morning of Saturday the 18th.

Ariel Sharon's libel suit against *Time* magazine once again touched on many of the issues initially raised at the time of the massacre and again when the Kahan Commission delivered its report. In spite of this extensive attention, a number of points have been overlooked in the discussion of this question. One is the matter of Israel's commitment not to enter Beirut in the first place, and the guarantees the United

States received from Israel as to the safety and security of the civilian population of the refugee camps.

According to Ze'ev Schiff's account of the discussion of Israel's entry into Beirut which took place between Sharon and Habib's replacement, Ambassador Morris Draper, on September 16, the Defense Minister stated that "new circumstances" made it necessary for the IDF to violate its pledge and enter the city. Draper apparently made no mention of Israeli promises regarding the welfare of Palestinian civilians, nor of the U.S. commitments to the P.L.O. in this regard.[22] This is not surprising, and not only because the burly Israeli general seems to have been his usual intimidating self during this interview. Since his own government gave these U.S. commitments virtually no public attention in the aftermath of the August 20 accords, Draper can be forgiven for failing to mention the matter to Sharon. Even after Israel entered Beirut, there is no reference to U.S. commitments to the P.L.O. in the context of the evacuation accords in six statements by the State Department, the White House, and the President himself.[23]

The language of the U.S. pledges to the P.L.O. is clear and damning: "Regarding U.S. Government guarantees as regards security . . . of the camps, . . . We will provide these guarantees"; "We appear to be in agreement on U.S. assurances about the safety of . . . the camps"; and "We also reaffirm the assurances of the United States as regards safety and security . . . for the camps in Beirut."[24] More unequivocal language would have been impossible. Yet these were confidential commitments, offered during the bargaining process, recorded on plain white paper rather than official stationery, and never made public by the United States. (Copies were later given to foreign journalists by P.L.O. leaders, and can be found in the P.L.O. archives.[25])

In public, the clear and explicit U.S. guarantee of the safety of the Palestinian civilian population embodied in the published August 20 evacuation agreement was virtually ignored in U.S. official statements at the time and afterward.[26] Furthermore, no mention was made by anyone on the U.S. side of any of the confidential pledges to the P.L.O. in this regard. Instead, in August there was self-congratulation and satisfied mutual backslapping in Washington over the fact that the United States had finally solved the core of the problem as described by itself and Israel—the presence of the P.L.O. in Beirut—by obtaining its evacuation.

Then, when reality intruded itself, when Israel did what so many had feared it would and had tried to obtain guarantees against, when Israel's allies were sent into the camps to perpetrate the very acts the P.L.O. had negotiated for weeks to try to avoid, there was apparent shock and surprise in Washington. Although a series of statements was made concerning the situation, and commenting—lukewarmly at first, and then increasingly stiffly—on the Israeli occupation of the Lebanese capital, there seems to have been little realization on the part of U.S. officials in Washington of the enormity of what was happening.[27] In the event, no practical measures were taken by the U.S. to stop the tragedy of the massacres until it was too late. And at no stage did any U.S. official in the many statements made at this time admit that the U.S. had promised to prevent just such an eventuality, that it had broken its word, and that it bore a major share of responsibility for what had happened.

In addition to the clear American responsibility for what happened, several other parties must share the blame. Israel's role goes far beyond the indirect responsibility and sins of omission attributed to seven Israeli officials by the Kahan Commission. No Israeli official who had had anything to do with the Phalangists could possibly have had any illusions as to what they would do if introduced into a Palestinian refugee camp; moreover, the historical record was full of bloody examples. The most notable of these, Tal al-Za'tar, had been witnessed by two IDF liaison officers, according to a statement by Sharon in the Knesset in reply to the attacks of his critics after Sabra and Shatila.[28] The Kahan report itself is replete with testimony regarding Phalangist intentions and actions regarding the Palestinians as they were revealed to Isreali officers in 1982.

The argument that the camps were full of "terrorists" left behind by the P.L.O. is often adduced in explanation of Israel's actions. It requires an assumption of gross incompetence on the part of Israeli military intelligence to believe that the IDF did not know that there were no P.L.O. fighters there. In fact, as is acknowledged by most sources,[29] there were none. Those men who had remained behind in the camps were Palestinians legally resident in Lebanon, many of whom were part-time members of camp self-defense militias. The Israelis knew perfectly well that they were incapable of offering serious resistance, as is evidenced by the introduction into the camps of a tiny force of a few hundred Phalangists. Clearly, the P.L.O. combatants who for two months had held several divisions of the IDF at the gates of Beirut would have made short work of such a force. But these battle-hardened fighters were gone, as the Israelis knew well. Sending the Phalangists into the camp could only have had one logical objective: the perpetration of a massacre.

Much can be said about the responsibility of others for Sabra and Shatila. Sharon and his accomplices are not the only ones who have gotten off easily: those Lebanese who actually perpetrated the massacre have never been fully identified, let alone made to pay for their crimes. In addition to those bearing direct responsibility, there are others indirectly at fault. Among them are the French, who saw this tragedy coming more clearly than any other external power, and warned against it in vain, but in the event were powerless to stop it. Many Arab states interceded with Washington at various stages of the war, and played a role in obtaining some of the U.S. guarantees which were violated. They were in a position to know what Sharon and the Phalangists were capable of, and had been repeatedly warned of the possibility of a massacre. None of them did anything effective to intercede with their friends in Washington in the more than two days after Bashir Gemayel's assassination and before the massacres began.

There remains one more party whose responsibility must be defined: this is the P.L.O. itself. It can be argued, and has been by many Palestinian critics, that the P.L.O. leadership was remiss in accepting U.S. guarantees from Habib which were flimsy, and ultimately proved worthless. Further, the massacres raise the question of whether the P.L.O. would not have been better off holding out for better terms no matter how great the Israeli pressure. The argument is that however much more human suffering might have been incurred during a continuation of the fighting, it could not have been greater than that inflicted during the massacres.

These questions have not, by and large, been raised in the course of the public disputes within the P.L.O. since 1982. The reason is simple: every major Palestinian leader, from the traditional Fateh leadership to Habash, Hawatmeh, Jibril, Abu Saleh, and Abu Musa, was in Beirut and played a role in the decisions which led to the P.L.O.'s withdrawal. Not all were satisfied with the results of the negotiations with Habib, but none raised his voice in opposition at the time, and little has been heard from any of them in this regard since. These criticisms of the failure of the P.L.O. leadership to protect their defenseless civilian followers left behind in Beirut have come rather from some of those who remained in Lebanon, or from Palestinians living far away and who could not understand why the P.L.O. ever agreed to leave Beirut in the first place.

Were the decisions taken by the P.L.O. during the 1982 war justified? Could another outcome have been achieved? There is no easy answers to these questions, and there can be no definite ones. In view of what we have already seen, all that can be said with certitude is that the P.L.O.'s original June 1982 decision in principle to withdraw from Beirut was taken under the most intense pressure. This came not only from Israel, the United States, the Lebanese government, and the Phalangists. According to those who took the decision, the most significant pressure came from the P.L.O.'s Lebanese allies on the left and among the Muslims. The effect of this pressure was powerfully reinforced by the almost complete lack of Arab support for the P.L.O. It is difficult to see how the P.L.O. leadership could simply have resisted such pressure in June 1982 without making any concessions whatsoever.

Should the P.L.O. have held firm to the position that having conceded the principle of withdrawal it would withdraw only under certain circumstances? This is an even more difficult question to answer. For over a month, the P.L.O. tenaciously insisted on just such a position. From late June until the end of July, the Palestinians attempted to achieve as a *quid pro quo* for their withdrawal both concessions "on the ground" (matching Israeli withdrawals, a U.N. buffer force, and binding international guarantees), and political compensation in the form of P.L.O. involvement in Middle East peacemaking efforts based on a modified version of SC 242 (the Franco-Egyptian draft resolution) or at least a dialogue with the United States (the efforts made by Khaled al-Hassan in Washington). As we have seen, these efforts failed: Israel was intransigent about the terms being demanded on the ground, the United States was insistent on refusing any U.N. involvement or any political compensation for a P.L.O. withdrawal, and the Arab states which were necessary intermediaries in this process proved to be less than whole-hearted in their support of the P.L.O. negotiating position.

In view of all this, should the P.L.O. simply have tried to hold out longer, rejecting those elements of the Habib terms which were unsatisfactory, and gambling on its ability to resist and on the possibility that U.S., or Israeli, or international, or Arab public opinion would force a change in the situation? A few in Beirut argued for this at the time. But to most it did not appear to be a viable option, and the decision of the P.L.O. leadership not to risk such a choice was generally, if unenthusiastically, approved.

In favor of such an option were a number of factors, among them the high state of morale of the Joint Forces and their plentiful supplies of food, fuel, and ammunition; the difficulties faced by the IDF in fighting in heavily built-up areas (its only advances on August 4 had been in the last remaining open areas around Beirut not yet occupied, while all the attacks along built-up axes had failed); the deep divisions inside Israel over the war, and the conflicts which had already arisen even within the Cabinet about Sharon's waging of it; and finally the growing unease of American public opinion over the failure of the Reagan administration to restrain Israel.

Other factors mitigated against such a choice, among them: after their advance of August 4, the Israelis were perilously close to dividing Beirut up into a number of separate islands of resistance; the IDF had shown itself willing to inflict enormous damage to the city and suffering on its inhabitants; Sharon was apparently impervious to domestic Israeli restraints, as was Israel itself to American pressure; the Reagan administration was highly reluctant to put effective pressure on Israel; and most importantly, the P.L.O. would be running a tremendous risk if the gamble failed.

Although many Palestinians asserted that a continuation of the conflict without a resolution was in the P.L.O.'s favor, by early August it was clear that this was a shortsighted argument. The West Beirut siege perimeter was not large, nor were there indefinite resources to defend it; and there were limits to the support such a last-ditch stand would have had from various constituencies, whether Palestinian, Lebanese, Arab, or international. Via the Habib accords, at least the P.L.O. leadership was assured of the continuation of the core of the Palestinian national movement and the safety of its leading members. The spreading out of the departure of P.L.O. forces over many days ensured that even a major Israeli violation of the agreement would not have affected more than a fraction of the P.L.O.'s manpower. Turning their backs on the accord and holding out for better terms would have risked not only the lives of those in the camps of Beirut (who in the end did suffer) but also the fighters, the cadres, the documents, the leaders, and the symbols accumulated by the Palestinian people for well over a decade. It is difficult to see how responsible political leaders could have made any choice other than the one they did, cruel though its results proved to be in the end.

Appendix

The 11 Points

Text of 11 point P.L.O. position, as distributed to offices abroad, July 8, 1982. (Passages in square brackets supplied by author.)

From Ch[airman] Arafat
To Souss, Tarazi, Ramlawi, Abu Shaker and Abu al-Tayyeb*
July 8, 1982.†

It is clear that there has been confusion about our stand and what we are keen to adhere to:

    1. Cease fire.
    2. Disengagement between the Palestinian and Israeli forces.
    3. International forces (U.N.) are to supervise the disengagement. We do not mind the Lebanese government choosing the composition of these forces to be [deployed] with the Lebanese army.
    4. Israeli troops to withdraw 5 repeat 5 miles.
    5. The Palestinian forces are to withdraw to the Palestinian camps.

---

  * These were the P.L.O. representatives in Paris, New York and London, Fateh Central Committee member Rafiq al-Natshe, located in Saudi Arabia, and P.L.O. Executive Committee member Dr. Ahmed Sidqi Dajani, located in Egypt at the time.
  † This message was repeated to Abu Maher in Damascus on July 11, 1982, and later to other stations.

6. The security of the Palestinian camps will be ensured by the international force and guaranteed internationally. This shall be coordinated with the P.L.O. in order to avoid what happened in the Palestinian camps of the South of Lebanon, and in Tal al-Zaatar camp [in 1976], at hands of Israeli and Phalangist forces.

7. Any Palestinian forces that are assigned to move from Beirut shall move with their full complement of arms by land with international guarantees.

8. The Palestinian forces that will stay in Lebanon will be agreed upon within context of the general agreement.

9. It should be well understood that the rights of the Palestinian people [in Lebanon] are to be preserved and that the international forces shall guarantee these rights, that are recognized by the Lebanese government and the United Nations.

10. Concerning the [P.L.O.] leadership, their movement will be according to what has been agreed upon with the Lebanese government, and such a move should be guaranteed internationally.

11. D-day is the day when the commander of the international force notifies us of his forces' readiness to execute their mission, this being:

   a. protecting the Palestinian camps against any aggression.

   b. taking up positions in the disengagement area and securing routes, including Beirut-Damascus international highway.
end.

List of Abbreviations

ADF	Arab Deterrent Forces.
DFLP	Democratic Front for the Liberation of Palestine.
IDF	Israel Defense Forces.
JF	Joint Forces (of the P.L.O. and the Lebanese National Movement).
LF	Lebanese Forces.
LNM	Lebanese National Movement.
MNF	Multi-National Force.
PFLP	Popular Front for the Liberation of Palestine.
PFLP-GC	Popular Front for the Liberation of Palestine-General Command.
PGM	Precision-guided munition.
PLA	Palestine Liberation Army.
PFL	Palestine Liberation Front.
PLO	Palestine Liberation Organization.
PNC	Palestine National Council.
PRCS	Palestine Red Crescent Society.
PSF	Popular Struggle Front.
PSP	Progressive Socialist Party.
UNIFIL	United Nations Interim Force in Lebanon.
UNRWA	United Nations Relief and Works Agency.
SC	Security Council
WAFA	The Palestine News Agency.

Cast of Characters
and Their Posts
During the 1982 War

'Abd al-Rahman, Hassan. P.L.O. representative in Washington.

'Abed Rabbo, Yasser. DFLP Deputy Secretary General; Head of P.L.O. Information Department.

Abu al-'Abbas (Muhammad 'Abbas). Deputy Secretary-General, PLF.

Abu 'Ali Mustafa (Mustafa al-Zibri). Deputy Secretary-General, PFLP.

Abu al-Hol (Hayel 'Abd al-Hamid). Fateh Central Committee member.

Abu Iyyad (Salah Khalaf). Chief, P.L.O. Unified Security; Fateh Central Committee member.

Abu Jihad (Khalil al-Wazir). Deputy Commander-in-Chief of P.L.O. forces; Fateh Central Committee member.

Abu Khaled al-'Amleh, Col. Commander of Fakhani sector.

Abu Lutf (Farouq al-Qaddoumi). Head, P.L.O. Political Department; Fateh Central Committee member.

Abu Maher (Muhammad Ghunaym). Fateh Central Committee member.

Abu Maher al-Yamani (Ahmed al-Yamani). PFLP Politbureau member.

Abu Mazin (Mahmud 'Abbas). Fateh Central Committee member.

Abu Musa, Col. (Sa'id Musa Maragha). Deputy Chief of P.L.O. Operations.

Abu Saleh (Nimr Saleh). Fateh Central Committee member.

Abu Shakir (Rafiq al-Natshe). Fateh Central Committee member.

Abu Sharif, Bassam. PFLP Politbureau member, official spokesman.

Abu al-Walid, Brig. (Sa'ad Sayel). Chief of P.L.O. Operations; Fateh Central Committee member.

Abu al-Za'im, Col. ('Atallah 'Atallah). Chief, Fateh Military Intelligence.

Adam, Maj. Gen. Yekutiel. Former Deputy Chief of Staff, IDF; Director-designate of Mossad killed in Damour, June 1982.

'Amr, Nabil. Director, "Voice of Palestine" Radio.

'Arafat, Yasser (Abu 'Ammar). Chairman, P.L.O. Executive Committee; Commander-in-Chief of P.L.O. forces; Fateh Central Committee member.

al-Asad, Lt. Gen. Hafez. President of Syria.

Bandar Ibn Sultan, Prince. Saudi Military Attaché in Washington.

Begin, Menachem. Prime Minister of Israel.

Belyayev, Dr. Igor. Soviet journalist and Middle East specialist.

Berri, Nabih. President, Amal Command Council.

Butros, Fu'ad. Foreign Minister of Lebanon.

Chehabi, Maj. Gen. Hikmat. Chief of Staff, Syrian Army.

Cheysson, Claude. Foreign Minister of France.

Clark, Judge William. Advisor to the President for National Security Affairs.

de Laboulaye, François. French Ambassador to the U.S.

Dillon, Robert. U.S. Ambassador to Lebanon.

Draper, Morris. U.S. Special Envoy to Middle East in succession to Philip Habib.

Eagleburger, Lawrence. U.S. Under Secretary of State.

Eytan, Gen. Rafael. Chief of Staff, IDF.

Fahd Ibn 'Abd al-'Aziz. King of Saudi Arabia; acceded to throne June 1982.

Gemayel, Bashir. Commander, LF; President-elect of Lebanon August 1982; assassinated September 1982.

Ghosheh, Dr. Samir. Secretary-General, PSF.

Gromyko, Andrei. Foreign Minister of the U.S.S.R.

Gur, Gen. Mordechai. Chief of Staff, IDF, during 1978 invasion of Lebanon.

Gutman, Francis. Secretary-General, French Foreign Ministry.

Habash, Dr. George. Secretary-General, PFLP.

Habib, Philip. U.S. Special Envoy to the Middle East.

Haig, Gen. Alexander. U.S. Secretary of State; resigned June 25, 1982.

Hamadeh, Marwan. Lebanese Minister of Tourism; member of LNM leadership.

al-Hassan, Hani. Fateh Central Committee member.

al-Hassan, Khaled (Abu Sa'id). Fateh Central Committee member.

Hawatmeh, Nayef. Secretary-General, DFLP.

al-Hoss, Dr. Salim. Former Prime Minister of Lebanon.

al-Hout, Shafiq. P.L.O. Beirut representative.

Isma'il, Col. Hajj. P.L.O. Commander, southern region.

Jibril, Ahmed. Secretary-General, PFLP-GC.

Jumblatt, Walid, Secretary, LNM; Secretary-General, PSP.

Karami, Rashid. Former Prime Minister of Lebanon.

Khaddam, 'Abd al-Halim. Foreign Minister of Syria.

Kirkpatrick, Jeane. U.S. Ambassador to the U.N.

Mauroy, Pierre. Prime Minister of France.

Pakradouni, Karim. Phalangist Party Politbureau member.

Primakov, Dr. Yevgeny. Director, Institute of Oriental Studies, U.S.S.R. Academy of Sciences.

Quleilat, Ibrahim. Secretary-General, Murabitun Movement.

Qureitem, Brig. Nabil. Lebanese Army liaison officer with P.L.O.

Sakhr Abu Nizar (Sakhr Habash). Secretary, Fateh Revolutionary Council.

Salam, Sa'eb. Former Prime Minister of Lebanon.

Sarkis, Elias. President of Lebanon.

Sa'ud al-Faisal, Prince. Foreign Minister of Saudi Arabia.

Schultz, George. U.S. Secretary of State, appointed June 1982.

Sghayir, Lt. Col. 'Azmi. P.L.O. Commander, Tyre district. Killed in action, 1982.

Shams al-Din, Shaykh Muhammad Mehdi. Vice Chairman, Higher Shi'ite Council.

Sharon, Gen. Ariel. Defense Minister of Israel.

Shultz, George. U.S. Secretary of State, appointed June 1982.

Siyam, Col. 'Abdullah. P.L.O. Commander, Khaldeh region, killed in action, June 1982.

Souss, Ibrahim. P.L.O. representative in Paris.

Tarazi, Zuhdi. P.L.O. Observer at the U.N.

Tueni, Ghassan. Lebanese Ambassador to the U.N.

al-Wazzan, Shafiq. Prime Minister of Lebanon.

Notes

Introduction

1. Books by journalists predominate. These include: Dan Bavly and Eliahu Salpeter, *Fire in Beirut: Israel's War in Lebanon with the P.L.O.*; John Bulloch, *Final Conflict: The War in Lebanon*; Tony Clifton and Catherine Leroy, *God Cried*; Alain de Chalvron, *Le piege de Beyrouth*; Michael Jansen, *The Battle of Beirut: Why Israel Invaded Lebanon*; Amnon Kapeliouk, *Sabra and Shatila: Inquiry into a Massacre*; Selim Nassib with Caroline Tisdall, *Beirut: Frontline Story*; Jonathan Randal, *Going All the Way: Christian Warlords, Israeli Adventurers, and the War in Lebanon*; and Ze'ev Schiff and Ehud Ya'ari, *Israel's Lebanon War*. Several other books are devoted wholly or in part to the war: Richard A. Gabriel, *Operation Peace for Galilee*; Chaim Herzog, *The Arab-Israeli Wars: War and Peace in the Middle East from the War of Independence through Lebanon*; Raphael Israeli, ed., *P.L.O. in Lebanon: Selected Documents*; and Itamar Rabinovich, *The War for Lebanon 1970-1983*. For a full listing, see bibliography.

2. Costs of occupation are cited in the *New York Times*, September 25, 1984, p. A8. Israel reported casualties until mid-August 1982 of 368 killed and 2383 wounded (*The Jerusalem Post*, October 10, 1983). Israeli figures since then do not include 75 soldiers killed in the destruction of the military headquarters in Tyre on November 11, 1982 (attributed to the accidental explosion of gas bottles). The number of killed recently reached 655.

3. Their situation 18 months after the war is described in Rashid Khalidi, "The Palestinians in Lebanon: The Social Repercussions of the Israeli Invasion."

4. Details can be found in articles by Thomas Friedman in the *New York Times*, May 30 and 31 and June 1, 1984. See also the article on the Lebanese economy by Nora Boustany in the *Washington Post*, February 23, 1985, p. A10.

5. The U.S. has successfully resisted Soviet involvement in the resolution of the crisis since the beginning of the war. For an assessment of how the war has provoked

"a qualitative change" in superpower roles in the Middle East, see Mahmoud Soueid, "L'invasion israelienne du Liban: causes et consequences."

6. That this did not initially seem to be the case can be seen from early appraisals by two of the best analysts of Soviet Middle East policy: Galia Golan, "The Soviet Union and the Israeli Action in Lebanon," and Karen Dawisha, "The U.S.S.R. in the Middle East: Superpower in Eclipse."

7. For discussion, see Rashid Khalidi, "Problems of Foreign Intervention in Lebanon."

8. A notable book in Arabic is *Lubnan 1982: Yawmiat al-Ghazw al-Israeli, Watha'iq wa Suwar*, published by the Arab Information Center of the *al-Safir* daily newspaper (Beirut, 1982). Its 491 pages contain a detailed chronology, numerous documents, and striking photographs taken during the siege. Also significant are the book by Phalange Party politburo member Karim Pakradouni, that by former Lebanese U.N. Ambassador Ghassan Tueni, the articles by P.L.O. Beirut representative Shafiq al-Hout, and the book by Col. Abu Musa, all cited in the bibliography.

9. Alexander Haig's *Caveat* is the sole exception so far. It is full of distortions and omissions regarding the Lebanese war (see chapter 5).

10. Virtually all of the P.L.O.'s central archives were removed from Beirut at the end of the war. These are not to be confused with the primarily historical archives of the P.L.O. Research Center, which were seized by the Israeli army when it entered Beirut in September 1982, and returned as part of the November 1983 prisoner exchange.

11. Interview, in Tunis, with Ibrahim Souss, P.L.O. representative in Paris, July 31, 1984.

12. According to James Bamford's book on the U.S. National Security Agency, *The Puzzle Palace*, p. 468, the "Agency can program its high-speed computers and 22,000 line-per-minute printers to kick out every telegram or telex containing the word *oil* or the word *Democrat* . . . " Since most international telex traffic (i.e., that carried by RCA, WUI and ITT) is necessarily routed via the U.S., most P.L.O. communications were undoubtedly intercepted. In *Le Nouvel Observateur*, May 23, 1983, p. 123, Josette Alia cites Israeli intelligence claims that they were intercepting P.L.O. wartime telephone communications.

13. The P.L.O. knew that Israeli intelligence had a major listening post at a school in East Beirut and assumed U.S. interception of international communications: interview with communications consultant to P.L.O. Chairman's Office, Tunis, September 25, 1982.

14. According to Hani al-Hassan, the first contacts with the French were "initiated by myself with the consent of Abu 'Ammar," and only later sanctioned by the P.L.O. leadership: interview, Tunis, July 31, 1984.

15. In the words of a French official deeply involved in the U.S.-French-P.L.O. negotiations, the Lebanese intermediaries were "*pas désinteressés*": interview, French Foreign Ministry, Paris, March 8, 1984.

16. This was reported by most Western journalists in Beirut during the war, and is repeated by many of those whose works are cited in note 1.

1. P.L.O. in Lebanon

1. Originally, the Palestinian commandos were known in Lebanon as "*fida'iyeen*" (self-sacrificers) and the P.L.O. as "*al-muqawama*" (the resistance), which

symbolized their positive image with Lebanese public opinion. By the 1980's, they were known as "al-munazameh" (the Organization), a far less favorable, if completely accurate, appellation.

2. Details on important wartime changes from positions critical of the P.L.O. to ones supportive of it by key Lebanese Muslim and leftist leaders like Walid Jumblatt and Nabih Berri can be found in chapter 3.

3. The Lebanese press in April and May was full of veiled and not-so-veiled criticisms of the P.L.O. by Lebanese public figures. This coincided with a growing anti-P.L.O. line in the government media.

4. The weaknesses of the Lebanese political system are ably discussed in the standard work on the subject: Michael Hudson, The Precarious Republic. Good accounts of modern Lebanese politics include: P. Edward Haley and Lewis Snider, eds., Lebanon in Crisis; Walid Khalidi, Conflict and Violence in Lebanon; and Kamal Salibi, Crossroads to Civil War: Lebanon 1958-1976.

5. It was based on the British policy of blowing up homes of suspected resistance members during the Palestine revolt of 1936-39: see J.C. Hurewitz, The Struggle for Palestine, pp. 83-84; and Walid Khalidi, From Haven to Conquest, pp. 357-67. With a new variation—buildings were now blown up while their occupants were still within—it was incorporated into Israeli army practice by Unit 101 (which was established by Gen. Ariel Sharon) in the Qibya and Samu' massacres of 1955 and 1966, among others. For the "thesis underlying most of Israel's retaliatory actions since the early 1950s" see Rabinovich, The War for Lebanon, p. 41. The origins of this entire approach are analyzed in Avi Shlaim, "Conflicting Approaches to Israel's Relations with the Arabs: Ben Gurion and Sharett, 1953-1956," 180-201

6. 'Al-Hamishmar, May 10, 1978, cited in Edward Said, The Question of Palestine, pp. xi-xii.

7. Cited in John Kifner, "Southern Lebanon: A Trauma for Both Sides," New York Times, July 22, 1984, p. 10.

8. Gur's comment, cited earlier, is evidence of such coexistence. While most attacks on Israeli forces since 1982 have been the work of Lebanese, the P.L.O. is credited for provision of arms, organization, and training which made many of them possible. As a result, in the words of an "American intelligence analyst" cited by Drew Middleton (New York Times, October 14, 1984, p. 23), "the P.L.O. today 'is alive and kicking in southern Lebanon.' "

9. See Rashid Khalidi, "L'impact du mouvement national palestinien sur le Liban"; and "The Palestinians and Lebanon." As'ad Abu Khalil's "Ideology and Practice of a 'Revolutionary' Marxist-Leninist Party" is a study of the effect of the P.L.O. on the Lebanese left.

10. This phenomenon was also observable among Palestinians who had left the ranks of the P.L.O. and returned in times of crisis.

11. Photographs of the mourners in the Lebanese daily papers of April 12, 1973—particularly al-Nahar and al-Muharrir—indicate that this figure is probably not exaggerated.

12. The 1975-76 war is covered in the works of Haley and Snider, Walid Khalidi, and Kamal Salibi, cited in note 4, and in John Bulloch, Death of a Country; Marius Deeb, The Lebanese Civil War; and Roger Owen, ed. Essays on the Crisis in Lebanon.

13. For the Syrian role see Adeed Dawisha, Syria and the Lebanese Crisis. Schiff and Ya'ari, Israel's Lebanon War; Jonathan Randal, Going All the Way; and Rabinovich,

The War for Lebanon, deal with Israel's involvement. Its covert intervention is covered in "Military Intelligence against the Mossad: The Inside Story," by *Kol Israel* reporter Haim Hecht in *Monitin* (April 1983), reprinted in the *Journal of Palestine Studies* (Summer 1983) 12(4): 178-185. See also Rashid Khalidi, "Problems of Foreign Intervention in Lebanon".

14. This can best be followed in Schiff and Ya'ari, *Israel's Lebanon War*, and Dawisha, *Syria and the Lebanese Crisis*.

15. The 1976-77 period is covered in Lawrence Whetten's essay in Haley and Snider, *Lebanon in Crisis*, pp. 82-90, and Khalidi, *Conflict and Violence in Lebanon*, pp. 103-121.

16. Figures on this growth can be found in Rashid Khalidi, "The Palestinians in Lebanon," p. 257, and Cheryl Rubenberg, *The Palestine Liberation Organization*. Several sections of the project "The Economic and Social Situation and Potential of the Palestinian Arab People in the Region of West Asia" undertaken for the U.N. Economic Commission on West Asia (ECWA) by TEAM International analyze performance of branches of the P.L.O. para-state.

17. Many such services were systematically taken over in East Beirut by the right-wing militias, which did not relinquish them after the 1975-76 war was over and retain control over them to this day.

18. There are no reliable figures on P.L.O. finances: all published estimates on its budget are based on speculation. This is an area where a large measure of secrecy has been maintained.

19. Figures from tables T8, T9, T11 and T13 on pp. 27, 29, 33, and 36 of the paper "Health Services for Palestinians in Lebanon," Doc. Ref. No. TEAM/SD1/WP17 presented to ECWA as part of the project cited in note 16.

20. Statements by P.L.O. leaders that the Israelis were preparing an invasion, and aimed to reach the outskirts of Beirut, were numerous in the year before the war. 'Arafat in particular repeatedly used the concept of an accordion to describe how he expected the P.L.O. to be squeezed between Israeli forces coming up from the south and areas controlled by the LF. Information to this effect was received from numerous reliable sources in the months preceding the war, and was generally believed. See the section on "P.L.O. Expectations" in chapter 3, particularly note 20.

21. At a meeting in Moscow with a P.L.O. delegation headed by 'Arafat in November 1979, Soviet Foreign Minister Gromyko at no point offered Soviet assistance in spite of the intense Israeli attacks on Lebanon described by 'Arafat, who stated, "We fought alone, and still do." Cited on Israeli, *P.L.O. in Lebanon*, p. 40. Senior Soviet Middle East specialists Dr. Yevgeny Primakov and Dr. Igor Belyayev explicitly stressed the limitations on Soviet aid in meetings with Palestinian re-searchers: Institute for Palestine Studies, Beirut, July 11, 1979; Belyayev spoke similarly at an American University of Beirut seminar, May 15, 1980.

22. A critical perspective on P.L.O. preparations can be found in Yezid Sayigh, "Palestinian Military Performance in the 1982 War", especially pp. 22-24. Ze'ev Schiff, "The Palestinian Surprise," gives a more positive view of some aspects of P.L.O. military performance.

23. Israel exaggerated both the scale of the P.L.O. military build-up and the number of weapons captured during the war. This was confirmed in *Haaretz* by its military editor, Ze'ev Schiff, on July 18, 1982. He pointed out that barely enough weapons had been seized to equip one division (not the five claimed by some Israeli

accounts), and that while Israel had asserted the P.L.O. had over 400 tanks before the war, only 38 T-34's had been captured, as well as 46 T-55's, most of the latter Syrian. As for artillery, far from a claimed 300-plus guns captured, only 51 had actually been taken, of which two were old French 155 mm howitzers, 32 Soviet 130 mm guns and the rest shorter-range Soviet 122 mm pieces. Many of the 130 mm guns were Syrian, Schiff added. The only weapons captured in quantity, he noted, were 26,000 rifles, of which 3500 were private and hunting weapons, and 4000 a mixed bag of modern and obsolete Western military rifles and automatic weapons; just 10,000 were P.L.O. standard-issue Kalashnikovs.

24. P.L.O. acceptance of the ceasefire was challanged by a Fateh faction linked to the Baghdad-based Abu Nidal group, leading to a military confrontation, many arrests, and two executions, the latter unprecedented in P.L.O. internal disputes. Thereafter, firing across the Lebanese frontier took place only in direct response to prior Israeli actions, except for a few failed operations by splinter groups not under P.L.O. control. This led to bitter criticism of the P.L.O. leadership by their opponents. See for example Hashim 'Ali Muhsin's *al-Intifada: Thawra Hatta al-Nasr*, pp. 226-29, distributed after 1983 by the Fateh dissidents, where pre-war P.L.O. policy, including acceptance of the 1981 ceasefire, is called "capitulationist" and is compared to Sadat's acceptance of the post-1973 war disengagement accords. This phase is covered in Helena Cobban, *The Palestinian Liberation Organization*, pp. 95-98; and Walid Khalidi, *Conflict and Violence in Lebanon*, pp. 133-139.

25. From mid-March until the end of August 1979, official UNIFIL press releases enumerated 148 Israeli-initiated attacks, mostly in the UNIFIL area of operations, involving the firing of over 19,000 artillery and mortar rounds, while the Joint Forces were listed as responsible for initiating 10 attacks and firing just over 2800 shells. Not counted by UNIFIL were Israeli operations launched outside its area, which included 13 Israeli air raids, 14 naval and amphibious attacks, and heliborne and other assaults.

26. Insights into the origins of this crisis are given in Hecht, "Mossad," pp. 182-83, and Schiff and Ya'ari, *Israel's Lebanon War*, pp. 31-35.

27. A good account of these attacks is in Schiff and Ya'ari, pp. 35-37.

28. The extent of this problem was recognized in the Israeli press, as is indicated by the titles of these analytical articles: "The Problem of the Israeli Army: How to Silence the Sources of Fire in Lebanese Territory" (Eitan Haber, *Yediot Aharanot*, July 22, 1981); "Into 'Arafat's Trap" (Haim Herzog, *Ma'ariv*, July 24, 1981); "The Military Balance in the North: Israel Lost Points" (Ze'ev Schiff, *Ha'aretz*, July 24, 1981); "The Military Balance in the North: Artillery Question Marks" (Ze'ev Schiff, *Ha'aretz*, July 27, 1981); "A Different War" (Yoram Pe'eri, *Davar*, July 24, 1981); "A Quick Blow and We Got Stuck" (Yu'eel Marcos, *Ha'aretz*, July 24, 1981): all translated in the Institute for Palestine Studies' *Bulletin*, (August 1981) vol. 11(8) [Arabic]. In the second of his articles cited above, Schiff stated that the P.L.O.'s 1200 rockets and shells hit 33 settlements, as well as "other targets."

29. This is brought out by Avi Shlaim in "Conflicting Approaches to Israel's Relations". See also the selections from former Israeli Prime Minister Moshe Sharett's diaries in Livia Rokach, *Israel's Sacred Terrorism*.

30. Sharon revealed his strategic vision in a speech prepared for delivery at Tel Aviv University in which he declared that beyond the Arab confrontation states, "Israel's security concerns should expand to include two other geographic regions

which have great security importance: . . . the more distant Arab states . . . [and] those foreign countries which . . . could pose a threat to Israel's security in the Middle East and on the shores of the Mediterranean . . . and the Red Sea. Thus we must expand the area of Israel's strategic and security concerns in the 1980's to include states like Turkey, Iran and Pakistan, and the areas like the Persian Gulf and Africa, particularly the states of North and Central Africa." *Ma'ariv*, December 18, 1981.

31. For a more extensive discussion of this subject, see Rashid Khalidi, "The Asad Regime and the Palestinian Resistance."

32. For the U.S. role, see Schiff and Ya'ari, *Israel's Lebanon War*, pp. 62-77, and Haig, *Caveat*, pp. 310-312, 317-352.

2. The Fall of South Lebanon and the Siege of Beirut

1. Figures from International Institute for Strategic Studies (I.I.S.S.) annual reference work, *The Military Balance 1982-1983*, pp. 56-57.

2. These include several works cited in ch. 1, n. 1 and: Sami' al-Banna, "The Defense of Beirut"; James Bloom, "From the Litani to Beirut"; and "Six Days-Plus-Ten-Weeks War"; W. Seth Carus, "The Bekaa Valley Campaign"; Anthony Cordesman, "The Sixth Arab-Israeli Conflict"; Maj. Richard Gabriel, "Lessons of War: The IDF in Lebanon"; Chris Giannou, "The Battle for South Lebanon"; Meir Pa'il, "A Military Analysis"; M. Richards, "The Israeli-Lebanon War of 1982"; Yezid Sayigh, "Palestinian Military Performance in the 1982 War"; and "Israel's Military Performance in Lebanon, June 1982"; Ze'ev Schiff, "The Palestinian Surprise"; and Clifford Wright, "The Israeli War Machine in Lebanon."

3. For how many Israelis now assess the war, see Edward Walsh, "Rockets in Galilee Symbolize Futility of Israel's Role in Lebanon," *Washington Post*, February 13, 1984, p. A19. Rockets were fired at Galilee in February, March, April, and August 1984, while Israelis planes hit targets in Lebanon 15 times in the first nine months of 1984, and repeatedly in early 1985. An early assessment of Israel's new problem with the Shi'a is by John Kifner, "Southern Lebanon: A Trauma for Both Sides," *New York Times*, July 22, 1984, p. 1.

4. Ehud Yarri, "Israel's Dilemma in Lebanon." See also Anthony Lewis, "The Lebanon Debacle," *The New York Times*, June 4, 1982, p. A19, who cites Eban, for a devasting critique of what he calls Israel's "misbegotten war."

5. Israel's basic war aims are ably analyzed and documented in Noam Chomsky, *The Fateful Triangle: The United States, Israel and the Palestinians*, pp. 198-207. Two chapters, totaling 259 pages, are devoted to the 1982 war and its aftermath.

6. See Schiff and Ya'ari, *Israel's Lebanon War*, and Schiff's "The Green Light," for more on war planning and the extent to which prior knowledge of it was widespread in Washington.

7. The I.I.S.S. ranked Israel as the world's fourth military power, after the U.S., USSR, and China (reported in *Time*, October 11, 1982), but it could be argued that on the basis of number of criteria it should be listed ahead of China.

8. Schiff, "The Palestinian Surprise," p. 43.

9. According to Herzog, currently President of Israel and former Chief of Military Intelligence in *The Arab-Israeli Wars*, pp. 344-45: "The strategic purpose of

the central advance was to reach the Damascus-Beirut road, turn eastwards along that road, and by feinting in the direction of the Syrian border to cause the Syrian forces in the Beqa'a Valley, who would thus be in danger of being outflanked, to withdraw eastwards towards the Syrian border." This purpose was not achieved.

10. Schiff, "The Palestinian Surprise," p. 43.

11. Early official P.L.O. military communiques, issued by the Palestine News Agency, WAFA, stressed intense resistance to Israeli advances, while admitting deep penetrations. See, e.g., "Israeli Advance Along Six Axes into South Lebanon Halted" (WAFA no. 90/82, item 3, 6 June 1984). WAFA reports concurred with Israeli accounts in describing intense fighting around Sidon, particularly at 'Ain al-Hilweh camp, and in the eastern 'Arqoub region: e.g. "Fierce Fighting North & South of Sidon, Around Tyre" (WAFA no. 91/82, item 7, 7 June 1984).

12. By the morning of June 9, 1984, WAFA tacitly admitted the loss of Tyre, reporting only partisan activity behind enemy lines, such as "continuous raids on enemy positions" (WAFA no.93/82, item 1, 9 June 1982), the ambush of two Israeli tanks inside Burj al-Shemali camp (WAFA No.93/82, item 2, 9 June 1982), and the ambush of a tank inside Tyre (WAFA no. 94/82, item 6, 10 June 1982). The fall of Tyre was admitted later in the day at a press conference given by Col. Abu al-Za'im (WAFA no.93/82, item 7). P.L.O. estimates of Israeli losses in the Tyre area given on June 11 (no.95/82, item 2) were 200 casualties and 60 vehicles destroyed.

13. Schiff, "The Palestinian Surprise," p. 43.

14. Ibid. See also Schiff's impressive eyewitness article on the 'Ain al-Hilweh battle: Ha'aretz, June 15, 1984.

15. Herzog records in The Arab-Israeli Wars, pp. 346-347, that the IDF "advanced slowly along narrow roads and gorges which were easily defensible," and faced "heavy fighting"; their advance was "very slow." He incorrectly credits most initial resistance to Syrian forces, which were only engaged on the 10th, after four days of fighting. An Israeli officer said his unit's advance toward Hasbaya was the most violent battle he had witnessed during his military career: Amnon Kapeliouk in 'Al Hamishmar July 9, 1982.

16. In 1982, according to the I.I.S.S., the IDF had over 125 helicopters capable of moving 3500 men, and 12 naval vessels capable of putting an armored battalion and its vehicles ashore. Using all its transport aircraft (22 C-130s, 21 C-47s and others), the IDF could perhaps sustain logistically one, or at most two, brigades without land supply lines.

17. Amnon Kapeliouk, 'al-Hamishmar, July 9, 1982. In an August 6, 1982 interview in Davar an Israeli officer stated that three brigades backed by nine warships and four squadrons of planes took this long to take complete control of Damour, as resistance reappeared after it was "cleared." He adds that Sharon and Eytan were "constantly and violently shouting that the alotted time was up, and Damour had still not fallen."

18. Foreign journalists traveling under Israeli escort in South Lebanon were not permitted to approach the camp, but could hear combat from a distance. See, e.g., David Shipler, "In Lebanon, White Flags Fly Amid the Misery and Rubble," The New York Times, June 15, 1982 (Shipler witnessed shelling of the camp on June 14) and Eric Pace, "In Sidon, 80 More Bodies for a Vast Bulldozed Pit," The New York Times, 17 June, 1982. On the 16th Pace was forbidden by an Israeli guide from entering the camp because of the "risk of booby-traps."

19. WAFA devoted extensive attention to details of the siege until June 17, sometimes issuing two or three reports per day, and quoting foreign and Israeli press accounts; al-Safir and other Beirut dailies also covered the siege closely.

20. In a speech on March 16, 1982, on the anniversary of the assassination of Kamal Jumblatt, 'Arafat specifically predicted that the P.L.O. would soon have to fight at Khaldeh (al-Safir, March 16, 1985, p. 1). Exactly three months later, Khaldeh fell to the IDF after a fierce battle.

21. Conversation with American informant, Institute for Palestine Studies, Beirut, April 27, 1982. In interviews in Tunis, Fateh Central Committee members Abu Jihad (Khalil al-Wazir) and Abu Iyyad (Salah Khalaf) confirmed that the P.L.O. had reliable information from many sources on the imminence of the attack: Abu Jihad, March 13, 1984; Abu Iyyad: March 14 and August 31, 1984.

22. Herzog, Arab—Israeli Wars, p. 341. Rabinovich, The War for Lebanon, p. 125, states that in November 1981 and February 1982 "the United States acted to prevent an attack on Lebanon." The P.L.O. expected a February attack.

23. Sayigh, "Israeli Military," p. 43.

24. Sayigh, "Palestinian Military," p. 10.

25. Ibid., p. 10.

26. Schiff, "Palestinian Surprise," p. 43. Rabinovich, The War for Lebanon, p. 151, has a higher estimation of P.L.O. military performance. He praises its strategy in the south, and states: "The P.L.O. performed quite well in the limited fighting that took place during the siege."

27. Interview with P.L.O. information official, Tunis, September 2?. 1982.

28. "Fighting Intensifies on all Fronts" (WAFA no. 95/82, item 4, 11 June 1982), describes how heliborne forces landed north of Rafid in the Biqa' were attacked by P.L.O. units they had cut off. Many similar accounts by Israeli soldiers can be found in the Israeli press.

29. Schiff, "Palestinian Surprise," p. 42.

30. Ibid., p. 42; Herzog, Arab-Israeli Wars, p. 345, states: "The policy laid down was for the forces to advance and reach the final objectives as rapidly as possible." Note also Sharon and Eytan's concern with the slowness of the advance, cited in n. 17.

31. Hajj Isma'il's flight, quickly publicized by Israel, had a detrimental impact on P.L.O. morale, and confirmed pre-war criticisms of him. In an interview in Tunis on March 9, 1984, Yasser 'Arafat agreed that there were serious lapses in his performance of his duty. Major Salah Ta'mari, who remained in Sidon until after the city's fall, stated that the Israeli bombardment was so intense that there was little more that the defenders of the city could have done, even with greater central direction: interview, Washington D.C., May 3, 1984.

32. Schiff's assertion that "Their death served no apparent purpose," and was "heroism that serves no end" ("Palestinian Surprise," p. 43) is belied by these achievements of the defenders of 'Ain al-Hilweh. In addition to the time they and the forces which fought at Khaldeh and Damour gained for preparing the defenses of Beirut, it is questionable whether the I.D.F. would have been so reluctant to enter Beirut had it not faced such intense resistance in these built-up areas further south.

33. Al-Banna, "Defense of Beirut," pp. 109-110. He considers the resistance to the Israelis at Khaldeh a major factor in Beirut's steadfastness. Rabinovich, The War for Lebanon, pp. 135, 151, is one of the few Israeli works to give the P.L.O. credit for deciding to withdraw combat forces to Beirut.

34. An Israeli engineering officer's statement to Israeli radio on August 8, 1982, "I hope we never have to enter Beirut," was due to his high regard for P.L.O. engineering capabilities. He noted: "There are some spheres, such as obstacles and mine fields, in which their military experience is no less than that of the Israeli army . . . Beirut can be thought of as one great obstacle, added to which are the various obstacles which have been erected by the terrorists. These are formidable obstacles indeed, and are not simple constructions at all." Cited in WAFA no.156/82, item one, August 11, 1984.

35. These offices, in the Arab University section of the Fakhani district, had underground shelter facilities, but were semi-public, having been used in the past for meetings, interviews, and administrative purposes. All were destroyed or rendered unusable by PGMs, one being hit with a "shelter-busting" weapon which penetrated thick reinforced concrete to explode several meters underground. Four floors were blown off the top of another building. Key personnel had been moved elsewhere by the time all were hit.

36. Those most at risk were radio operators, of whom seven were killed during the war (four men and three women: 'Imad al-Far, Muhammad Hishmeh, Jum'a Salem, Bilal Minawi, Nadia Abu 'Isa, Iman 'Isa and 'Aiysha Yunis), five of them while at their posts: interview with the Chief of the Fateh General Wireless Section, Tunis, March 14, 1984.

37. For the impact in Beirut of this see "Al-Kata'ibiyun yuwasilun majazirihim al-fashiya fil-jabal" [The Phalangists continue their Fascist massacres in the mountains], al-Ma'raka, no. 8, 1 July 1982, p. 1 headline. The Lebanese press prominently featured the Shouf killings.

38. Archives of the Office of the Chairman of the Executive Committee of the P.L.O., Tunis (hereafter P.L.O. Archives), Chairman's office to P.L.O./Paris, repeated to P.L.O./N.Y., June 30, 1982.

3. P.L.O. Decisions

1. An example is Bavly and Salpeter, Fire in Beirut, pp. 108-109, which greatly overemphasizes the military factor.

2. Truckloads of diesel fuel needed for the generators at the main Beirut telephone exchange, not far from the IDF lines, often had to be moved there under heavy shelling. Frequently, fuel was siphoned out of the supply stored for winter heating in abandoned apartment buildings. In one case, a vital underground telephone cable between the front lines had to be repaired by a P.L.O./LNM crew working under fire.

3. An example of how rapidly and accurately bad news on the battlefield was communicated can be seen from a listing of 20 radio messages sent by the various local commands to Central Operations from 10:10 P.M. on June 12 until 12:05 P.M. on June 13, 1982 detailing the critically important Israeli advances from Qabr Shmoun toward Souq al-Gharb (and later sent to the P.L.O. U.N. representative for submission to the Security Council as evidence of Israeli ceasefire violations): P.L.O. Archives, Chairman to P.L.O./N.Y., June 13, 1982 (copy of original log of radio messages attached to telex in Archive).

4. The IDF appears to have downplayed its own casualties. One example was the initial statement after Israel's ground offensive of August 4, 1982 that total IDF

casualties were only 65 wounded, four of them "critically." Two days later a spokesmen admitted 19 killed and 146 wounded in the same attack (WAFA quoted a P.L.O. Military Spokesman's estimate on August 4 of 100 Israeli casualties). On the basis of obituaries published in the Israeli press, WAFA published names of 453 Israeli soldiers killed in Lebanon until August 12 (WAFA no.159/82, item 2, August 14, 1982), for which period the official IDF figure was 368. The discrepancy may be explained by the IDF practice of counting only soldiers killed by enemy action as combat deaths (rather than those killed in any way in a combat theater, or who died later of their wounds), a distinction not made in private obituaries.

5. The best figure on wartime casualties is 19,085 killed and 30,302 wounded, according to an official Lebanese police report: *Washington Post*, December 2, 1982. No official count of P.L.O. casualties was ever issued; according to the police report, 84% of casualties in Beirut were civilians. Of 1100 combatants killed there, 45.6% were Palestinian, 37.2% Lebanese, 10.1% Syrian, and 7.1% other nationalities.

6. *Ma'ariv* on June 17, 1982 quoted the head of *Kol Israel*'s Network D, which broadcasts in Arabic, as saying: "At one time the Voice of the Phalange was actually a branch of the Israeli broadcasts . . . an indirect link was actually formed with them, I was told." A direct telex line existed between Israel and the "Voice of Lebanon," according to information available to the P.L.O. a year before the 1982 war.

7. Brig. Abu al-Walid said this at pre-war meetings attended by a consultant to the Chairman's office: interview, Washington D.C., August 6. Until the invasion began, WAFA (June 5 and 6, no.89/82, item 2 and no.90/82, item 1) pointed to the likelihood of a major offensive involving landings to cut the Beirut–Ras al-Naqoura coast road, interruption of communications, and capture of Beaufort and the Nabatiyeh area, none of which had been attempted in 1978.

8. "5 June 1967: 15 Years of Israeli Aggression and Palestinian Resistance," WAFA no.88/82, item 2. It concluded: "[The P.L.O.'s] response cannot by itself deter Israel. But it shows that the Palestinians themselves are undeterred, that they will not lie back passively like the Arab states and take blow after Israeli blow."

9. Al-Banna, "Defense of Beirut," p. 108, suggests that "a conservative estimate of the firepower ratio between defenders and attackers was 1:5000."

10. WAFA commentary: "Israel's True Objectives in Lebanon," WAFA no.91/82, item 4.

11. These raids and their results, discussed in note 35 in chapter 2, were well reported in Beirut. See *al-Safir*, June 8, 1982, p.1, especially the photos of some of the buildings hit, two of them in particular known as P.L.O. headquarters.

12. Abu Jihad interview, Tunis, March 13, 1984. "Military Spokesman: Israeli Entry to Shouf Transcends Palestinian-Israeli Conflict," WAFA no. 92/82, item 6, June 8, 1982.

13. "Israeli Landing Attempt at Khaldeh Foiled, Ship Hit," WAFA no.93/82, item 4.

14. "P.L.O. Press Conference: Israel's Aims in Lebanon," WAFA no.93/82, item 7. Col. Abu al-Za'im also admitted the loss of Sidon, Tyre, and Nabatiyeh, while affirming that none of them had been cleared fully of combatants of the Joint Forces.

15. "Khaldeh Landing Force Wiped Out, 6 Tanks Destroyed, 2 Captured," WAFA no.93/82, item 8, 9 June 1982. The vehicles were M-113 APCs, not tanks: photos of those captured, and of the bodies of their crews, were featured in the next morning's

papers: al-Safir, June 10, 1982, pp. 1 and 5. Some are reproduced in Lubnan 1982: yawmiyyat al-ghazw al-isra'ili: watha'iq wa suwar, p. 57. It was rumored at the time that a few Israelis were killed after capture, although the photos indicate that most died when their vehicles were hit by antitank weapons.

16. Abu Iyyad remonstrated with Walid Jumblatt after the war, noting the problems created for the Druze by Israel allowing the LF into the Shouf, and adding that had they allowed P.L.O. bases there, the result might have differed. Jumblatt demurred, saying, "Don't blame the Druze, blame me; perhaps we were short-sighted, but we simply didn't want the P.L.O. in our area.": interview, Tunis, March 14, 1984

17. Abu Jihad interview, Tunis, March 13, 1984. He added that 2500 RPG-7's delivered in Syria for the P.L.O. on June 28 and never received would have been of great utility, since even in the worst days of the siege weapons were being smuggled into the city by boat, infiltration, or bribery of Lebanese and Israelis on the siege perimeter.

18. Ibid.

19. "Landing Attempt Foiled between Damour and Khaldeh," WAFA no.94/82, item 4, June 10, 1982; "Israeli Tank Destroyed in Khaldeh Area—Air Raids in Southern Beirut," WAFA no.94/82, item 7, June 10, 1982.

20. Adam was killed in the IDF regional HQ (in an area which was believed to be pacified) by commandos who were apparently hidden in the buildings: see "Maj. Gen. Adam Highest Ranking Israeli Officer ever Killed in Action," WAFA no.95/82, item 6, June 11, 1982.

21. The P.L.O. claimed that a fresh armored division and two new paratroop battalions had been brought into Lebanon, raising the total of Israeli troops in the country to 120,000: "120,000 Israeli Troops in Lebanon", WAFA No.95/82, item 1, June 11, 1982.

22. Ibid.

23. "P.L.O. Official Statement," WAFA, no.95/82, item 7, June 11, 1982. The P.L.O. had already privately confirmed its acceptance of a ceasefire. It refused to announce this publicly because Israel had excluded the P.L.O. from the ceasefire, and the IDF was still advancing: P.L.O. Archives, Abu Lutf to Political Dept./Abu Ammar/ Abu Jihad, telex no. 221/PLO-NY/82, June 11, 1982. There were differences within the P.L.O. leadership over the matter, according to an advisor to the Chairman present at a heated discussion of it: interview, Washington D.C., July 28, 1984.

24. "Israeli Attacks Continue," WAFA no.96/82, item 1, June 12, 1982. Col. Siyam was killed on the night of June 11-12. Before he died, he managed to get off an inspirational radio message, the last from his command post. A communique quoting from it spoke of a "hand-to-hand battle," and concluded, "our men have chosen to fight until the enemy is stopped in his tracks," the first time during the war that such language had been used, clearly implying a critical battlefield situation: WAFA no. 96/ 82, item 14, June 11, 1982.

25. WAFA, no.96/82, item 9, June 12, 1982. The first siege was from June to October 1976.

26. Interview, Tunis, August 31, 1984.

27. A similar tone characterized a "WAFA Analysis of the Situation" (no. 95/82, item 10, June 11, 1982), which asked "Where did Israel go wrong?" noting that the invasion had lasted eight days, instead of a planned three; that Israeli casualties were

"already beyond politically acceptable levels" (an IDF spokesman announced casualties as of the 11th of 91 killed, 220 wounded and 19 missing); and that most P.L.O. forces had not yet been engaged, but were awaiting the enemy in Beirut, a city eight times as big as Sidon, with four times the population and five times the regular P.L.O. forces stationed there.

28. The three denials were issued on June 17, the same day Yasser 'Arafat declared that the battle of Beirut had not yet begun, and that the city would be "the Stalingrad of the Arabs" (WAFA, no. 101/82, item 7): "P.L.O. Official Statement about American-Israeli Lies," WAFA no. 101/82, item 6; "Official Palestinian Information Spokesman," no. 100/82, urgent flash; and "Abu Iyyad Statement to WAFA," no. 100/82, item 11.

29. "Arafat Inspects Positions of Joint Forces," WAFA no. 98/82, item 3, June 14, 1982; "Arafat Visits Forces for Second Day," WAFA, no. 98/82, item 4, June 15, 1982; "Abu Jihad Visits Southern Suburbs Positions," WAFA, no. 98/82, item 6, June 14, 1982. The rumors had a strong effect on P.L.O. supporters abroad: see, e.g., P.L.O. Archives, P.L.O./N.Y. to Chairman, June 14, 1982, telex no. 246.

30. The reasons for this are unclear: the most likely is the lack of a cabinet decision to enter the city, combined with a fear of casualties. Schiff and Ya'ari, *Israel's Lebanon War*, p. 181, argue that the Israeli Cabinet "never ordered or sanctioned the IDF's entry into Beirut."

31. "Battle for Mountains Begins: Israeli Attack on Aley Repulsed," WAFA no. 101/82, item 2, June 17, 1982.

32. "Brig. Abu al-Walid: Resistance has no Option but Self-Defence," WAFA no. 103/82, item 4, June 19, 1982.

33. "Abut Iyyad Statement Spells out Palestinian Position," WAFA no. 102/82, item 5, June 18, 1982. He said much the same thing here as he had on June 16 (cited in note 28), but more aggressively and in a far more confident tone. A major press furore arose over al-Hassan's statement and the denials, which will be treated more fully in the next chapter.

34. "Harakat al-insihab al'an: harakat al-insihab munthu zaman," al-Ma'raka, no. 25, July 19, 1982, p. 3.

35. The Israelis paid for their victory: "some thirty dead" according to Bavly and Salpeter, *Fire in Beirut*, p. 103.

36. "Arafat in TV Interview: Our Situation is Stronger than Ever," WAFA no. 105/82, item 1, June 21, 1982.

37. "The Palestinian 'Red Line,'" WAFA no. 108/82, item 1, June 24, 1982.

38. P.L.O. Archives, Chairman to P.L.O./Paris, June 27, 1982.

39. Several groups of drivers were captured and spoke at press conferences held by the West Beirut Higher Security Committee: "Car bombs linked to Israelis," Beirut, Reuters, *The Guardian* (London), July 8, 1982; "Begin and Sharon: The Car Bomb Murderers," WAFA no. 112/82, item 2, June 28, 1982; and "Car Bombs from Israel via the 'Good Fence,'" WAFA no. 122/82, item 3, July 8, 1982. *Newsweek* correspondent Tony Clifton reported seeing Hebrew-marked wrappings on explosives in a car meant to explode inside the Lebanese Information Ministry: *God Cried*, p. 45.

40. "Berri: 'Lebanon is Indeed a Target of the Invasion,'" WAFA no. 111/82, item 3, June 27, 1982; "Strengthening of Lebanese National Position Accompanies Phalangist Massacres in Mountains," WAFA no. 114/82, item 2, June 30, 1982; and "Lebanese Nationalist Opposition to Palestinian Withdrawal," WAFA no. 115/82, item

1, July 1, 1982. Jumblatt's statement was seen as so important it was telexed to offices abroad: P.L.O. Archives, Chairman's Office to P.L.O./Paris, June 25, 1982. A Central Operations situation report noted that support for the P.L.O. resulted from these Phalangist actions (P.L.O. Archives, Central Operations to all offices, June 30, 1982, 6:00 P.M. local time). Berri's remarks about "the new Palestinians" are in WAFA no. 121/82, item 6, July 7, 1982.

41. E.g. P.L.O. Archives, P.L.O./Paris to Chairman, July 5, 1982, reporting French officials' "apprehensions of a severe and heavy Israeli assault against Palestinian positions in West Beirut."

42. The P.L.O. Military Spokesman reported that "intensive counter-battery fire of the Joint Forces" had scored direct hits on Israeli artillery positions and armored vehicles in Ba'abda and Shweifat, WAFA no. 119/82, item 3, July 5, 1982, a claim which was corroborated at the time by foreign reporters on the spot.

43. The police figures were reported by Chris Drake, in "Battered Beirut Cries for its Dead," *The Guardian*, July 13, 1982. The P.L.O. estimated more than 300 casualties: "Beirut an Inferno: Three Hundred Civilian Casualties," WAFA no. 125/82, item 9, July 11, 1982.

44. The P.L.O. claim regarding IDF casualties is in WAFA, ibid. Reuters reported that "Palestinian fighters scored direct hits on Israeli positions in the hills and correspondents yesterday [July 11] saw Israeli armoured units pulling back from exposed forward positions," *The Guardian*, July 13, 1982.

45. "Abu Iyyyad: We Will Not Surrender"; "Arafat: P.L.O. to Remain in Beirut," both in WAFA no. 116/82, items 5 and 4 respectively, July 2, 1982.

46. "Abu Iyyad: No Climb Down from Bottom Line Defined in PLO Document," WAFA no. 131/82, item 5, July 17, 1982. The 11 points were first sent to Paris on July 8: P.L.O. Archives, Chairman to Souss, July 8, 1982. Hani al-Hassan stated that the P.L.O. consciously toughened its stand when Israeli military pressure was applied: interview, Tunis, August 31, 1984.

47. "Israeli Attacks Thrown Back as Battle of Beirut Begins," WAFA no. 119/82, item 3, July 5, 1982.

48. "Abu Iyyad Explains P.L.O. Negotiating Position"; "Brig. Abu al-Walid: No Departure from Beirut by Land, Sea or Air," both in WAFA no. 123/82, items 4 and 2 respectively, July 9, 1982. There is a striking contrast between Brig. Abu al-Walid's confident statement of July 9 and the subdued tone of that of June 19, cited in note 32 above.

49. "WAFA Comment: The Balance Sheet after 5 Weeks of War," WAFA no. 125/82, item 4, July 11, 1982.

50. "Arafat Attacks Silence, Impotence of Arabs over Lebanon War," WAFA no. 125/82, item 2, July 11, 1982.

51. "WAFA Commentary: Israel's Losses after 5 Weeks of War," WAFA no. 126/82, item 1, July 12, 1982.

52. "WAFA Military Analysis: Israel's Vietnam or Israel's Verdun?", WAFA no. 128/82, item 5, July 14, 1982.

53. After some confusion at P.L.O. offices abroad (and in the Western media) regarding the P.L.O. negotiating position, the 11 points received general distribution by telex and radio beginning on July 11, 1982: P.L.O. Archives, Abu 'Ammar to Abu Maher (Damascus), July 11, 1982, later repeated to other offices.

54. This fact was extensively reported by foreign and Lebanese reporters on the

spot, and was the subject of a protest by the Canadian Ambassador, whose residence was damaged in the bombing, as were several other embassies. His comments are quoted in R. Wright, et al., "Beirut: The Liquidation of a City," *The Sunday Times*, August 8, 1982.

55. P.L.O. Archives, P.L.O. Central Operations to all offices, July 25, 1982, 6:00 P.M. local time.

56. Interview with Abu Iyyad, Tunis, March 14, 1984.

57. These citations are taken from the following situation reports: P.L.O. Archives, Central operations to all offices, July 26, 1982, 2:00 P.M. local time; ibid.; July 27, 1982, 5:00 P.M. local time; July 31, 1982, 2:00 P.M. local time.

58. "WAFA Commentary: 242 Revisited," WAFA no. 144/82, item 6, July 30, 1982.

59. "Israeli Savagery Pours 80,000 Shells into West Beirut," WAFA no.145/82, item 4, July 30, 1982.

60. P.L.O. Archives, Central Operations to all offices, August 1, 1982, 7:00 P.M. local time.

61. The text, part of an exchange of letters between the U.S. and Lebanon on August 18 and 20 which constituted an agreement between the two governments, was published in the *Department of State Bulletin* (September 1982) 82 (2066), pp. 2-5.

62. "Abu Iyyad: Where are the Arabs?" WAFA no. 145/82, item 4, July 31, 1982. He later repeated these demands, adding that Egypt should abrogate its peace treaty with Israel.

63. "WAFA Commentary: The Battle of Beirut Airport," WAFA no. 147/82, item 1, August 2, 1982.

64. "Israel Admits 165 Casualties Wednesday," WAFA no. 151/82, item 4, August 6, 1982, reports an August 4 P.L.O. estimate of 100 Israeli casualties, the IDF spokesman's initial admission of only 64 wounded, and the later revision upward to 19 killed and 146 wounded. Other sources give the casualties as 18 killed and 76 wounded: Bavly and Salpeter, *Fire in Beirut*, p. 108.

65. WAFA report cited in preceding note; Yasser 'Arafat and Abu Iyyad interviews, Tunis, March 9 and 14, 1984.

66. Tony Clifton and photographer Catherine Leroy give vivid eyewitness accounts of the Sanaye' bombing in *God Cried*, pp. 45-46. Another is that of John Bulloch, who was 100 yards away when the building was hit: *Final Conflict*, pp. 132-33.

67. The P.L.O. estimate of casualties on August 12 was 300: "P.L.O. Military Spokesman: 300 Casualties in 9 Hours of bombing," WAFA no. 157/82, item 6, August 12, 1982, while the Lebanese police counted "at least 128" killed and 400 wounded, according to an AP report in *The New York Times*, August 13, 1982.

68. "WAFA Commentary: Israel's Seventy Day War," WAFA no. 157/82, item 7, August 12, 1982.

69. "Abu Iyyad Condemns U.S. as Responsible for Israel's War," WAFA no. 157/82, item 9, 12 August 1982.

70. P.L.O. Archives, Central Operations to all offices, August 12, 1982, 6:30 P.M. local time.

71. "WAFA Editorial: All Options are Still Open," WAFA no. 154/82, item 1, August 9, 1982.

72. Interview, Tunis, March 9, 1984.

4. The Decision To Leave Beirut

1. For an excellent study of the subject, see Nadine Picaudou, "La bourgeoisie palestinienne et l'industrie: étude socio-historique".

2. This emerges clearly from the standard works on the pre-1984 period, Ann Mosely Lesch, *Arab Politics in Palestine, 1917-1939: The Frustration of a Nationalist Movement*, and Y. Porath's *The Emergence of the Palestinian-Arab National Movement 1918-1929*, and *The Palestinian Arab National Movement 1929-1939: From Riots to Rebellion*.

3. The P.L.O.'s organizational structure is depicted in the chart in the frontispiece and is described in C. Rubenberg, *The Palestine Liberation Organization,* pp. 7-17 and Helena Cobban, *The Palestinian Liberation Organisation* (which focuses on Fateh) pp. 3-18, and in Aaron David Miller, *The P.L.O. and the Politics of Survival.*

4. Both these feelings towards 'Arafat were evident during a March 14, 1984 interview with Abu Iyyad, notwithstanding his differences at that time with 'Arafat over his visit to Cairo. The early ties between the historic leaders of Fateh are described in Abu Iyyad, *My Home, My Land,* pp. 19-37.

5. Interviews with Abu Sa'id are the source of most of the considerable amount of previously unpublished original material about Fateh and the P.L.O. in H. Cobban, *The Palestinian Liberation Organisation.*

6. The P.L.O. telex traffic between Beirut and New York was extremely heavy at the beginning of the war. Between June 11 and 26, 89 messages were sent by the P.L.O.'s U.N. mission, an average of six per day, nearly all of them dealing with the Security Council's deliberations on the Lebanese war: P.L.O. Archives, Abu Lutf (N.Y.) to Political Department, Abu 'Ammar, Abu Jihad, no. 221, June 11, 1982; P.L.O./N.Y. to Abu 'Ammar, no 310, June 26, 1982.

7. Ample evidence for the existence of crossed signals within the administration during the first few days of the war can be found in Alexander Haig's *Caveat,* pp. 337-339, dealing with the internal debate over the U.S. veto of June 8, for which Haig takes credit.

8. Ibid., pp. 318-319; and Henry Kissinger, "From Lebanon to the West Bank to the Gulf," *The Washington Post,* June 16, 1982.

9. P.L.O. Archives, Abu Lutf (N.Y.) to Political Department/Abu 'Ammar/Abu, no. 221, June 11, 1982; Ibrahim Souss, P.L.O. Paris, to Chairman, June 11, 1982.

10. P.L.O. Archives, Abu Lutf to Pol. Dept., June 11. The Saudi prince also asked 'Arafat to agree to postponement of an Arab League foreign ministers or summit meeting, "until the international situation clears up." The meeting was postponed indefinitely.

11. Daily situation reports are replete with comment on U.S.-Israeli-Lebanese rightist collusion: e.g. P.L.O. Archives, Central Operations to all offices, June 30, 1982, which makes this reference and another to "American-Israeli-isolationist pressures" preventing an accord with the Lebanese government.

12. This new situation led P.L.O. leaders to take Saudi claims regarding their influence on the United States less seriously than in the past. This is confirmed by a study of the telex traffic and interviews with P.L.O. leaders (notably with 'Arafat, Tunis, March 9, 1982), and flatly contradicts the claims by Haig that the P.L.O. was

strongly reinforced in holding out against U.S.-Israeli demands by Saudi encouragement from June 13 onward (Haig, *Caveat*, pp. 343-345).

13. P.L.O. Archives, Chairman to Abu Lutf (N.Y.), June 13, 1982. The Central Operations list is cited in note 3 in chapter 3.

14. P.L.O. Archives, Chairman to Zuhdi/Abu Lutf, urgent, June 13, 1982.

15. In an interview at the Quai d'Orsay on March 8, 1984, an official in the Cabinet du Ministre stated that as of June 15, 1982, France began to attempt to achieve a settlement on this basis after a P.L.O. request conveyed by Hani al-Hassan to a French emissary in Beirut, Francis Gutman, the Secretary-General of the Foreign Ministry. This was confirmed by Hani al-Hassan, interview, Tunis, August 31, 1984, and by Ibrahim Souss, interview, Tunis, August 31, 1984.

16. At the very outset, according to Hani al-Hassan in an interview, ibid., the idea of negotiations via the French on this basis were "initiatied by myself with Abu 'Ammar," and only later approved by the rest of the leadership. Criticism of this approach, expressed most forcefully in public by Abu Iyyad, was referred to in section II C of the preceding chapter, and is discussed further below.

17. Much of the following paragraph is based on details provided by Abu Iyyad in an interview in Tunis, March 14, 1984.

18. Interview on August 6, 1984 in Washington D.C. with Advisor to Chairman's Office who attended several meetings of the P.L.O. Higher Military Council throughout April and May 1982, and the meeting of the night of June 6-7, 1984.

19. Abu Iyyad interview, March 14, 1984. See note 20 for Jumblatt's confirmation of this.

20. In an August 1 interview with Jumblatt by Selim Nassib cited in his *Beirut: Frontline Story* (London: Pluto Press, 1983), p. 106. In answer to a question about "a certain wavering" in the postion of the LNM at the beginning of the war, Jumblatt replied: "Yes, that's true. At one point we were completely lost. We did not expect such a rapid development of events, nor such a spread-out operation. The invasion was a shock." (ibid., p. 104).

21. Interview with Yasser 'Arafat, Tunis, March 9, 1984. This was confirmed by Abu Iyyad: Tunis, 14 March 1984.

22. Selim Nessib, *Beirut*, p. 106.

23. *Al-Safir*, July 3, 1982, p. 1 for Wazzan's statement. Summaries of the pledge can be found in P.L.O. Archives, Chairman to P.L.O./N.Y., copy to Souss/Paris, July 2, 1982, and a Central Operations situation report of July 4, 1982. Several individuals besides the recipients saw the text briefly at the time, but no copy could be found in the Archives of the Chairman's Office.

24. The effect on Palestinian opinion in Beirut was discussed in the preceding chapter; that on offices abroad can be seen from a telex from Tarazi to WAFA on June 14, asking for information on some of the more outrageous rumors about the situation of the P.L.O. in Beirut, and from a telex two days later from the P.L.O. New York office to Chairman 'Arafat (no. 246) reporting that comments attributed to Hani al-Hassan had caused concern among P.L.O. supporters.

25. P.L.O. Archives, memo to Chairman 'Arafat from P.L.O. Unified Information official (unnamed in text), June 17, 1982, annotated as having been read by 'Arafat. The memo was later passed on by 'Arafat to al-Hassan: interview with Hani al-Hassan, Tunis, August 31, 1984.

26. Three of these statements were issued in the WAFA bulletin of June 17,

although two were actually made late on the night of the 16th; the fourth, made late on the 17th, appeared in the bulletin of the 18th: "Official Palestinian Spokesman," urgent flash [no number]; "Abu Iyyad Statement to WAFA," WAFA no. 100/82, item 10; "P.L.O. Official Statement about American-Israeli Lies," WAFA no. 101/82, item 6; "Nobody Can Disarm the Joint Forces," WAFA no. 102/82, item 1.

27. "Arafat: This Battle will be the Stalingrad of the Arabs," WAFA no 101/82, item 7, June 17, 1982.

28. The matter was public knowledge within the P.L.O. in Beirut at the time, as was the news of the resolution of these differences the following day: interview on July 28, 1984 in Washington D.C. with Advisor to Chairman's Office who attended the meeting at which the disagreement took place.

29. In interviews, Yasser 'Arafat and Abu Iyyad (Tunis, March 9 and 14, 1984, respectively) confirmed that it was the position of their Lebanese allies which forced the P.L.O. to make this commitment. Abu Iyyad termed this "a surprise," and said it was the most important factor in the June decision. Other P.L.O. sources confirm this: e.g., Abu Lutf interview, Tunis, August 31, 1984; Hani al-Hassan interview, Tunis, August 31, 1984; Ibrahim Souss interview, Tunis, August 30, 1984.

30. The first discussion of this took place at a meeting on the night of June 26-27: "P.L.O. Leadership to Discuss U.S. Proposals," WAFA no. 109/82, item 8, June 26, 1982 notes that "The P.L.O. leadership tonight received via the French Foreign Ministry a number of important proposals regarding the situation in Beirut. WAFA has learned that the Palestinian leadership will meet tonight to study these proposals and present a reply. Similar messages had been received from the Indian Foreign Ministry." The document finally agreed on was the result of deliberations during this and several later meetings.

31. In the P.L.O. Archives, Arabic originals of outgoing telexes are kept together with the English versions actually sent, while incoming texts are filed with their Arabic translations.

32. In one of his first messages to the French, 'Arafat said, "I wish to extend our gratitude to President Mitterand, the French government and people for their friendly and solid stand.": P.L.O. Archives, Chairman to Souss, June 24, 1982, 10:00 P.M. Beirut time.

33. Interviews with official of Cabinet du Ministre, French Foreign Ministry, Paris, March 8, 1984, and official of French Foreign Ministry, Beirut, January 12, 1983.

34. P.L.O. Archives, Souss to Chairman, June 19, 1982.

35. Haig, Caveat, p. 345.

36. Ibid., pp. 345-46.

37. P.L.O. Archives, Souss to Chairman, urgent, June 25, 1982.

38. Cited in Rashid I. Khalidi, British Policy towards Syria and Palestine 1906-1914, pp. 184, 199.

39. Interview with official of Cabinet du Ministre, French Foreign Ministry, Paris, March 8, 1984.

40. Interview with Director of the Archives, Office of the Chairman of the P.L.O. Executive Committee, Tunis, March 11, 1984.

41. On June 26, 1984, for example, the P.L.O. received an analysis of the situation within the administration from a source in Washington which clearly outlined the differences between Haig and the National Security Council over the handling of

the Lebanese crisis: P.L.O. Washington to Chairman's Office, June 26, 1982. The conflict between Haig's approach and that of Judge William Clark, the President's National Security Advisor, can be seen, e.g. in Haig, *Caveat*, pp. 338-341. The Chairman's Office also received complete and extensive media reports from P.L.O. offices in the U.S. and major world capitals.

42. P.L.O. Archives, Souss to Chairman, very urgent, June 26, 1982.

43. P.L.O. Archives, Chairman to Souss, urgent and secret, June 25, 1982.

44. P.L.O. Archives, Chairman to Souss, June 27, 1982.

45. P.L.O. Archives, Souss to Chairman, urgent, June 28, 1982.

46. P.L.O. Archives, Chairman to Souss, June 28, 1982.

47. P.L.O. Archives, Souss to Chairman, urgent, June 29, 1982, no. 1; and Souss to Chairman, June 29, 1982, no. 2, which contained a similar message after a second meeting with French Foreign Ministry officials that evening.

48. P.L.O. Archives, Souss to Chairman, urgent, June 29, 1982, no. 3; Souss to Chairman, most urgent, June 29, 1982, no. 4 (the second dispatch contains an English translation of the American note, which had been sent immediately in French "as it was submitted to me by the Foreign Minister" in the first); and Souss to Chairman, most urgent, June 30, 1982. Souss was usually invited to the Foreign Ministry to receive messages from Washington, some of which he saw in the original French, and which he and Ministry officials translated into English for transmission to Beirut: interview, Tunis, August 30, 1984.

49. P.L.O. Archives, Chairman to Souss (copy to Zuhdi/N.Y.), June 30, 1982, 1:30 P.M. local time, no. 1; Chairman to Souss, (copy to Zuhdi/N.Y.), June 30, 1982, no. 3. In Chairman to Souss (copy to Zuhdi/N.Y.), June 30, 1982, no. 4, 'Arafat informed both that he had just learned, via Habib and Wazzan, of the dropping of the U.S. condition regarding light weapons which had previously been transmitted by the French. This is an early example of the delays inherent in the roundabout lines of communication between Habib and the P.L.O. when compared with the French channel.

50. P.L.O. Archives, Chairman to Souss (copy to Zuhdi/N.Y.), June 30, 1980, no. 3.

5. The Decision To Accept the Habib Plan

1. See, e.g., the statements of Wazzan, Salam, Jumblatt, and Berri on 5 July (al-Safir, July 6, 1982, p. 1), the first of many in this regard.

2. Interview with Abu Iyyad, Tunis, March 14, 1984.

3. Harrison Salisbury, *The 900 Days: The Siege of Leningrad*; Dov Joseph, *The Faithful City: The Siege of Jerusalem, 1948*.

4. For the quintessential expressions of these allegations, see Martin Peretz, "Lebanon Eyewitness," *The New Republic*, August 2, 1982, and Norman Podhoretz, "J'Accuse, " *Commentary*, December 1982.

5. New York: Stein and Day, 1984.

6. Interview with Nabil 'Amir, Director of "The Voice of Palestine" Radio, Tunis, March 18, 1984. He describes the wartime problems faced by the radio, especially that of finding new sites for it, in his *Ayyam al-hub wal-hisar*, pp. 41-45.

7. Interview with Director of the Office of the Chairman, Tunis, March 7, 1984.

8. Interview with Director of the PRCS's Gaza Hospital, Washington D.C., March 16, 1985. Every book by a Western journalist actually in West Beirut during the siege confirms that shelling was indiscriminate. See, e.g., those by Bulloch, Randal, Clifton and Leroy, Jansen, and Nassib cited in note 1 of chapter 1. Use of the word "indiscriminate" by Tom Friedman of the *New York Times* to describe the Israeli bombardment of August 4 led to a clash with his editors, who saw fit to excise the word. The text of an angry telex by Friedman to them is reproduced in full in an article by P.L.O. Alexander Cockburn, "A Word Not Fit to Print" *The Village Voice*, September 22, 1982. (Cockburn later had to leave the *Voice* after accusations about money he received from the Institute for Arab Studies.) For a survey of the controversy over press coverage of the war, see Roger Morris, "Beirut—and the Press—Under Seige."

9. In the words of a French Foreign Ministry official, Habib's plan was already fully formed by June 15, and its essentials never changed: interview, March 8, 1984.

10. The text was transmitted to 'Arafat in P.L.O. Archives, Souss to Chairman, July 2, 1982; a detailed AFP summary can be found in *Revue d'Etudes Palestiniennes*, (Autumn 1982), no. 5 p. 145. Details in this and the following three paragraphs are based on this text. On the same day, *Le Monde* published an appeal for Palestinian self-determination and mutual recognition and negotiations between the P.L.O. and Israel by former French Premier Pierre Mendes-France, former World Zionist Organization President Nahum Goldmann, and former World Jewish Congress President Philip Klutznick, which was publicly welcomed by 'Arafat, who invited the three to travel to besieged Beirut. Mendes-France and Goldmann died before this could be arranged. See M. Merhav, P. Klutznick and H. Eilts, *Facing the P.L.O. Question*, pp. 14–15.

11. In a later message (P.L.O. Archives, Souss to Chairman, July 13, 1982, 8:00 P.M.), a Foreign Ministry official told the P.L.O. this language was also included in the draft out of fear that Bashir Gemayel might stage a putsch at the time of the Presidential elections on September 23. According to a reliable Israeli account, this concern was not far-fetched: Schiff and Ya'ari, *Israel's Lebanon War*, pp. 231-232.

12. *The Washington Post*, June 16, 1982.

13. P.L.O. Archives, Souss to Chairman, July 5, 1982, no. 1.

14. Ibid., no. 2.

15. Haig, *Caveat*, p. 348.

16. Ibid.

17. P.L.O. Archives, Souss to Chairman, July 8, 1982, no. 1. The Saudi Military Attaché in Washington, Prince Bandar Ibn Sultan, told the French Ambassador to the United States François de Laboulaye that he had been instructed by phone by King Fahd to help obtain French participation in a force "not essentially placed under U.N. supervision." Souss reported that "The French do not seem to be very reassured by the Saudi position": P.L.O. Archives, Souss to Chairman, July 10, 1982, no. 2, 2:30 P.M.

18. These telexes were the following: P.L.O. Archives, Chairman to P.L.O.-N.Y./Souss-Paris, July 2, 1982, 10:00 P.M.; Souss to Chairman, July 3, 1982, no. 1; Chairman to Souss, July 3, 1982, no. 1; Souss to Chairman, July 3, 1982, no. 2; Chairman to Souss, July 3, 1982, no. 2; Souss to Chairman, July 8, 1982, nos. 1, 2, 3; Chairman to Souss, July 8, 1982, no. 1. 10:00 P.M.; Chairman to Souss, July 8, 1982, no. 2. The latter was the 11 points, which were repeated to P.L.O. offices abroad on July 9, 1982, and to Damascus (Abu 'Ammar to Abu Maher, July 11, 1982).

19. P.L.O. Archives, Souss to Chairman, July 8, 1982, no. 4.

20. Ibid., July 9, 1982, no. 2.

21. Ibid., July 10, 1982, no. 1.

22. Ibid., July 10, 1982, no. 2, 2:30 P.M.

23. Ibid., July 12, 1982, 5:45 P.M.

24. P.L.O. Archives, Chairman to Souss, July 11, 1982, 3:00 P.M.

25. Z. Schiff & E. Ya'ari, *Israel's Lebanon War*, p. 211.

26. See, e.g., ibid., pp.212-213, 222-227.

27. P.L.O. Archives, Souss to Chairman, July 19, 1982, 8:15 P.M.

28. Ibid., July 21, 1982, 8:30 P.M.

29. Z Schiff & E. Ya'ari, *Israel's Lebanon War*, pp. 42-44. Other key points made by the French find support in this book.

30. P.L.O. Archives, Souss to Chairman, July 21, 1982, 8:30 P.M.

31. Examples of such warnings are ibid., July 11, 1982, 1:45 P.M. hrs; and ibid., July 17, 1982, 7:45 P.M.

32. The French query was in ibid., July 14, 1982, 1:00 P.M.; 'Arafat replied describing Habib's offer in P.L.O. Archives, Chairman to Souss, July 14, 1982, 2:30 P.M. Some of Wazzan's points were confirmed by Habib in an interview, Washington D.C., December 3, 1984.

33. P.L.O. Archives, Souss to Chairman, July 24, 1982, 7:30 P.M.

34. Ibid., July 27, 1982, 2:30 P.M.

35. Ibid., July 24, 1982, 7:30 P.M.

36. Ibid., July 15, 1982, 8:30 P.M. The Algerian and United Arab Emirates Foreign Ministers, Souss, and the Arab League Ambassador in Paris were present at the one-hour meeting.

37. Ibid., July 30, 1982, 2:00 P.M.

38. S Nassib, *Beirut*, p. 126.

39. "WAFA Commentary: Israel's Seventy Day War," WAFA No. 157/82, item 7, August 12, 1982.

40. Interview, Tunis, March 10, 1984.

41. P.L.O. Archives, Chairman to Abu Tayeb (Cairo), July 11, 1982, 5:30 P.M.

42. P.L.O. Archives, Zuhdi to Chairman, July 5, 1982. This is confirmed by the envoy, who was then in the P.L.O. delegation at the U.N.: Hassan 'Abd al-Rahman interview, Washington D.C., October 26, 1984.

43. Syrian policy towards the P.L.O. and the region since 1970 are discussed in R. Khalidi, "The Asad Regime and the Palestinian Resistance".

44. P.L.O. Archives, Abu Maher to Abu 'Ammar, July 11, 1982. Details of these meetings were confirmed by Abu Mazin, who participated in them: interview, Tunis, August 30, 1984.

45. The French reported the result of many of their contacts with the Soviets to the P.L.O., at times asking that it also take the matter up with Moscow: P.L.O. Archives, Souss to Chairman, July 5, 1982, no. 1; ibid., July 9, 1982, no. 1; ibid., July 9, 1982, no. 2; ibid., July 13, 1982, 8:00 P.M. ibid., July 24, 1982, 7:30 P.M. Abu Mazin stated that at a July 5 meeting with an Arab League delegation visiting Moscow, Foreign Minister Andrei Gromyko had expressed anger at Syrian claims that Soviet weapons were defective, while other Soviet officials expressed dissatisfaction about Syria's posture during the war: interview, Tunis, August 30, 1984.

46. P.L.O. Archives, Abu Maher to Abu 'Ammar, July 13, 1982.

47. P.L.O. Archives, Souss to Chairman, July 13, 1982, 8:00 P.M.

48. P.L.O. Archives, Chairman to Abu Maher, July 13, 1982.

49. P.L.O. Archives, Abu Maher to Abu 'Ammar, July 17, 1982. The Syrian position was apparently based on the belief that in a Reagan–Asad exchange of letters on June 10, the U.S. had committed itself to obtaining a complete Israeli withdrawal from Lebanon. This was indirectly confirmed by Philip Habib in response to a question at a talk at the American Enterprise Institute, Washington D.C., November 15, 1984.

50. P.L.O. Archives, Chairman to Souss, copy to Zuhdi, July 16, 1982, 8:03 P.M.

51. P.L.O. Archives, Abu Sa'id to Chairman, July 17, 1982, via P.L.O./N.Y., no. 483/82.

52. P.L.O. Archives, Abu Sa'id memo to Chairman, July 19, 1982 no. 1.

53. Interview with P.L.O. official present at July 19, 1982 meeting of the P.L.O. leadership, Tunis, March 14, 1984.

54. P.L.O. Archives, Chairman to Abu Sa'id, July 19, 1982, 3:30 A.M.

55. P.L.O. Archives, Abu Sa'id to Chairman, July 19, 1982, no. 1.

56. Ibid., July 19, 1982, no. 2. Khaled al-Hassan explained the reasons for the seemingly conflicting signals sent to Beirut in interviews in Tunis on August 29 and 31, 1984.

57. P.L.O. Archives, Chairman to Abu Sa'id, July 20, 1982, 2:45 P.M.

58. Ibid., July 22, 1982, 11:30 A.M., no. 1; and ibid, July 22, 1982, 9:45 P.M., no.2.

59. P.L.O. Archives, Abu Sa'id to Abu Lutf, July 22, 1983, via P.L.O./N.Y., no 510/82; enclosed in Zuhdi to Chairman, July 22, 1982, no 513/82.

60. Ibid.

61. This was confirmed by the Arab journalist in Washington who received the original document from the Saudi diplomat.

62. A telex from Abu Jihad to New York on July 23, 1982, reporting an "American-Saudi-Syrian agreement on the method of resolution under an Arab scenario (*ikhraj Arabi*)", is evidence that this was the initial understanding in Beirut.

63. P.L.O. Archives, Souss to Chairman, July 28, 1982, 7:30 P.M.

64. French perplexity at Khaled al-Hassan's apparent opposition to the Franco-Egyptian resolution, and 'Arafat's efforts to reassure them, including a directive to al-Hassan to support the French initiative can be followed in P.L.O. Archives: Souss to Chairman, July 22, 1982, 11:30 P.M.; Chairman to Souss, July 22-23, 1982, 2:00 A.M.; Chairman to Abu Sa'id, July 24, 1982, 11:30 A.M.; Chairman to Souss, July 17, 1982, 6:30 P.M., urgent. In an interview, Khaled al-Hassan denied this was his fault: Tunis, August 29, 1984. This is confirmed by Hassan 'Abd al-Rahman: interview, Washington D.C., October 26, 1984.

65. P.L.O. Archives, Chairman to P.L.O. offices in Paris, N.Y., Bonn, Vienna, London, Geneva, representatives in Washington and Cairo, July 29, 1982.

66. The P.L.O. delegation headed by Abu Lutf included Fateh Central Committee members Abu Mazin, Khaled al-Hassan, Abu Shakir (Rafiq al-Natshe), and P.L.O. Executive Committee member Yasser 'Abed Rabbo. In interviews in Tunis, the first three confirmed details regarding this meeting (August 31, 1984; August 30, 1984; and August 29, 1984 respectively).

67. P.L.O. Archives, Central Operations to all offices, August 1, 1982, 7:00 P.M.; and Chairman to Souss, August 2, 1982, contain the first references to the decision which could be found, but specify that it was taken several days earlier.

68. Abu Iyyad interview, Tunis, March 14, 1984. None of these messages could be found in the P.L.O. archives, since none were issued by the Chairman's office (causing problems with the Soviets, who would accept communications only from 'Arafat, in his capacity as Chairman). The message to the Soviets was drafted by Abu Iyyad, Abu Saleh, Nayef Hawatmeh of the DFLP and Abu Maher al-Yamani of the PFLP, while Abu Saleh wrote the one to Asad.

6. Decisions and Consequences

1. For details of the massacre see J. Randal, *Going All the Way*, 90-91, 130; and H. Cobban, *The Palestinian Liberation Organization*, 73-74. Both were present at the fall of the camp.

2. P.L.O. Archives, Chairman to Souss, August 1982.

3. P.L.O. Archives, "U.S. Comments on Palestinian Proposal of 3 August," typed memo on plain paper, n.d. [3-4 August 1982]; P.L.O. response, August 4.

4. P.L.O. Archives, Brig. Qureitem to Hani al-Hassan, August 4, 1982; Sa'eb Salam to Hani al-Hassan, August 4, 1982.

5. P.L.O. Archives, "U.S. Comments on Palestinian Views of 4 August," typed memo on plain paper, n.d. [August 4, 1982]; "American Point of View on Palestinian note of 6 August," typed memo on plain paper, n.d. [August 6, 1982].

6. P.L.O. Archives, Chairman to Souss, August 11, 1982. The final text of the accords and the notes exchanged between Lebanese Foreign Minister Fu'ad Butros and U.S. Ambassador to Lebanon Robert Dillon are in the *Department of State Bulletin*, (September 1982) 82 (2066): 2-5.

7. Philip Habib interview, Washington D.C., December 3, 1984. Sharon's ambitious war aims are confirmed by another U.S. diplomat privy to the negotiations: interview, Washington D.C., March 27, 1985, as well as by the retiring U.S. Ambassador to Israel, Sam Lewis, and a State Department spokesman: *The Washington Post*, May 25, 1985, pp. A1, A15.

8. Ibid.

9. Ibid.

10. Ibid. Habib indicated that both Haig and Sharon were less than truthful in their dealings during the war: "Haig was lying; Sharon was lying," he said.

11. Ibid., and Philip Habib interview, Washington D.C., November 15, 1984.

12. See, e.g., D. Bavly and E. Salpeter, *Fire in Beirut*, 112-113.

13. Hani al-Hassan interview, Tunis, August 31, 1984.

14. Interviews in Tunis with: Yasser 'Arafat, 9 March 1984; Abu Jihad, 13 March 1984; Abu Iyyad, March 14 and August 13, 1984; Abu Lutf, August 31, 1984; Hani al-Hassan, August 31, 1984.

15. Yasser 'Arafat interview, Tunis, March 9, 1984.

16. Abu Iyyad interview, Tunis, March 14, 1984.

17. P.L.O. Archives, Souss to Chairman, August 11, 1982, 3:40 P.M.

18. P.L.O. Archives, Chairman to Souss, August 12, 1982.

19. For the view in Washington of the mission of the MNF in Beirut, see the Department of State "Fact Sheet on the Departure," which was "made available to news correspondents Acting Department Spokesman Alan Romberg" in the *Depart-*

ment of State Bulletin (September 1982) 82 (2066): 5-7, especially p. 6, where this mission is described without specific reference to the Palestinian camps.

20. Philip Habib interview, Washington D.C., December 3, 1984.

21. Department of State Bulletin (November) 82 (2068): 48.

22. Schiff and Ya'ari, Israel's Lebanon War, 258-260.

23. These are the White House statement of September 15; the State Department statement of the 15th; the White House statement of the 16th; the President's statements of the 18th and 20th; and the White House statement of the 23d, all in the Department of State Bulletin (November) 82 (2068): 47-50.

24. "U.S. Comments" of August 3 and 4, and "American Point of View" of August 6, cited in notes 3 and 5.

25. My attention was first drawn to these documents by Loren Jenkins of the Washington Post and Tom Friedman of the New York Times, who received copies of them from P.L.O. leaders soon after the massacres. A knowledgeable U.S. diplomat confirmed that these documents originated with the U.S. mediator: interview, Washington D.C., March 27, 1985.

26. See, e.g., all the documents in the Department of State Bulletin (September 1982) 82 (2066): 1-27; and ibid. (November 1982) 82 (2068): 46-51.

27. The President's statement of September 14, 1982, cited in ibid., p. 47, and those cited in note 23. U.S. officials on the spot were late to realize what was happening. One stated: "Even Friday [September 17] we didn't believe a massacre to be possible. Once we realized, and got nervous, we did everything we could. We had taken Begin at his word." Interview, Washington D.C., March 27, 1985.

28. The Jerusalem Post October 15, 1982.

29. See, e.g., Schiff and Ya'ari, Israel's Lebanon War, p. 257; and Zakaria al-Shaikh, "Sabra and Shatila 1982: Resisting the Massacre," by a Palestinian present during the massacres.

Bibliography

A. Unpublished Documentary Sources

Archives of the Office of the Chairman of the Executive Committee of the Palestine Liberation Organization, Tunis: telex files.

"The Economic and Social Situation and Potential of the Palestinian Arab People in the Region of West Asia." Study presented to the United Nations Economic Commission for West Asia by TEAM International, March 1983.

B. Interviews

Unpublished
Following interviews took place in 1984:

'Abbas, Mahmud (Abu Mazin): Tunis, August 30.
'Abd al-Rahman, Hassan: Washington DC, October 26.
'Amr, Nabil: Tunis, March 18.

'Arafat, Yasser (Abu 'Ammar): Tunis, March 9; Amman, November 24.

Armali, Shawqi: Tunis, March 16.

Draper, Morris: Washington D.C., December 14.

Habib, Philip: Washington D.C., November 15, December 12.

al-Hassan, Hani: Tunis, August 31.

al-Hassan, Khaled (Abu Sa'id): Tunis, August 29, 31.

Khalaf, Salah (Abu Iyyad): Tunis, March 14, August 31.

Qaddoumi, Farouq (Abu Lutf): Tunis, August 31.

Souss, Ibrahim: Tunis, August 31.

Ta'mari, Salah, Washington D.C., May 3.

al-Wazir, Khalil (Abu Jihad): Tunis March 10, 13.

Following interviewees declined to be cited by name:

Chief, Fateh General Wireless Section: Tunis, March 14, 1984.

Consultant to Chairman's Office: Washington D.C., July 28, August 6, 1984.

Communications Consultant to Chairman's Office: Tunis, September 25, 1982.

Deputy Chief, Occupied Homeland Affairs Office: Tunis, August 20, 1984.

Director, Gaza Hospital, Palestine Red Crescent Society (PRCS), Washington D.C., March 16, 1985.

Director, Office of the Chairman: Tunis, March 7, 1984.

Director of Archives, Chairman's Office: Tunis, March 11, 1984.

Official of Cabinet du Ministre: French Foreign Ministry, Paris, March 8, 1984.

Official of French Foreign Ministry, Beirut, January 12, 1983, New York, March 29, 1985.

Official of U.S. State Department, Washington DC, March 27, 1985.

P.L.O. Information Official: Tunis, September 28, 1982 March 14, 1984.

Published

Abu Musa, Col., int. Mahmud Ma'rouf. "Al-Haqa'iq al-mansiyya 'an harb Beirut" [Forgotten truths about the battle of Beirut]. *al-Mawqif al-'Arabi* (March 21-27, 1983) 127:11-15.

_____ int. Salwa al-'Amad. "Layt al-'arab, kul al-'arab, a'tou nisf ma a'tatahu Beirut" [If only all the Arabs had offered half what Beirut offered]. *Shu'un Filastiniyya* (January 1983) 134:53-69.

'Arafat, Yasser, int. Salwa al-'Amad. "Shahada hawl ma'rakat Beirut" [Testimony on the battle of Beirut]. *Shu'un Filastiniyya* (March/April 1983) 136/137:19-28.

_____ int. Uri Avnery. "A Meeting with Arafat." *New Outlook* (August/September 1982) 25(6):47-49, 63.

_____ int. Amnon Kapeliuk. "A Chance for Dialogue - Interview with Arafat." *New Outlook* (August/September 1982) 25(6):9-11.

Hawatmeh, Nayef. "Maham al-thawra ba'd ijtiah lubnan wa ma'rakat Beirut al-butuliyya" [The tasks of the revolution following the invasion of Lebanon and the heroic battle of Beirut]. *Shu'un Filastiniyya* (February 1983) 135:3-26.

Nawfal, Mamduh. "Shahadat Mamduh Nawfal hawl al-harb" [Testimony of Mamduh Nawfal on the war]. *Shu'un Filastiniyya* (February 1983) 135:27-39.

Tlas, Lt. Gen. Mustafa, int. Siegesmund von Ilsemann and Adel Elias. "'War of Liberation': A Talk with the Syrian Defense Minister". *Der Spiegel* interview, translated and reprinted in the *New York Review of Books* (November 22, 1984):36-40.

C. Books

'Abd al-Fattah, Ziyad, ed. *al-Ma'raka* [The battle]. Tunis: Maghreb Editions, 1983.

'Abd al-Haqq, Badr, and Ghazi al-Sa'di, ed. and trans. *Shahadat maydaniyya li-dubbat wa junud al-'aduw* [Testimonies from the field by enemy officers and soldiers]. Amman: Dar al-Jalil, 1982.

Abu 'Arafa et al., comp. *al-Harb al-filastiniyya al-isra'iliyya: atwal hurub isra'il ma' al-'arab* [The Palestinian-Israeli war: the longest of Israel's wars with the Arabs]. Jerusalem: Abu 'Arafa Agency, 1982.

Abu Iyad, with Eric Rouleau. *My Home, My Land: A Narrative of Palestinian Struggle*. New York: Times Books, 1981.

Abu Khater, Joseph Ibrahim. *Lubnan wal-'arab: min mu'tamar al-*

Ta'ef ila qimmat Fas [Lebanon and the Arabs: From the Ta'ef conference to the Fez summit]. Beirut: Dar Iqra', 1984.

Abu Musa, Col., with Hashim 'Ali Muhsin. *al-'Aqid Abu Musa yatakalam 'an al-harb al-khamisa wa sumud Beirut* [Col. Abu Musa speaks of the fifth war and the steadfastness of Beirut]. Damascus: Dar al-Jalil. 1984.

Abu al-Tayyeb. *al-Qati' al-thalith min zilzal Beirut* [The third sector of the Beirut earthquake]. Amman: al-Dustour Commercial Press, 1983.

'Amr, Nabil. *Ayyam al-hub wal-hisar* [Days of love and siege]. Tunis: n.p., 1983.

'Arafat, Fathi. *al-Sahha wal-harb* [Health and the war]. Nicosia: The Palestinian Red Crescent Society, Central Information and Orientation Bureau, 1984.

'Arafat, Yasser. *'Am al-jamara wal-nar wal-amal* [The year of embers, fire and hope]. Cairo: Dar al-Mawqif al-'Arabi, 1983.

_____ *Abu 'Ammar: hiwarat wa mawaqif* [Abu 'Ammar: dialogues and positions]. Tunis: P.L.O. Unified Information, n.d. [1983].

'Ayyid, Khalid. *Qitar al-mawt: ma'rakat Beirut fi siyaq al-irhab wal-tawassu' al-sihyuni* [The train of death: the battle of Beirut in the context of Zionist terror and expansion]. Beirut: Dar al-Sharq al-Awsat, 1984.

Ball, George W. *Error and Betrayal in Lebanon: An Analysis of Israel's Invasion of Lebanon and the Implications for U.S.-Israeli Relations*. Washington D.C.: Foundation for Middle East Peace, 1984.

Bamford, James. *The Puzzle Palace: A Report on America's Most Secret Agency*. Rev. ed. Harmondsworth and New York: Penguin Books, 1983.

Bashur, Ma'an. *Beirut: min al-hisar ila al-intifada* [Beirut: from the siege to the uprising]. Beirut: Dar al-Kitab al-Hadith, 1984.

Bavly, Dan and Eliahu Salpeter. *Fire in Beirut: Israel's War in Lebanon with the P.L.O.* New York: Stein and Day, 1984.

Bourgi, Albert and Pierre Weiss. *Liban: la cinquieme guerre du Proche-Orient*. Paris: Editions Publisud, 1983.

Bulloch, John. *Death of a Country: The Civil War in Lebanon*. London: Weidenfeld and Nicolson, 1977.

_____ *Final Conflict: The War in Lebanon*. London: Century Publishing, 1983.

Chomsky, Noam. *The Fateful Triangle: The United States, Israel & the Palestinians*. Boston: South End Press, 1983.

Clifton, Tony, and Catherine Leroy. *God Cried*. London: Quartet Books, 1983.

Cobban, Helena. *The Palestinian Liberation Organization: People, Power and Politics*. Cambridge: Cambridge University Press, 1984.

Corm, Georges. *Le Proche-Orient éclaté: de Suez à l'invasion du Liban, 1956-1982*. Paris: La Decouverte/Maspero, 1983.

Les Crises du Liban 1958-1982: Chronologie commentée. Paris: Documentation française, 1983.

Dawisha, Adeed. *Syria and the Lebanese Crisis*. London: Macmillan, 1980.

de Chalvron, Alain. *Le piège de Beyrouth*. Paris: Editions Le Sycomore, 1982.

Deeb, Marius. *The Lebanese Civil War*. New York: Praeger, 1980.

Eshel, Lt. Col David. *The Lebanon War, 1982*. 2d ed. Hod Hasharon: Eshel-Dramit, 1983.

Freedman, Robert O., ed. *The Middle East Since Camp David*. Boulder, Colo.: Westview Press, 1984.

Gabriel, Richard A. *Operation Peace for Galilee*. New York: Hill & Wang, 1984.

Gavron, Daniel. *Israel After Begin: Israel's Options in the Aftermath of the Lebanon War*. Boston: Houghton Mifflin, 1984.

Gilmour, David. *Lebanon: The Fractured Country*. New York: St. Martin's Press, 1984.

Gordon, David C. *The Republic of Lebanon: Nation in Jeopardy*. Boulder, Colo.: Westview Press, 1983.

Haig, Alexander M. Jr. *Caveat: Realism, Reagan and Foreign Policy*. New York: Macmillan, 1984.

Haley, P. Edward, and Lewis Snider, eds. *Lebanon in Crisis*. Syracuse: Syracuse University Press, 1979.

Hart, Alan. *Arafat: Terrorist or Peacemaker?* London: Sidgwick and Jackson, 1984.

Henry, Paul-Marc. *Les jardiniers de l'enfer*. Paris: Olivier Orban, 1984.

Herzog, Chaim. *The Arab-Israeli Wars: War and Peace in the Middle East from the War of Independence Through Lebanon*. Rev. ed. New York: Vintage, 1984.

Hirokawa, Ryuichi, ed. *Beirut 1982: From the Israeli Invasion to the Massacre of Palestinians at Sabra and Chatila Camps*. Damascus: P.L.O. Central Council Ad Hoc Committee on Sabra and Chatila, 1982.

Hirst, David. *The Gun and the Olive Branch: The Roots of Violence in the Middle East.* 2d ed. London: Faber & Faber, 1984.

Hudson, Michael. *The Precarious Republic: Political Modernization in Lebanon.* New York: Random House, 1968.

Hurewitz, J.C. *The Struggle for Palestine.* New York, Norton, 1950.

Hussein, Sa'doun. *100 yawm fi mu'taqal Ansar: mu'anat sahafi lubnani kharij min al-asir* [100 days in Ansar camp: experiences of a Lebanese journalist released from prison]. Beirut: Muassassat al-Rou'i, 1983.

Ibrahim, Muhsin. *Qadaya nathariyya wa siyasiyya ba'd al-harb* [Postwar theoretical and political problems]. Beirut: Beirut al-massa', 1984.

al-Ijtiah al-isra'ili li-lubnan, 1982: dirasat siyasiyya wa 'askariyya [The Israeli invasion of Lebanon, 1982: political and military studies]. Beirut: Institute for Palestine Studies, 1984.

Israel in Lebanon: The Report of an International Commission to Enquire Into Reported Violations of International law by Israel During Its Invasion of the Lebanon. Sean MacBride, Chairman. London: Ithaca Press, 1983.

Israeli Commission of Inquiry into the events at the Refugee Camps in Beirut. *The Beirut Massacre: the Complete Kahan Commission Report.* Yitzhak Kahan, Chairman, with an introduction by Abba Eban. Tel Aviv: Kohl-Carz, 1983.

Israeli, Raphael, ed. *P.L.O. in Lebanon: Selected Documents.* London: Weidenfeld & Nicolson, 1983.

'Issa, Fayez Rashid. *Wal-jarrah tashhad: mudhakkirat tabib fi zaman al-hisar* [And the surgeon testifies: memoirs of a doctor during the siege]. Damascus: General Union of Palestinian Writers and Journalists, 1983.

'Itani, Layla, ed. *Harb Lubnan: suwar, watha'iq, ahdath* [The Lebanon war: photographs, documents, events]. Beirut: al-Masira Publishers, 1982.

Jansen, Michael. *The Battle of Beirut: Why Israel Invaded Lebanon.* London: Zed Press, 1982.

Joseph, Dov. *The Faithful City: The Siege of Jerusalem, 1948.* New York: Simon and Schuster, 1960.

Kapeliouk, Amnon. *Sabra and Shatila: Inquiry into a Massacre.* Belmont, Mass.: Association of Arab-American University Graduates, 1984.

Khalaf, 'Ali 'Isa. *al-Hisar: yawmiyat Beirut 82* [The siege: Beirut dairy 82]. Amman: Dar Ibn Rushd, 1983.

Khalidi, Rashid I. *British Policy Towards Syria and Palestine, 1906-1914.* London: Ithaca Press for the Middle East Centre, St. Antony's College Oxford, 1980.

Khalidi, Walid. *Conflict and Violence in Lebanon: Confrontation in the Middle East.* Cambridge: Harvard Center for International Affairs, 1979.

_____ ed. *From Haven to Conquest.* Beirut: Institute for Palestine Studies, 1970.

Kriegel, Annie. *Israel est-il coupable?* Paris: R. Laffont, 1982.

Lamb, Franklin P., comp. and ed. *Reason Not the Need: Eyewitness Chronicles of Israel's War in Lebanon.* London: Spokesman, 1984.

Lebanese Republic. *Watha'iq: ittifaq jala' al-quwwat al-isra'iliyya* [Documents: Agreement for the evacuation of Israeli forces]. Beirut: Foreign Ministry, Ministry of Information, 1983.

Lebanon: The Summer of '82. Athens: Express International, 1985.

Lesch, Ann Mosely. *Arab Politics in Palestine 1917-1939: The Frustration of a National Movement.* Ithaca: Cornell University Press, 1979.

Lubnan 1982: yawmiyat al-ghazw al-isra'ili, watha'iq wa suwar [Lebanon 1982: diary of the Israeli invasion, documents and photographs]. Beirut: al-Markaz al-'Arabi lil-Ma'lumat, 1982.

Lubnan bayna al-wujud al-filastini wal-ghazw al-sihyuni [Lebanon between the Palestinian presence and the Zionist invasion]. Cairo: al-Mawqif al-'Arabi Publishers, 1983.

Mallison, Sally V. *Armed Conflict in Lebanon, 1982.* Washington D.C.: American Educational Trust, 1983.

Mas'ad, Raouf. *Sabah al-Khair ya watan: shahada min Beirut al-muhasara* [Good morning homeland: Testimony from besieged Beirut]. Cairo: Cairo Press, 1983.

Matar, Ahmed. *Beirut 82: wa'i al-dhat* [Beirut 82: Self-consciousness]. Damascus: Secretariat General of The General Union of Palestinian Writers and Journalists, n.d.

Mikdadi, Lina. *Surviving the Siege of Beirut: A Personal Account.* London: Onyx Press, 1983.

The Military Balance 1982-1983. London: The International Institute for Strategic Studies, 1983.

Miller, Aaron David. *The P.L.O. and the Politics of Survival.* New York: Praeger, 1983.

Muhsin, Hashim 'Ali. *al-Intifada: thawra hatta al-nasr* [The uprising: Revolution until victory]. 2nd ed. Damascus: Dar al-Jalil, 1984.

Nakhleh, Khalil and Clifford A. Wright. *After the Palestine-Israel War: Limits to U.S. and Israeli Policy.* Belmont, Mass.: Institute of Arab Studies, 1983.

Nassib, Selim, with Caroline Tisdall. *Beirut: Frontline Story.* London: Pluto Press, 1983.

Owen, Roger, ed. *Essays on the Crisis in Lebanon.* London: Ithaca Press, 1976.

Paix en Galilee, Beyrouth. Paris: Editions du Minuit, 1983.

Pakradouni, Karim. *La Paix manquée: Le mandat d'Elias Sarkis, 1976-1982.* Beirut: Editions Fiches du Monde Arabe, 1983.

Peck, Juliana S. *The Reagan Administration and the Palestinian Question: The First Thousand Days.* Washington, D.C.: Institute for Palestine Studies, 1984.

Porath Y. *The Emergence of the Palestinian-Arab National Movement, 1918-1929.* London: Frank Cass, 1974.

_____ *The Palestinian Arab National Movement, 1929-1939: From Riots to Rebellion.* London: Frank Cass, 1977.

al-Qadiyya al-filistiniyya: al-'adwan wal-muqawama wa subul al-taswiya [The Palestine problem: aggression, resistance and paths to a settlement]. Moscow: Soviet Academy of Sciences, 1983.

Rabinovich, Itamar. *The War for Lebanon 1970-1983.* Ithaca: Cornell University Press, 1984.

Randal, Jonathan. *Going all the Way: Christian Warlords, Israeli Adventurers, and the War in Lebanon.* Rev. ed. New York: Vintage Books, 1983.

Rasa'il min qalb al-hisar: min Abu 'Ammar ila al-jami' [Messages from the heart of the siege: from Abu 'Ammar to all stations]. Amman: Dar al-Jalil, 1983.

Racz, Juraj, and Janata, Michael. *From Camp David to Beirut: An Outline of the Fifth Israeli-Arab-War—Its Roots and Results.* Prague: International Organization of Journalists, 1983.

Rashid, Fawziyya. *al-Hisar* [The siege]. Beirut: Dar al-Farabi, 1983.

Rikhye, Maj. Gen. (ret.) Indar Jit. *The Theory and Practice of Peacekeeping.* New York: St. Martin's Press for the International Peace Academy, 1984.

Rokach, Livia. *Israel's Sacred Terrorism: A Study Based on Moshe Sharett's Personal Diary and Other Documents.* Belmont, Mass.: AAUG, 1980.

Rosenblatt, R., Safa Zeitoun, and Mahgoub 'Umar. *al-Atfal wal-harb* [The children and the war]. Cairo: Dar al-Fata, 1984.

Rouleau, Eric. *Les Palestiniens: d'une querre á l'autre.* Paris: Editions La Decouverte et Le Monde, 1984.

Rubenberg, Cheryl. *The Palestine Liberation Organization: Its Institutional Infrastructure.* Belmont, Mass.: Institute of Arab Studies, 1983.

Sabbagh, Zuheir. *Sabra, Shatila, al-majzara: bahth fi khalfiatiha wa dawafi'iha* [Sabra, Shatila, the massacre: A study in its background and motivations]. Jerusalem: Salah al-Din Publications, 1983.

Sabra, Chatila in memoriam. Tunis: Sud Editions, 1983.

Said, Edward. *The Question of Palestine.* New York: Times Books, 1980.

Salem, Hilmi. *al-Thaqafa taht al-hisar* [Culture under the siege]. Cairo: Shuhdi Publishers, 1984.

Salibi, Kamal. *Crossroads to Civil War: Lebanon 1958-1976.* New York: Caravan Press, 1976.

Salisbury, Harrison. *The 900 Days: The Siege of Leningrad.* New York: Harper and Row, 1969.

al-Sawahiri, Khalil, ed. *Ahadith al-ghuzat: shahadat min al-harb al-filastiniyya al-israi'liyya al-thalitha* [Testimonies of the invaders: Eyewitness accounts of the third Palestinian-Israeli war], Kuwait: General Union of Palestinian Writers and Journalists, Kuwait Branch, 1982.

Schenker, Hillel, ed. *After Lebanon: The Israeli-Palestinian Connection.* New York: The Pilgrim Press, 1983.

Schiff, Ze'ev, and Ehud Ya'ari. *Israel's Lebanon War.* New York: Simon and Schuster, 1984.

Schiffer, Shimon. *Kurat al-thalj: asrar al-tadakhul al-isra'ili fi lubnan* [Snowball: Secrets of the Israeli intervention in Lebanon]. Beirut: al-Watan al-'Arabi, 1984.

Shahin, Mahmoud, comp. *Harb al-muwajaha fi lubnan: kama yarwiha dubbat wa junud al-'aduw* [The war of confrontation in Lebanon: As described by enemy officers and soldiers]. Damascus: P.L.O. Unified Information, n.d.

Silver, Eric. *Begin: The Haunted Prophet.* New York: Random House, 1984.

Timerman, Jacobo. *The Longest War: Israel in Lebanon*. New York: Vintage, 1982.

Tlas, Lt. Gen. Mustafa, comp. *al-Ghazw al-isra'ili li-lubnan* [The Israeli invasion of Lebanon]. Damascus: Tishrin Institute for Journalism and Publishing, 1983.

Trabulsi, Fawwaz. *'An amal la shifa minhu: min dafatir hisar Beirut* [About incurable hope: From notebooks of the siege of Beirut]. Beirut: Arab Research Institute, 1984.

Tueni, Ghassan. *Une guerre pour les autres*. Paris: J.C. Lattès, 1985.

'Umar, Mahgoub. *al-Nas wal-harb: Beirut 82* [The people and the war: Beirut 82]. Cairo: al-'Arabi Publishing and Distribution, 1982.

Witness of War Crimes in Lebanon: Testimony Given to the Nordic Commission, Oslo, October 1982. London: EAFORD and Ithaca Press, 1983.

Yermiya, Dov. *My War Diary: Lebanon June 5-July 1 1982*. Boston: South End Press, 1984.

Zeitun, Safa al-Din. *Sabra wa Shatila: al-madhbaha* [Sabra and Shatila: the massacre]. Cairo: al-Fata al-'arabi, 1983.

D. Articles, Monographs and Theses

Abu Khalil, As'ad. "Ideology and Practice of a 'Revolutionary' Marxist-Leninist Party: The Socialist Arab Action Party—Lebanon." M.A. Thesis, Political Studies and Public Administration Department, American University of Beirut, 1983.

Abu Lughod, Ibrahim. "The Meaning of Beirut, 1982." *Race & Class* (Spring 1983) 24(4):345-360.

Ahmad, Eqbal. "The Public Relations of Ethnocide." *Journal of Palestine Studies* (Spring 1983) 12(3):31-40.

Ajami, Fouad. "The Shadows of Hell." *Foreign Policy* (Fall 1982) 48:94-110.

Akins, James E. "The Flawed Rationale for Israel's Invasion of Lebanon." *American-Arab Affairs* (Fall 1982) 2:32-39.

Alia, Josette. "Liban: Ce que Sharon ne dira jamais." *Le Nouvel Observateur* (November 6, 1982):116-123; 129-134.

Anon. "Israel's New Order in Lebanon." *Arab Studies Quarterly* (Fall 1982) 4(4):309-323.

al-Banna, Sami'. "The Defense of Beirut." *Arab Studies Quarterly* (Spring 1983) 5(2):105-115.

Bar-on, Mordechai. "The Palestinian Aspect of the War In Lebanon." *New Outlook* (October 1982) 25(7):30-34, 49.

Bechtoldt, Heinrich. "Post-Sinai and the Attack on the P.L.O. State." *Aussenpolitik* (1982) 33(3):273-281.

Bloom, James J. "From the Litani to Beirut: A Brief Strategic Assessment of Israel's Operations in Lebanon, 1978-82." *Middle East Insight* (November/December 1982) 2(4):37-45.

_____ "Six Days-Plus-Ten-Weeks War: Aspects of Israel's Summer Campaign in Lebanon, 1982." *Middle East Insight* (January/February 1983) 2(5):45-55.

Bourgi, Albert, and Pierre Weiss. "Israel et le Sud-Liban." *Peuples Méditerranéens/Mediterranean Peoples* (July/September 1982) 20:93-104.

Bruzonsky, Mark A. and Dale Gavlak. "Review article: Israel's War in Lebanon." *Middle East Journal* (Winter 1984) 38(1):115-119.

Carus, W. Seth. "The Bekaa Valley Campaign." *The Washington Quarterly* (Autumn 1982) 5(5):34-41

Chomsky, Noam. "The Sabra/Shatila Whitewash." *Inquiry* (June 1983) 6:27-31.

Cody, Edward. "Covering the Invasion of Lebanon." *Washington Journalism Review* (September 1982) 4:18-21

Cohen, Eliot A. "Peace for Galilee: Success or Failure?" *Commentary* November 1984) 78:24-30.

Cordesman, Anthony H. "The Sixth Arab-Israeli Conflict: Military Lessons for American Defense Planning." *Armed Forces Journal International* (August 1982) 120(1):28-32.

Dawisha, Adeed. "The Motives of Syria's Involvement in Lebanon." *The Middle East Journal* (Spring 1984) 38(2):228-236.

Dawisha, Karen. "The U.S.S.R. in the Middle East: Superpower in Eclipse?" *Foreign Affairs* (Winter 1982-83) 61:438-452.

Dorman, William A. and Mansour Farhang. "The U.S. Press and Lebanon." *SAIS Review* (Winter-Spring, 1983) 3(1):65-81.

Duclos, L.J. et al. "La Guerre d'Israel au Liban." *Maghreb-Machrek* (1983) 98:66-115.

Ewig, Mark A., Maj. "Surprise from Zion: The 1982 Israeli Invasion of Lebanon." *Air University Review* (September–October 1984) 35:48-57.

Eytan, Ze'ev. "The Palestinian Armed Forces After Beirut." *The Jerusalem Quarterly* (Summer 1984) 32:131-139.

Falk, Richard. "Rethinking U.S.-Israeli Relations after the Lebanon War." *SAIS Review* (Winter-Spring 1983) 3(1):43-63.

Farjoun, Emmanuel. "Pax Hebraica." *Khamsin* (1983) 10:4-12.

Filiu, Jean-Pierre. "Un Moment de l'Errance." *Peuples Méditerranéens/Mediterranean Peoples* (July-September 1982) 20:39-58.

Frankel, J. "Israel: The War and After." *Dissent* (Winter 1983) 30(1):7-14.

Freedman, Robert O. "The Impact of the Israeli Invasion of Lebanon on Soviet Middle East Policy." *Middle East Focus* (May 1983) 6(1):9-13.

_____ "The Soviet Union, Syria and the Crisis in Lebanon: A Preliminary Analysis." In *The Middle East Annual 1983*. Cambridge: Harvard University, in press.

Furlong, R.D.M. "Israel Lashes Out." *International Defence Review* (August 1982) 8:1001-1007.

Gabriel, Richard A., Maj. (ret). "Lessons of War: The IDF in Lebanon." *Military Review* (August 1984) 64(8):47-65.

Garfinkle, A.M. "Sources of the Al-Fatah Mutiny." *Orbis* (Fall 1983) 27(3):603-640.

Genet, Jean. "Four Hours in Shatila". *Journal of Palestine Studies* (Spring 1983) 12(3):3-22.

Gervasi, Frank. *Media Coverage: The War in Lebanon.* Washington D.C.: The Center for International Security, 1982.

Ghalioun, Burhan, Ilan Halevi, Souheil Al Kache, and Elias Sanbar. "Stratégies." *Peuples Méditerranéens/Mediterranean Peoples* (July-September 1982) 20:3-38.

Giannou, Chris. "The Battle for South Lebanon." *Journal of Palestine Studies* (Summer/Fall 1982) 11(4)/12(1):69-84.

Gichon, Mordechai, Lt. Col. (Res.). "The Campaign." *IDF Journal* (December 1982) 1(2):11-29.

Golan, Galia. "The Soviet Union and the Israeli Action in Lebanon." *International Affairs* (Winter 1982/83) 59(1):7-16.

Gross, Laurence M. "The Legal Implications of Israel's 1982 Invasion into Lebanon." *California Western International Law Journal* (Summer 1983) 13:458-492.

Hagopian, Elaine. "Redrawing the Map in the Middle East: Phalangist Lebanon and Zionist Israel." *Arab Studies Quarterly* (Fall 1983) 5(4):321-336.

Harkabi, Yehosofat. "The Intelligence-Policymaker Tangle." *Jerusalem Quarterly* (Winter 84) 30:125-131.

Heiberg, M. "Lebanon and Premonitions of Battles to Come." *Journal of Peace Research* (1983) 20(4):293-298.

Hourani, Faisal. "Harb al-shuhur al-thalatha wal-raqm alladhi istahal shatbahu" [The three-month war and the factor which could not be eliminated]. *Shu'un Filastiniyya* (August/September/October 1982) 129/130/131:5-17.

al-Hout, Shafiq. "Lahadhat laha tarikh" [Moments of history] 20 semi-weekly installments, *al-Sharq al-Awsat* (June 9, 1984/August 15, 1984).

Hudson, Michael C. "The Palestinians After Lebanon." *Current History* (January 1983) 82:5-9.

Inbar, Efraim. "Israel and Lebanon, 1975-1982." *Crossroads* (Spring 1983) 10:39-80.

Ja'far, Qasim. "al-Mawajaha al-jawiyya al-suriyya al-isra'iliyya fi 1982" [The Syrian-Israeli aerial confrontation in 1982]. *al-Fikr al-Istratiji al-'Arabi* (January-May 1983) 6/7:59-106.

Jalbert, Paul. "'News Speak' about the Lebanon War." *Journal of Palestine Studies* (Fall 1984) 14(1):16-35.

Jiryis, Sabri. "Malamih al-marhala al-jadida" [Outlines of the new phase]. *Shu'un Filastiniyya* (August/September/October 1982) 129/130/131:18-25.

Khalidi, Rashid. "The Asad Regime and the Palestinian Resistance." *Arab Studies Quarterly* (Fall 1984) 6(4):259-266.

_____ "L'impact du mouvement national palestinien sur le Liban." *Revue d'Etudes Palestiniennes* (Summer 1984) 12:3-14.

_____ "The Palestinians and Lebanon." In Halim Barakat, ed. *Towards a Viable Lebanon.* Washington: Center for Contemporary Arab Studies, Georgetown University, forthcoming.

_____ "The Palestinians in Lebanon: Social Repercussions of Israel's Invasion." *The Middle East Journal* (Spring 1984) 38(2):225-266.

_____ "Problems of Foreign Intervention in Lebanon." *American-Arab Affairs* (Winter 1983-84) 7:24-29.

La Gorce, Paul-Marie de. "Anatomie d'une crise (juin-aout 1982)." *Politique Etrangère* (October 1982) 47(3):583-593.

Lambeth, Benjamin S. *Moscow's Lessons from the 1982 Lebanon Air War*. Santa Monica: Rand Corporation, 1984.

"Liban: une guerre en question." *Les Nouveax Cahiers* (Fall 1983) 70:2-27.

Mallison, Sally V. and Thomas Mallison. "Israel in Lebanon, 1982: Aggression or Self-Defnese?" *American-Arab Affairs* (Summer 1983) 5:39-49.

Mansour, Camille. "Les Palestiniens apres la guerre du Liban." *Politique Etrangère* (Summer 1983) 48(2): 447-460.

Merhav, Meir, Philip M. Klutznick and Herman F. Eilts. *Facing the P.L.O. Question*. Washington D.C.: Foundation for Middle East Peace, 1985.

Miller, Aaron David. "Lebanon: One Year After." *Washington Quarterly* (Summer 1983) 6(2):129-141.

_____ "The P.L.O.: What Next?" *Washington Quarterly* (Winter 1983) 6(4):116-125.

Morris, Roger. "Beirut—and the Press—under Siege." *Columbia Journalism Review* (November-December 1982) 21:23-33.

Morrison, M. "Over There - Scotching the PLO." *Policy Review* (Fall 1982) 22:55-66.

Moughrabi, Fouad. "Lebanon: The Shameless Silence." *Arab Studies Quarterly* (Fall 1982) 4(4):350-357.

_____ "The Palestinians After Lebanon." *Arab Studies Quarterly* (Summer 1983) 5(3):211-219.

Muir, Jim. "Lebanon: Arena of Conflict, Crucible of Peace." *The Middle East Journal* (Spring 1984) 38(2):204-219.

Muravchik, Joseph. "Misreporting Lebanon." *Policy Review* (Winter 1983) 23:11-66.

Nakhleh, Khalil. "The Invasion of Lebanon and Israel's Imperial Strategy." *Arab Studies Quarterly* (Fall 1982) 4(4):324-335.

Nassib, S. "Dispatches from the War." *Race & Class* (Spring 1983) 24(4):361-390.

Natour, Souheil. "Hal kana min al-mumkin an tamna' al-tanazalat al-filastiniyya al-ijtiah al-isra'ili li lubnan? [Could Palestinian concessions have prevented the Israeli invasion of Lebanon?] *Shu'un Filastiniyya* (March-April 1983) 136/137: 29-42.

Naylor, R.T. "From Bloodbath to Whitewash: Sabra-Shatila and the Kahan Commission Report." *Arab Studies Quarterly* (Fall 1983) 5(4):337-361.

Neumann, Robert G. "Assad and the Future of the Middle East." *Foreign Affairs* (Winter 1983-1984) 62(2):237-256.

Norton, Augustus R. "Instability and Change in Lebanon." *American-Arab Affairs* (Fall 1984) 10:79-88.

_____ "Israel and South Lebanon." *American-Arab Affairs* (Spring 1983) 4:23-31.

Picard, Elizabeth. "La bourgeoisie palestinienne et l'industrie: etude socio-historique." In A. Bourgey et al *Industrialisation et changements sociaux dans l'Orient arabe*, pp. 347-400. Beirut: Editions du Centre d'Etudes et Recherches sur le Moyen Orient Contemporain, 1982.

_____ "From 'Community-Class' to 'Patriotic Struggle': An Analysis of the Role and Influence of the Shi'a in the Lebanese Political System (1970-1984)." Paper presented to Middle East Studies Association annual meeting, San Francisco, November 1984.

Pa'il, Meir. "A Military Analysis." *New Outlook* (August/September 1982) 25(6):18-28.

Peretz, Martin. "Lebanon Eyewitness." *The New Republic* (August 2, 1982):15-23.

Perlmutter, Amos. "Begin's Rhetoric and Sharon's Tactics." *Foreign Affairs* (Fall 1982) 61(1):67-83.

Podhoretz, Norman. "J'accuse." *Commentary* (December 1982) 74(3):21-31.

Porat, Ben. "L'Histoire secrète de la guerre du Liban." *Paris-Match* (June 24, 1983):3-9, 88.

Quandt, William B. "Reagan's Lebanon Policy: Trial and Error." *The Middle East Journal* (Spring 1984) 38(2):237-254.

Rabinovich, Itamar. "The Foreign Policy of Syria: Goals, Capabilities, Constraints and Options." *Survival* (July/August 1982) 25(4):175-183.

_____ "Seven Wars and One Peace Treaty." In Alvin Z. Rubinstein, ed. *The Arab-Israeli Conflict: Perspectives*, pp. 41-68. New York: Praeger, 1984.

Rahall, Nick J. II. "Lebanon and U.S. Foreign Policy towards the Middle East." *American-Arab Affairs* (Fall 1982) 2:40-50.

Ramzy, Ameen I. "The Medical Impact of the Siege of Beirut." *Race & Class* (Spring 1983) 24(4):411-414.

Rasler, K. "Internationalized Civil War: A Dynamic Analysis of the Syrian Intervention in Lebanon." *Journal of Conflict Resolution* (September 1983) 27(3):421-456.

Richards, Martin. "The Israeli-Lebanon War of 1982." *Army Quarterly and Defence Journal* (January 1983) 113(1):9-19.

Rondot, Phillipe. "Palestiniens: l'après Beyrouth." *Défense Nationale* (January 1983) 39:125-140.

Rouleau, Eric. "The Future of the P.L.O." *Foreign Affairs* (Fall 1983) 62(1):138-156.

Rubenberg, Cheryl. "Beirut under Fire." *Journal of Palestine Studies* (Summer/Fall 1982) 11(4)12(1):62-68.

Rubinstein, C. L. "The Lebanon War: Objectives and Outcomes." *Australian Outlook* (April 1983) 37:10-17.

Ryan, Sheila. "Israel's Invasion of Lebanon: Background to the Crisis." *Journal of Palestine Studies* (Summer/Fall 1982) 11(4)/12(1):23-37.

Said, Edward W. "Palestinians in the Aftermath of Beirut: A Preliminary Stocktaking." *Arab Studies Quarterly* (Fall 1982) 4(4):301-308.

Sanbar, Elias. "The Long Return to the Homeland." *Arab Studies Quarterly* (Fall 1982) 4(4):291-300.

Sanin, V. "The Lesson of the Lebanon Tragedy." *International Affairs* (Moscow) (November 1982) 11:106-110.

Saunders, Harold H. "An Israeli-Palistinian Peace". *Foreign Affairs* (Fall 1982) 61(1):101-121.

Sayigh, Yezid. "Israel's Military Performance in Lebanon, June 1982." *Journal of Palestine Studies* (Fall 1983) 13(1):24-65.

_____ "Palestinian Military Performance in the 1982 War." *Journal of Palestine Studies* (Summer 1983) 12(4):3-24.

Schiff, Ze'ev. "Dealing with Syria." *Foreign Policy* (Summer 1984) 55:92-112.

_____ "The Green Light." *Foreign Policy* (Spring 1983) 50:73-85.

_____ "Lebanon: Motivations and Interests in Israel's Policy." *The Middle East Journal* (Spring 1984) 38(2):220-227.

_____ "The Palestinian Surprise." *Armed Forces Journal International* (February 1984) 131(7):42-43.

_____ "Who Decided, Who Informed." *New Outlook* (October 1982) 25(7):19-22.

_____ and Hirsch Goodman. "The Road to War: Ariel Sharon's Modern Day 'Putsch''. *Spectrum* (April/May 1984) 2(4):8-13.

Schocken, Gershom. "Israel in Election Year 1984." *Foreign Affairs* (Fall 1984) 63(1):77-92.

Schueftan, Dan. "The P.L.O. after Lebanon." *Jerusalem Quarterly* (Summer 1983) 28:1-11.

Shaheen, Ahmed. "Hajm al-musharaka al-'arabiyya fi harb lubnan wa dawafi'ihi" [The extent of Arab participation in the Lebanese war and its motivations]. *Shu'un Filastiniyya* (August/September/ October 1982) 129/130/131:33-37.

al-Shaikh, Zakaria. "Sabra and Shatila 1982: Resisting the Massacre." *Journal of Palestine Studies* (Fall 1984) 14(1):57-90.

Shlaim, Avi, and Yaniv, Avner. "Domestic Politics and Foreign Policy in Israel." *International Affairs* (Spring 1980) 56:242-262.

Soueid, Mahmoud. "L'invasion israelienne du Liban: causes et conséquences." *Revue d'Etudes Palestiniennes* (Winter 1984) 10:81-88.

Stein, Kenneth W. "The P.L.O. After Beirut." *Middle East Review* (Spring-Summer 1983) 15:11-17.

Stevens, Janet. *The Israeli Use of U.S. Weapons in Lebanon.* Belmont, Mass.: AAUG Press, 1983.

Stork, Joe and Jim Paul. "The War in Lebanon." *MERIP Reports* (September/October 1982) 108/109:3-7.

Thimmesch, Nick. "The Media and the Middle East." *American-Arab Affairs* (Fall 1982) 2:79-88.

Tucker, Robert W. "Lebanon: The Case for the War." *Commentary* (October 1982) 74(4):19-30.

van Creveld, Martin. "Not Exactly a Triumph." *Jerusalem Post Magazine* (December 10, 1982):5-10.

Verrier, June. *Israel's Lebanon War and Its Aftermath.* Canberra: Australian Department of the Parliamentary Library, 1982.

Wagner, Donald. "Lebanon: An American's View." *Race & Class* (Spring 1983) 24(4):401-410.

Wrong, Terence H. "The Sideshow in Lebanon." *SAIS Review* (Winter 1981-1982) 3:73-92.

Wright, Claudia. "The Turn of the Screw - The Lebanon War and American Policy." *Journal of Palestine Studies* (Summer/Fall 1982) 11(4)/12(1):3-22.

Wright, Clifford A. "The Israeli War Machine in Lebanon." *Journal of Palestine Studies* (Winter 1983) 12(2)38-53.

Yaniv, Avner, and Robert J. Lieber, "Personal Whim or Strategic Imperative? The Israeli Invasion of Lebanon." *International Security* (Fall 1983) 8(2):117-142.

Yarri, Ehud. "Israel's Dilemma in Lebanon." *Middle East Insight* (April/May 1984) 3(4):18-23.

Yishai, Y. "Dissent in Israel: Opinion on the Lebanon War." *Middle East Review* (Winter 1983-84) 16(2):38-44.

Zagorin, Adam. "A House Divided." *Foreign Policy* (Fall 1982) 48:111-121.

E. Collections of Press Reports

Claremont Research and Publications. *The Israeli Invasion of Lebanon, Press Profile: June/July 1982.* New York: Claremont Research & Publications, 1982.

_____ *The Israeli Invasion of Lebanon: Part II, Press Profile: August 1982/May 1983.* New York: Claremont Research & Publications, 1983.

_____ *The Beirut Massacre, Press Profile: September 1982.* New York: Claremont Research & Publications, 1982.

Morris, Claud, comp. & ed. *Eyewitness Lebanon: Evidence of 91 International Correspondents.* London: Morris International, 1983.

F. Journals—Special Issues

Abu Lughod, Ibrahim and Ahmad, Eqbal, eds. "The Invasion of Lebanon." *Race & Class* (Spring 1983) 24(4).

IDF Journal [special issue] (December 1982) 1(2).

"La guerre israelo-palestinienne." *Revue d'Etudes Palestiniennes* (Fall 1982) 5.

"Lebanon and Palestine 1982." *Arab Studies Quarterly* (Fall 1982) 4(4).

"Liban: Remises en Cause." *Peuples Méditerranéens/Mediterranean Peoples* (July-September 1982) 20.

"The War in Lebanon." *Journal of Palestine Studies* [double issue (Summer/Fall 1982) 11(4)/12(1).

"The War in Lebanon." *Journal of Palestine Studies* (Winter 1983) 12(2).

"War in Lebanon." *MERIP Reports* (September/October 1982) 108/109.

G. Newspapers and Periodicals

'Al Hamishmar
Bulletin of the Institute for Palestine Studies
Davar
Department of State Bulletin
Davar
Filastin al-Thawra
The Guardian
Ha'aretz
The Jerusalem Post
Ma'ariv
al-Ma'raka
al-Mawqif al-'Arabi
al-Mitras
al-Muharrir
al-Nahar
New Outlook
The New Republic
The New York Times
Le Nouvel Observateur
Paris-Match
al-Safir
Time Magazine
The Sunday Times
United Nations Interim Force in Lebanon press releases
The Village Voice
WAFA English-language daily bulletin
The Washington Post

Index

This index lists people, places, events, and institutions which appear in the text. The reader is urged to consult the Cast of Characters on pp. 187–89 for capsule descriptions of individuals cited, and the List of Abbreviations on p. 185 for explanations of acronyms.